One of the wonderful gifts that immigrants bring to the United States is the gift of their cuisine. A cuisine reflects not just the ingredients that make up the food, but the entirety of a country's history and culture. Since the Philippines lie astride the main trade routes of Asia, ... by the Malays, who came to ... ars ago. In succession came the Chinese, the Spanish, the Mexicans, and, in this century, the Americans.

A surprise to those unfamiliar with the Philippines is the great geographical diversity of the Islands and their six major culinary regions. Gerry Gelle's contribution to our understanding of this diversity is his knowledge of these regions. His recipes include the mountain and coastal regions of Northern Luzon and the many islands of the Visayas and the island of Mindanao. We learn of the rich mixtures of people, from the Pangasinans of Luzon with their specialty of "cultured" fish, to the Tagalogs, who use vinegar and fruits to give their dishes the preferred sour taste. He explains the use of guinamos, a paste of fermented shrimp or fish, in the Visayas, and the use of hot chiles and spices to make curry in Mindanao. After cooking with these recipes, you will know the aromas and tastes of Filipino cooking.

E   S   I   A
IRIAN JAYA

FILIPINO Cuisine

RECIPES FROM THE ISLANDS

FILIPINO
Cuisine

RECIPES FROM THE ISLANDS

Gerry G. Gelle

RED
CRANE
BOOKS
SANTA FE

FIRST EDITION

Printed in the United States of America

Cover & inside photographs by Michael O'Shaughnessy
Maps and drawings by Deborah Reade
Book design by Beverly Miller Atwater

Library of Congress Cataloging-in-Publication Data

Gelle, Gerry G., 1965–
    Filipino cuisine : recipes from the islands / Gerry G. Gelle.
        p.   cm.
    1. Cookery, Philippine.   I. Title.
    TX724.5.P5G45   1997
    641.59599—DC21   97–13868
                                                            CIP

RED CRANE BOOKS
2008-B Rosina Street
Santa Fe, New Mexico 87505
http://www.redcrane.com
e-mail: publish@redcrane.com

On the cover: Sweet Marinated Pork: Tocino can be made with pork or chicken.
It can be served hot or cold with rice, bread or chopped and sprinkled over salad.

Table of Contents

Acknowledgments

This cookbook is dedicated to my father and mother, Gregorio and Asuncion, and to my brothers, Gaylord and Gilbert. It is their love and support that made my life and this book possible. I want to thank the Mariegold Bake Shop of Daly City, Baby's Eatery and Special Palabok of San Francisco and Mrs. Roxas of Alameda, who helped cook most of the dishes for the photographs. Henrydan "Chef Hen" Awayan and Blandon Yee helped arrange and decorate the photographed dishes. Michael and Marianne O'Shaughnessy of Red Crane Books believed in the book and published it. Cindy Barrilleaux did a fine and clarifying editorial job. Finally, I thank Elpidio "Uncle Bali" Balicudiong, his family and our many friends who served as the inspiration and resource for the recipes and ideas in this cookbook. *Salamat po sa inyong lahat!*

The meat market at Manila.
Woodcut. 1857.

Women wearing the traditional Balintawak dress.
Undated photo.

Introduction

Filipino cuisine is a blend of the exotic and familiar. Just as the Filipino people are part Malay, Chinese and Spanish, so is the cooking of the Philippines. And more recently other cultures have influenced Filipino food. These influences have come from the Americans, Japanese and Germans.

About 20,000 years ago the Ice Age reduced the levels of the oceans, creating bridges between land masses, making migration possible. The Malays were the first inhabitants of the Philippine Islands. The Malay influence on Filipino food can be found in the indigenous recipes such as *Kare-kare* (a meat and vegetable stew in a peanut sauce), *Pinakbet* (another meat and vegetable stew flavored with shrimp paste), and *Dinuguan* (a stew made from pork blood and spiced with chile peppers).

Chinese traders sailed across the South China Sea around 300 AD, and by the year 1000, trading was taking place on a regular basis with the coastal ports and colonies that the Chinese had established. By 1400, they had made their way inland and become established as part of the Philippine culture. Today, Filipinos, or *Pinoys,* of Chinese ancestry call themselves *Chinoy*. The Chinese contribution to Philippine cooking is in the noodle dishes, called *Pancit,* steamed dumplings or *Siomai,* and egg rolls or *Lumpia,* both the fresh and fried.

Foreign Influences

In 1521, Ferdinand Magellan discovered the Philippines, beginning a period of Spanish influence and domination that lasted over three hundred years. Magellan claimed the islands in the name of Spain and the ruler at that time, King Philip, thus the name Philippines. Also in the sixteenth century Pope Alexander VI, in an effort to quell the feuding between the major world powers—at this time Spain and Portugal—took a map of the known world and drew a line down the middle of the Atlantic Ocean. All that lay east of the line was given to Portugal and all that lay west of the line was given to Spain. Portugal's sphere of influence encompassed the eastern-most tip of South America—what is now part of Brazil—all of Africa, and eastern Asia. Spain's influence extended to most of South America, all of North and Central America and most of the lands bordering on the Pacific Ocean, including the Philippines. Historians point out that although Spain received more land, it was then mostly unexplored, while Portugal gained control of trade routes and bases that were already established. This division of the world explains why the people of Brazil speak Portuguese while the rest of South America speaks Spanish. And although tlhe Philippines are part of Asia, many of the Filipino languages and dialects are heavily studded with Spanish words and phrases.

Spanish additions to the Filipino cuisine predominate. It has been said that about 80 percent of the dishes prepared in the Philippines today can be traced to Spain. The Spaniards introduced tomatoes and garlic along with the technique of sautéing them with onions in olive oil.

Another significant addition to the Filipino cuisine by the Spanish was many baked goods and desserts, among them *Pan de Sal* (a crusty dinner roll), *Flan* (an egg custard), *Ensaymada* (cheese buns) and many, many other delicious foods. Most derive from Spanish recipes but have been adapted to Filipino tastes and ingredients.

Since the Spanish had to sail west to get to their Pacific possessions, the Philippine Islands were administered through Mexico for more than two hundred years. The Manila Galleons plied the waters between Acapulco and Manila, heavily laden with goods and treasures from Asia and Europe. Because of this connection, the cuisine of the Philippines has a strong Mexican influence, as in the use of bay leaves and annatto seeds. Such dishes as Adobo (braised pork and/or chicken in vinegar and soy sauce) and *Menudo* (a pork and liver stew) are found in both countries, and both undoubtedly originated in Spain. Annatto seeds, also known as *atsuete* or *achote*, are a natural food coloring that provides an orange color to dishes. Both Mexicans and Filipinos use it extensively, and Americans use it to color preserved meats and sausages.

In the 1890's, the Spanish-American War erupted and the once Spanish-held possessions, including the Philippines, became American territories. With the Americans came the introduction to the Philippines of potato and macaroni salads, baked fruit pies, and more recently, fast foods such as hamburgers, french fries and pizza.

The most significant influence of the Americans came after World War II, with the widespread distribution of canned foods. One of the results is Filipino fruit salad, which consists of American canned fruit cocktail, mixed with native sweet preserves of *buko* (young coconut), *kaong* (palm nuts) and bits of *langka* (jackfruit), giving it a Filipino taste and texture. Canned corned beef is another staple product found in most Filipino larders. In the United States, it is mixed with cubes of potatoes to make hash. In the Philippines, it is sautéed with onions and garlic and eaten with rice.

The most significant addition to the Philippine culture by the Americans has been the English language. It is not unusual for a Filipino to be speaking in a native dialect, such as Tagalog, and suddenly use English phrases and sentences. Official government broadcasts are made in English to overcome the barriers of regional dialects.

The most recent influences to the Filipino cuisine come from Japanese and German cooking. Today, Japanese and German tourists visit the Philippines and Filipinos are going to Japan and Germany as contract laborers, entertainers and professionals. With this exchange of people has come an exchange of cooking techniques. Many restaurants have opened to provide Japanese food--it is not unusual to go to the metropolitan areas of the Philippines and find *sushi* bars, tempura restaurants and fast food places serving rice and noodle bowls. And many hotel restaurants have added traditional German dishes to their menus. Filipinos found that both cultures' use of vinegar, spices and salt to flavor and preserve foods was similar. Vinegar, spices and salt were used in traditional German recipes to flavor and preserve food for the

Fish vendors bundle dried fish for sale at the market. 1995.

long cold winters in which fresh food became scarce. Filipinos have used these ingredients not to combat the cold but the tropical heat, in which food could easily spoil unless preserved with vinegar, spices and salt.

For example, German sauerkraut is shredded cabbage boiled and preserved with vinegar, usually eaten as a side dish or added to soups and stews. Filipino *Atsara* is shredded green papaya, also preserved with vinegar, and eaten as a side dish or added to soups and stews.

As an aside, one of the reasons Europeans originally came to Southeast Asia was to gather spices. Now it seems to have come full circle, in that the Spanish and German recipes have brought the use of these spices back to their place of origin. As more and more peoples and cultures visit the Philippines and as more and more Filipinos visit other peoples and cultures, the Filipino cuisine will continue to change and evolve taking the best from those cultures and adapting it to the Filipino taste.

Regional Influences

Not only have the influences of cultures outside the Philippines helped develop Filipino cuisine, but so have the geographical and cultural differences within the Philippines. There are six major culinary regions in the Philippines.

Northern Luzon

This coastal and mountainous region around the northern tip of Luzon Island is rugged and so is life. The people tend to be thrifty and live simply, traits well reflected in their style of cooking. This region is populated mainly by the Ilocanos and Pangasinans along with minority groups such as the Ifugaos, Bontocs, Ibanags and Kakingas.

The Ilocanos like their vegetables steamed or boiled and flavored with *bagoong*, a fermented paste derived from shrimp or fish. And to give their vegetables extra flavor, pork or a broiled fish is added, as in such Ilocano dishes as *Pinakbet*, *Dinengdeng* or *Inabraw*.

A vegetable particularly enjoyed in Northern Luzon is *saluyot* or okra leaves. Not related to okra at all, *saluyot* looks like spinach when it is cooked, but has a slippery texture like okra. The Japanese are starting to import *saluyot* in the form of a powder, as a healthful alternative to tea.

The Pangasinans are known for their cultured fish, in particular *bangus*. *Bangus*, also called milkfish, is a firm, white-fleshed fish that grows well in brackish water. In this area of Northern Luzon and along the central plains of Luzon, *bangus* is grown in an ancient system of fish ponds. Here, *bangus* fingerlings are grown to maturity under the expert watch and care of fish ranchers and then harvested.

Gobi (mudfish), *hito* (catfish), carp and *tilapia* are also starting to be grown under this system of aquaculture. But, instead of ponds used exclusively to grow fish, they are grown in rice paddies when the paddies are filled with water.

It is this use of native vegetables like *saluyot* combined with locally grown fish, poultry and meat, particularly pork, along with *bagoong* that gives the cooking of Northern Luzon a definite identity.

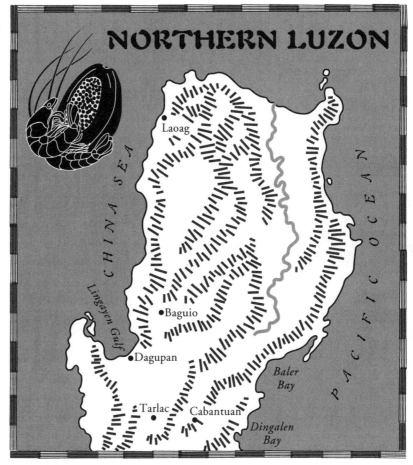

NORTHERN LUZON

CHINA SEA

Laoag

Lingayen Gulf

PACIFIC OCEAN

Baguio

Dagupan

Baler Bay

Tarlac

Cabantuan

Dingalen Bay

In the central part of Luzon, including the area directly surrounding the capital of the Philippines, Manila, the combination of an abundant and stable food supply and the influences of foreign peoples, particularly the Spanish and Chinese, has resulted in the most sophisticated cuisine in the Philippines. In *Rellenong Manok* (stuffed chicken), for instance, the

Central Plains

carcass of a chicken is removed from the intact skin. The skin is then stuffed in such a way that at the center is a sausage, often chorizo *de Bilbao*, surrounded by a layer of carrots, celery and eggs encased in a mixture of chicken, ground pork, raisins, peppers and spices. This is then stuffed back into the skin, sewn back up, steamed and baked to a golden brown. It is served with a spicy, tangy red sauce, creating a sweet and savory dish satisfying not only to the different tastes and textures of the mouth but to the senses of sight and smell as well.

Other delicacies in this area are *Morcon* (stuffed rolled beef) and *Embutido* (stuffed pork sausage). All are rich and served with interesting sauces.

Southern Tagalog

In this area, directly south of Manila, the people speak the major dialect of the Philippines, Tagalog. The region is noted for its contrast of tastes within the meal. The most preferred way of Tagalogs to flavor an entree is through the use of vinegar and fruits like *kamias*, tamarind and over-ripe guavas, which give the dishes a very sour taste. An example of this is *Sinigang,* in which fish, seafood, vegetables and/or meats are cooked in a broth heavily soured with tamarind and other sour fruits.

Another popular method of cooking is to marinate freshwater fish, which abound in the local streams and rivers, in vinegar seasoned with crushed garlic, salt and pepper. The marinated fish is then fried or broiled, and served with a dipping sauce, or *sawsaw*, of more vinegar, garlic, salt and pepper. This method of cooking is called *inihaw*.

Sweet fruits, such as bananas and melons, are served with the sour entrees to cleanse the sour taste from the palate. And to finish off the meal are native cakes and delicacies such as *Espasol*, *Suman* and *Bibingka*, made with glutinous rice and coconuts for which Southern Tagalog is the Philippines' major source.

Bicol

At the southern-most tip of Luzon Island is the region called Bicol. The Bicolanos are most noted for their use of coconut and hot chilies. For example, the popular dish called *laing* consists of meat or shrimp and vegetables flavored with *bagoong*, seasoned with hot chilies, wrapped in *gabi,* or taro leaves, and boiled in coconut milk until the coconut milk is reduced to a flavorful, spicy and thick sauce.

Visayas consists of the many islands that occupy the middle region of the Philippine archipelago along with the eastern parts of the island of

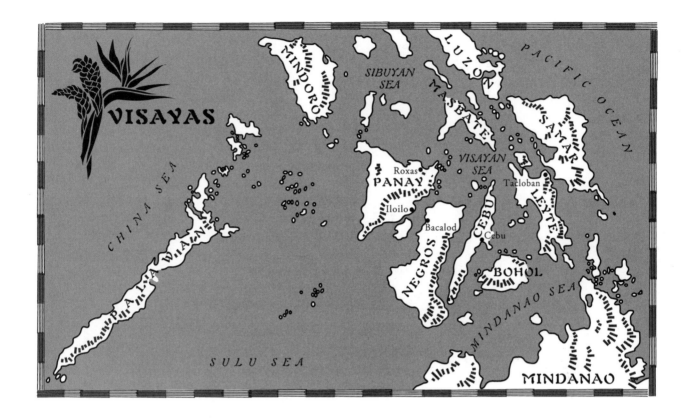

Mindanao. The two main dialects spoken here are Hiligaynon and Cebuano. What makes the cooking of Visayas distinctive is the availability of dried salted fish, the use of a distinctly different fermented fish or shrimp paste called *guinamos*, and the fact that Visayas is the Philippines' main producer of sugar.

Visayas is surrounded by the Sibuyan, Visayan, Sulu, Mindanao and China Seas as well as the Pacific Ocean. Saltwater fish is abundant here. Fish and seafood not consumed immediately are preserved in a brine of salt and water, and then dried in the sun. Visayas is noted for a variety of dried salted seafood, such as *daing* (refers to any small native fish), *tuyo* (sardines), *pusit* (squid) and *hipon* (shrimp). Because of the use of dried salted foods, Visayan cooking tends to be salty.

Visayas

Visayan cuisine is simple. The fish are broiled over live coals or boiled in a well-seasoned vinegar, a technique called *pinamarhan*. It is similar to the Tagalog's *paksiw na isda*, in which fish is boiled in vinegar with lots of pepper and some vegetables, for a rich sour broth. What makes Visayan *pinamarhan* different from Tagalog *paksiw* is that in *pinamarhan*, the dish is cooked until it is dry, concentrating the taste of the vinegar and spices in the meat of the fish.

Visayans also like to eat fish "raw" as in *kinilaw*. Unlike some Japanese dishes, such as some *sushi* and *sashimi* recipes, the sliced fish is marinated in a mixture of vinegar, garlic, onions and salt, sometimes with slices of tomatoes and unripe mango for extra taste and texture.

As mentioned, the use of *guinamos* is another distinctive aspect of Visayan cuisine. This is different from other fermented shrimp or fish pastes, known throughout the rest of the Philippines as *bagoong*, in which shrimp or fish is fermented with salt and cooked until a salty sauce rises to the top. This sauce is skimmed off and sold as *patis* or fish sauce. The sediment that settles to the bottom is the *bagoong*. With *guinamos*, shrimp or fish is fermented and then pounded together with lots of salt to form a paste and no sauce. Its flavor and odor are much stronger than the *bagoongs*.

Because Visayas is the Philippines' main producer of sugar, the region is well known for its native Filipino sweets, such as *pinasugbu* (sweetened pineapple), *turrones* (candies made with nuts), banana chips and traditional cookies and biscuits whose recipes may be of Spanish origin but have been adapted to the Filipino taste.

Mindanao

When referring to Mindanao in this context, we mean the western part of the island of Mindanao, which lies closest to Malayasia and the rest of the Southeast Asian continent. It is this proximity that differentiates this region from the rest of the Philippines. There are several group in this region: the Maranao live on the shore of Lake Lanao; the Maguinado occupy the province of Cotabato; the Tausags, Badjaos and other sea-faring groups live in the Sulu Sea area. Although ethnically diverse, what joins these groups in common cooking styles is a Malaysian import—the religion of Islam.

The Philippines is the only country in Asia that is predominantly Christian, particularly Catholic. The only exception is western Mindanao. Because of the Islamic edicts against eating pork, which is used extensively in the rest of the Philippines, the people of Mindanao have taken advantage of the cattle and fish grown in this area.

Mindanao cooking has borrowed from Indonesia and Malaysia the use of hot chilies and spices used to make curry, as in *Tiola Sapi,* a spicy boiled beef, *Piarun,* a fish entree heavily spiced with hot chilies, and *Lapua,* blanched native vegetables seasoned with salt and vinegar and *guinamos.*

As you can see, what makes the cooking of Mindanao distinct from the other regions of the Philippines is how it has been heavily influenced by Malaysia, Islam and the food products that are grown or gathered in this area. Being so close to the Equator, both the food and temperature in Mindanao are hot.

The Filipino attitude towards cooking and eating

As there are differences in regional cooking, there are differences in attitudes toward food. Of the foods used as staples, most Filipinos on the island of Luzon prefer rice. Visayans on the islands of Cebu, Leyte and Samar use corn extensively. People of Luzon and some in Visayas will eat root crops such as sweet potatoes, yams and cassava as a dessert or snack. But to eat them as a staple in these regions would indicate to others that one is desperately poor, whereas in Mindanao, cassava, or *panggi*, is the staple crop.

Bicolanos and Tagalogs of Southern Luzon, where coconut trees grow abundantly, use lots of coconut in their recipes.

Many varieties of hot chili peppers are found in the Philippines, the hottest and most popular being the *sili labuyo*. While they are available throughout the Philippines, only the people of Bicol at the southern tip of Luzon and the Muslims of western Mindanao use hot peppers extensively in their cooking.

The most popular meat for most Filipinos is pork. Other popular meats are beef and poultry. The people of Pampanga, along with the Igorots, Bontocs, Ifugaos and Ibanags in northern Luzon, are particularly fond of dog meat. The Tagalogs and Pampanguenos eat frogs as a delicacy, but the rest of the people of the Philippines rarely touch them.

Fish is also very popular and readily available. Visayans prefer saltwater fish like sardines, tuna, bonito and mackerel, which abound in the waters surrounding the Philippines. Tagalogs, Pampanguenos, Ilocanos, and Pangasinans prefer freshwater fish caught in the rivers, lakes and streams that are located within these areas. In Pangasinan and Pampanga, there is a system of fish farming or aquaculture in which *bangus*, mudfish, catfish, carp and *tilapia* are raised in artificially created ponds and rice paddies.

Traditional Filipinos rarely use cutlery for eating. Instead, they eat with their fingers and hands. The technique is called *kamayan* and the word for "to eat" is *kumain*. In this technique, small balls of rice are formed with the fingers while pressing them against the plate. Small pieces of fish, meat and vegetables can also be incorporated into this ball of rice. Then they are brought to the mouth with the finger tips and pushed in from behind with the thumb.

Sugpo

The western influence introduced forks, knives and spoons to the Philippines. In the West, the knife and fork are the primary pieces of cutlery, but in the Philippines, it is the spoon and fork. Here, the fork is held with the left hand and the spoon in the right. The fork is used to spear and hold the piece of food while the spoon is used to cut or tear off smaller pieces. The smaller piece of food is then placed in the spoon, and the fork is used to push rice into the spoon. The piece of food and rice are then brought to the mouth with the spoon and eaten.

In the West, dinner is sequential, starting with a soup and/or salad, an antipasto or appetizer, followed by the entree and finished off with a dessert. Planning a Filipino menu is based on contrasts of taste and texture rather than different courses. The taste sensations of sweet, sour, bitter and salty are introduced into the menu along with a variety of textures such as smooth, silky, crispy, crunchy, chewy. Rather than serving the individual components separately, they are all brought to the table at one time, and it is up to the guest to decide what combination they want to create. Dining at a Filipino table is more like eating at a buffet than a traditional western-style sit-down dinner.

Suahe

At the heart of any Filipino meal is a bowl of rice, short, long or medium grain. There are dozens if not hundreds of different varieties of rice, each of which gives a different "mouth-feel" and taste.

Served with the rice is a meat, fish or poultry, broiled, fried or roasted, giving the meal a crispy and chewy texture. Another way to include that texture is with some fried *lumpias,* or egg rolls. Both the meats and *lumpias* are then flavored with something salty, such as soy sauce, *bagoongs* (fish or shrimp paste) or *patis* (fish sauce). These salty sauces are then flavored with something sour such as *kalamansi,* lemon juice, or vinegar just before being served. A bowl or cup of soup, such as *sinigang,* is also served, to add a smooth and silky taste and texture to the meal.

Ulang

Many Filipinos also add a noodle dish, such as *pancit*, or a stew-like dish such as adobo or *caldereta* for an added savory taste.

Since the Filipino style of cooking lends itself to individuality, the cook who wishes to can choose dishes with an eye to richness and fat content. By varying recipes, the emphasis can be placed on healthy cooking. There are many products on the market now that contain reduced fat content and low-fat or no-fat coconut milk is also available.

No Filipino meal would be complete without dessert, whether it is simply fruit, like bananas, mangoes, papayas and melons, or sweets like *matamis na kamote* (sugar-glazed sweet potatoes) and *kaong* (palm nut) or true desserts like flan (egg custard) and native cakes like *biko* or *bibingka* made from rice and coconut milk. The dessert isn't served just at the end of the meal--it is not unusual to eat it as part of the meal, for not only extra texture but the sweetness needed to counteract the salty, sour and sometimes bitter tastes that are part of the meal.

As you can see, the cooking of the Philippines is a blend of traditional, native cooking and the best aspects of foreign influences. Recipes and techniques have been adopted and then adapted to the Filipino taste. Filipino cooking is tasty without being too spicy, simple but not sparse, different but not strange, and satisfying without being overwhelming. As Filipinos go out to the rest of the world and as the rest of the world visits the Philippines, new ideas will be brought to the Filipino kitchen. It is this meeting of the East and West with a steady and constant evolution of traditional dishes that is Filipino cuisine.

Traditional Filipino DISHES

Adobo

Popularly regarded as the Filipino national dish, adobo is both a specific dish and a method of cooking in which pork, chicken, fish, seafood or vegetables are braised in vinegar with garlic and pepper. The basic recipe is simple and allows for many variations, limited only to the imagination of the cook and the available ingredients. Pork Adobo *(adobong baboy)* is the basis of most variations.

Although adobo can be made quickly by omitting the marinating, the flavors are more subtle and complex if one takes the time to marinate the fish, meat or chicken first. When marinating, be sure to use a saucepan that is not aluminum, as the vinegar will discolor it and impart a strange flavor. Adobo is best when made a day or more before serving, allowing the flavors to mix and age. Just before serving, it can be reheated on the stove or in the microwave, and served on a bed of freshly cooked rice.

Leftover adobo is delicious and versatile. It can be mixed with leftover rice, heated and served either for lunch or as a great alternative breakfast dish with eggs. So make some adobo today, and eat it tomorrow. It is well worth the wait!

Beef Adobo
ADOBONG CARNE

½ cup cider vinegar

½ cup soy sauce

1 bay leaf

4 peppercorns, whole

1 clove garlic, minced

1 tablespoon ginger,
    julienned

¼ teaspoon salt

¼ teaspoon black pepper

2 pounds lean beef, cut
    into 2-inch cubes

2 tablespoons vegetable
    oil

Combine all the ingredients except the beef and oil in a saucepan that is not aluminum. Add the beef and marinate overnight.

Remove the beef and reserve the sauce. In a skillet, heat the oil and brown the beef on all sides.

Add the sauce and simmer, covered, for 45 minutes, or until the beef is tender.

Serve with rice. Makes 4–6 servings.

Beef Adobo with Coconut Milk
ADOBONG CARNE AT GATA

½ cup red wine vinegar or
    cider vinegar

½ cup water

2 cloves garlic, minced

6 peppercorns, crushed

1 teaspoon salt

1 teaspoon ginger,
    julienned

2 pounds stewing beef, cut
    into 2-inch cubes

2 jalapeño peppers, whole

1 12-ounce can coconut
    milk

Combine the vinegar, water, garlic, peppercorns, salt, ginger and beef in a pot and bring it to a boil. For medium or hot spiciness, add the jalapeño peppers at this point. For mild spiciness, add the peppers during the last 10 minutes of cooking. Lower the heat and simmer, covered, for 1 hour, or until the beef is tender. (For extra spiciness, when the meat is cooked, crush the jalapeño peppers against the side of the pan to release their full flavor.)

Add the coconut milk and simmer, uncovered, another 10–15 minutes, until the sauce has thickened.

Serve with rice. Makes 4–6 servings.

Pork and Chicken Adobo
ADOBONG BABOY AT MANOK

Combine the vinegar, salt, pepper, bay leaves and the 6 cloves of garlic in a pot that is not aluminum. Add the chicken and pork and marinate for 1 hour. After marinating, remove the chicken and set aside, leaving the pork in the pot.

Cover the pot, bring the sauce to a boil over medium heat, and simmer for 30–45 minutes, or until the pork is almost tender. Add the chicken and chicken livers and simmer, uncovered, for another 30 minutes, or until the pork and chicken are tender.

Add ½ cup of water to the sauce and bring it to a boil. Remove the pork and chicken and set aside. Remove the chicken livers and grind to a fine paste either in a mortar and pestle or blender or food processor. Add chicken liver paste back to the sauce. Allow the sauce to cool, and skim off any excess fat.

In another pot, sauté the minced garlic in the oil, add the chicken and pork, and brown. Add the soy sauce and reserved adobo sauce, and simmer, covered, for another 10–15 minutes, or until the meats are very tender.

Serve with rice. Makes 6–8 servings.

¾ cup native Philippine vinegar (*sukang paombong*) or ½ cup distilled white vinegar

1 teaspoon salt

1 teaspoon black pepper

3 bay leaves

6 cloves garlic, crushed

2 pounds chicken, cut up

1 pound pork shoulder or pork butt, cut into 2-inch cubes

½ cup water

2 cloves garlic, minced

3 tablespoons vegetable oil

2 tablespoons soy sauce

3 chicken livers, uncooked

Pork Adobo
Adobong Baboy

⅓ cup cider vinegar

2 tablespoons soy sauce

1 teaspoon salt

3 cloves garlic, minced

3 bay leaves

½ teaspoon black pepper

1 tablespoon sugar

½ cup water

1½ pounds pork shoulder or pork butt, cut into 2-inch cubes

2 tablespoons vegetable oil

Combine all the ingredients except the meat and oil in a medium saucepan that is not aluminum. Add the meat to the sauce and marinate for at least 30 minutes.

Simmer, covered, for 1 hour or until the meat is tender. Remove the meat and reserve the sauce.

Heat the oil in a skillet and brown the meat on all sides. Drain off the excess oil. Add the reserved sauce to the meat and heat for a few minutes, stirring and scraping the sides of the skillet.

Serve with rice. Makes 5–6 servings.

VARIATIONS: Let your imagination and creativity run wild. Using the basic recipe, after simmering the meat for an hour, follow the directions below:

Simple adobo: After the meat has marinated, sauté 1 chopped medium onion and 3 minced garlic cloves in the vegetable oil. Add the reserved sauce and cook until it is reduced by ¼. Add the meat and simmer, covered, for 1 hour, or until tender.

Garlic-lovers' adobo: In a skillet, brown 3 crushed garlic cloves in the oil. Add 1 medium onion, sliced thin, and cook until the onion is soft and translucent. Remove the onions and garlic and brown the meat in the same oil. Add the sauce, garlic and onions, and simmer until the liquid is reduced in volume by half, or for a very strong garlic taste, until it is almost dry.

Pork adobo with vegetables: Sauté in the oil 1 minced garlic clove, 1 medium onion, sliced, and 3 chopped medium tomatoes until the onions and tomatoes are soft. Add the meat and brown. Add ½ cup each chopped green and red bell pepper. Pour the sauce over the meat and vegetables and simmer until the peppers slightly wilt. Optional: Add 1 tablespoon shrimp paste.

Pork adobo with potatoes or plantains: Prepare adobo with vegetables, above, and instead of bell peppers, add either 1 cup sliced plantains that have been lightly fried in a small amount of oil, 1 cup of french-fried potatoes, or 1 cup of sliced raw potatoes to the simmering meat and cook for 40–45 minutes or until the potatoes are tender.

Tangy adobo: For extra tanginess, as much as ½ cup of cider vinegar can be used in the marinade.

Adobo fried rice: In a lightly oiled saucepan, heat the leftover rice for a few minutes, add the leftover meat and sauce and stir-fry over medium heat until warmed through.

Leftover adobo: Slice the leftover meat thin, pan fry or broil and serve with fried eggs and the leftover rice for breakfast. Or make a sandwich of the sliced meat and grill it in hot butter until golden brown on both sides.

Fish Adobo
ADOBONG ISDA

4 cloves garlic, crushed

1 tablespoon vegetable oil

2 pounds dressed whole
   catfish, bass or cod

⅓ cup white wine vinegar or
   distilled white vinegar

¼ cup water

1 teaspoon salt

¼ teaspoon black pepper

2 bay leaves

Sauté the garlic in oil (do not brown). Add the fish and all the rest of the ingredients. Bring to a boil over medium heat. Lower the heat and simmer, covered, for about 10 minutes, turning the fish once.

Uncover and continue simmering until the sauce is reduced by half.

Serve with rice. Makes 4 servings.

Squid Adobo
ADOBONG PUSIT

⅓ cup native Philippine vinegar
   or distilled white vinegar

¼ cup water

1½ teaspoons salt

¼ teaspoon black pepper

1 bay leaf

3 cloves garlic, crushed

1 teaspoon sugar

1 pound squid, cleaned and
   gutted, left whole

1 small onion, sliced thin

3 tablespoons vegetable oil

Combine the vinegar, water, salt, pepper, bay leaf, garlic and sugar in a saucepan that is not aluminum. Add the squid and marinate for 1 hour. Remove the squid and reserve the liquid.

In a skillet, sauté the onion in the oil. Add the squid and sauté for 2–3 minutes. Do not overcook.

Pour the reserved liquid over the squid, and simmer for 5 minutes.

Serve with rice. Makes 4–5 servings.

VARIATION:

—For more texture and a dimension of sweet and sour, add 2 quartered, medium tomatoes to the sauce after the squid is sautéed.

Chicken Adobo
ADOBONG MANOK

Heat the oil in a large pot and sauté the garlic and ginger. Add the chicken pieces and lightly brown. Add the vinegar, salt, pepper, water and bay leaves and simmer, covered, for 30 minutes, or until the chicken is tender.

Remove the cover and continue to simmer until the liquid is reduced by half.

Serve with rice. Makes 6–8 servings.

VARIATIONS:

—For more spice, add 1 whole jalapeño pepper to the liquid before simmering the chicken. For a really spicy chicken adobo, cut the pepper into small pieces before adding it to the liquid.

—For a sweet, thick sauce, add ½ cup of canned coconut milk after reducing the adobo sauce, and simmer, uncovered, for a few extra minutes.

—For extra texture and a sweet-and-sour taste, add 1 cup of drained pineapple pieces and 2 medium tomatoes, quartered, after the chicken has simmered and before the sauce has been reduced.

3 teaspoons vegetable oil

1 teaspoon ginger, grated

3 cloves garlic, minced

2½–3 pounds chicken, cut up

½ cup native Philippine vinegar (*sukang paombong*) or distilled white vinegar

1 teaspoon salt

¼ teaspoon black pepper

½ cup water

2 bay leaves

Pork and Shrimp Adobo with Bamboo Shoots
ADOBONG LABONG

2 tablespoons vegetable oil

5 cloves garlic, crushed

1 medium onion, chopped

½ pound pork, ground or minced

½ pound shrimp, shelled and peeled

⅔ cup chicken broth

2 tablespoons fish sauce

3 cups canned bamboo shoots, drained and sliced

4 tablespoons distilled white vinegar

Salt and pepper to taste

In a skillet, heat the oil and sauté the garlic and onions until brown. Add the pork and brown for 5–10 minutes. Drain off the excess oil. Add the shrimp and sauté for 1–2 minutes.

Add the chicken broth and fish sauce and bring to a boil. Add the bamboo shoots, lower the heat, and simmer, uncovered, for 3–4 minutes.

Add the vinegar and simmer for another 15–20 minutes, or until the liquid has reduced by half.

Season with the salt and pepper.

Serve with rice. Makes 3–4 servings.

Eggplant Adobo
ADOBONG TALONG

Cut the eggplants into 1-inch cubes, or if using Japanese eggplants, slice them lengthwise. In a skillet, fry the eggplant in hot oil until it is brown on both sides. Drain on paper towels.

Pour off the excess oil, add the remaining ingredients to the skillet, and simmer for 3–4 minutes. Add the eggplant to the sauce and simmer, covered, for another 5 minutes, stirring or turning the eggplant once.

Serve with rice. Makes 4–6 servings.

VARIATION:

Okra Adobo: Substitute 2 pounds of whole okra for the eggplant and parboil for 2 minutes. Drain well, and sauté the okra in ¼ cup oil for 3–4 minutes. Add the remaining ingredients and simmer for 6–8 minutes. Makes 6–8 servings.

Green Bean Adobo: Substitute 2 pounds of green beans, cut in half, for the eggplant, and parboil for 2–3 minutes. Drain well and sauté the beans in 2 tablespoons of oil for 2–3 minutes. Add the remaining ingredients and simmer for 6–8 minutes. Makes 6–8 servings.

2 medium eggplants or 6 Japanese eggplants
½ cup vegetable oil
½ cup white distilled vinegar
¼ cup soy sauce
¼ teaspoon salt
¼ teaspoon black pepper
4 cloves garlic, minced

Traditional Filipino DISHES

Guinataan
Filipino dishes cooked in coconut milk

The word "coconut" comes from the Portuguese word *"coco"*, meaning monkey or clown. Looking at the three black spots or "eyes" on the end of the nut, you will understand why this is so.

Not only are coconuts valued as the source of coconut milk, but every part of the coconut is useful—the shells are made into utensils and musical instruments; the hairy fibers can be woven into mats, hats, baskets and ropes or made into brooms; the fronds are layered together to make roofs; the oils are used for cooking, and are also made into soap, shampoos, perfumes and facial creams.

Coconut recipes often refer to coconut juice, coconut water, coconut milk and coconut cream. Coconut juice, or coconut water, is the sweet, clear liquid found in the center of fresh coconut. This is not the coconut milk that many people mistake this for. Coconut juice or water is not used for cooking, but is enjoyed fresh out of the coconut. In parts of Southeast Asia and Central America where coconuts grow, tourists are treated to coconuts freshly picked with either their tops lopped off or a hole poked into the top into which a straw is inserted, creating a quick refreshing drink of coconut water.

Then the coconut can be sliced open and the flesh scooped out like gelatin if the coconut is green, or the flesh can be separated from the shell if the coconut is older. The locals dry the meat into a coconut product called copra from which coconut oil is derived and turned into many useful products. Thus the locals not only get paid for opening the coconut for the tourists but for the copra also.

Coconut milk is made from the white meat that has been removed from the mature, brown, hairy coconut. The meat is grated and moistened with water, gathered in a cheesecloth and squeezed hard. This first pressing yields the thick coconut cream, which is used to make thick sauces for sweet and savory dishes and as a thickener for many coconut-based sauces. Coconut oil is derived from this cream and used for frying.

After the coconut cream is squeezed out, more water is added to the coconut meat, and the mixture is again wrung out through the cheesecloth. This second pressing produces thick coconut milk. A third pressing produces a thin coconut milk that takes a very long time to thicken to a proper consistency.

Most cooks in the United States use canned or frozen coconut milk, because it is more readily available and is easier to use in most recipes. The quality of most canned coconut milk is usually good if not excellent. The following are some guidelines for using canned coconut milk:

If a recipe calls for coconut cream, pour the contents of a can of coconut milk into a tall glass without shaking the can. Let it sit until the liquid separates. The coconut cream will float to the top, and can be skimmed off with a spoon. The liquid that settles to the bottom can be used as thin coconut milk.

If a recipe specifies thick coconut milk, shake the can of coconut milk and use as is. For coconut milk of medium thickness, dilute the can with half as much water.

Once opened, coconut milk will keep for only a few days in the refrigerator. The unused portion can be frozen.

Other by-products of coconut milk are *latik* and coconut oil, used in making many Filipino desserts and dishes. To make these, coconut milk is boiled, and then simmered for a long time. As it simmers, the coconut oil will rise to the top, and a cheese-like precipitate will form at the bottom and become a delicate brown color. This is the *latik*. The coconut oil is drained off and used to grease molds and plates, and for frying. The *latik*, with its concentrated coconut flavor, is used to flavor or top many Filipino dishes and desserts.

Crabs in Coconut Milk
GUINATAANG ALIMASAG

2 tablespoons vegetable oil

3 cloves garlic, crushed

1 teaspoon ginger, minced

2 12-ounce cans coconut milk

6 whole blue or rock crabs, well cleaned, or 1 pound crab legs

1 teaspoon salt

⅛ teaspoon ground white pepper

4 green onions, cut into 1-inch lengths

Heat the oil in a large pot and sauté the garlic and ginger.

Add the coconut milk, bring it to a boil, reduce the heat and cook for 15–20 minutes or until the liquid is reduced by half, stirring occasionally.

Add the crabs, salt and pepper to the pot and mix well. Cover the pot and cook for 5 minutes. Add the green onions and simmer for another 3 minutes or until the onions are just tender.

Serve with hot rice. Makes 3–4 servings.

Fish in Coconut Milk
GUINATAANG ISDA

2 pounds milkfish (bangus) or any fleshy fish such as cod or bass, cleaned and dressed

⅓ cup white distilled vinegar

1½ teaspoons salt

2 cloves garlic, crushed

½ teaspoon ginger, crushed

½ teaspoon peppercorns, whole

1 12-ounce can coconut milk

⅛ teaspoon red pepper flakes

Cut the fish into 4 pieces, put in a non-stick skillet, and add the vinegar, salt, garlic, ginger and peppercorns. Bring it to a boil, reduce the heat and simmer, covered, for 10 minutes, turning the fish once during cooking.

Add the coconut milk and red pepper flakes and cook over moderate heat for 5 more minutes. Makes 4 servings.

Shrimp in Coconut Milk
Guinataang Hipon

Using whole shrimp with the heads on gives this dish its extra flavor. If they are not available, be sure to leave the shells on while cooking to get a rich flavor.

Sprinkle the shrimp with the salt and set aside.

In a large pan or skillet, heat the oil and sauté the onion, garlic and ginger for a few minutes.

Add the coconut milk and bring to a boil. Reduce the heat and simmer for 10–15 minutes or until the liquid is reduced by half. Stir occasionally so as not to burn the coconut milk.

Add the unpeeled shrimp, pepper and bell pepper slices. Simmer for another 3–5 minutes, stirring occasionally and very gently, being careful not to damage the heads of the shrimp.

Serve with hot rice. Makes 3–4 servings.

1 pound shrimp, whole and heads on

¾ teaspoon salt

1 tablespoon vegetable oil

1 small onion, chopped

1 clove garlic, crushed

½ teaspoon ginger, minced

2 12-ounce cans coconut milk

⅛ teaspoon ground white pepper or crushed red pepper flakes, if more spice is desired

1 small red or green bell pepper, sliced into thin strips

Squash and Shrimp in Coconut Milk
GUINATAANG KALABASA AT HIPON

1 clove garlic, minced

1 medium onion, sliced

1 tablespoon vegetable oil

2 pounds Japanese, or kabocha, squash, thinly sliced

1 tablespoon fish sauce

¼ teaspoon white pepper

1 12-ounce can coconut milk

¼ cup water

1 tablespoon shrimp paste (*bagoong alamang*)

½ pound small shrimp, peeled

2 tablespoons green onions, finely chopped

The squash for this dish are the shape of a very small pumpkin, green, with a delicate flavor. They are available at Asian markets.

In a saucepan, sauté the garlic and onion in hot oil over medium heat. Add the squash slices, fish sauce and pepper. Stir to mix well and cook for 5 minutes.

Dilute ½ can of coconut milk with the ¼ cup of water (save the rest of the milk for use later). Add this mixture to the squash.

Stir in the shrimp paste, cover and simmer for 20 minutes or until the squash is tender.

Add the shrimp and the rest of the coconut milk. Simmer for 3–5 minutes more. Correct seasonings with more shrimp paste if desired.

Sprinkle with the chopped green onions. Makes 5–6 servings.

Eggplant in Coconut Milk
GUINATAANG TALONG

Roast the eggplants over charcoals or in a broiler until the skin burns on all sides. When the eggplant is cool, peel off any remaining burnt skin and chop it fine.

Add the chopped onion and the vinegar and mix well. Season with the salt and pepper.

Pour the coconut milk into a saucepan and bring to a light boil. Add the eggplant mixture and cook, covered, for 5 minutes.

Remove from heat and serve at room temperature. Makes 4–5 servings.

4 Japanese eggplants

1 small onion, chopped

1 tablespoon distilled white vinegar

½ teaspoon salt

½ teaspoon black pepper

½ cup coconut milk

Vegetables in Coconut Milk
GUINATAANG GULAY

1 clove garlic, minced

1 tablespoon ginger, julienned

1 small onion, chopped

1 tablespoon vegetable oil

2 Japanese eggplants or 1 medium eggplant (approx. 1 pound), cut into ½-inch cubes

½ pound green beans, cut into 2-inch lengths

2 tablespoons shrimp paste

1 12-ounce can coconut milk

½ pound small shrimp, peeled, deveined and chopped

1 jalapeño, finely chopped (optional)

In a medium saucepan, sauté the garlic, ginger and onion in the oil until the onion is translucent. Add the eggplant and green beans and cook for 2–3 minutes, stirring frequently.

Add the shrimp paste and coconut milk, stir well, cover and simmer for 5 minutes or until the vegetables are tender.

Add the shrimp and hot pepper if desired, and simmer, uncovered, for 2 more minutes. Correct the seasonings with more shrimp paste if desired. Makes 3–4 servings.

Traditional Filipino
DISHES

Kilawin

Kilawin, also known as *kinilaw,* comes from the root word *"hilaw,"* meaning raw. *Kilawin* are pickled meat or seafood dishes that are tangy and savory. The meat, fish or shellfish, which must be very fresh, is marinated in acids such as vinegar and *kalamansi* juice to "cook" the delicate flesh. Chopped raw onions, chili peppers and herbs such as cilantro are sometimes added to enhance the flavor. *Kilawin* is best made in advance and allowed to age and mellow in the refrigerator for a few days.

Pickled Pork Liver
Kilawin

1½ cups pork liver, diced

1 cup native Philippine vinegar *(sukang paombong)* or distilled white vinegar

1 teaspoon salt

1½ teaspoons black pepper

2 cups water

2 cups pork, diced

6 cloves garlic, crushed

2 tablespoons vegetable oil

1 medium onion, sliced

Marinate the liver in ½ cup of the vinegar, salt and pepper for 5 minutes.

Put the water in a saucepan and bring to a boil. Add the diced pork and cook over medium heat until the pork is tender, about 10 minutes. Remove the pork and reserve ½ cup of the pork broth.

In a skillet, sauté the garlic in the oil until it is light brown. Add the sliced onions and sauté until the onions are translucent.

Add the liver and marinade liquid to the onions and garlic, and stir-fry for about 3 minutes. Press the liver with the back of a wooden spoon to squeeze the juice out of the liver.

Add the pork and stir-fry another 2 minutes, pressing the pork to release any excess liquid.

Add ½ cup of vinegar and the ½ cup of the reserved broth and simmer for 3 more minutes.

Season to taste with salt and pepper. Makes 3–4 servings.

Pickled Tripe and Liver
KILAWIN GOTO AT ATAY

Place the tripe in a deep pot, cover with water and boil for 5 minutes. Drain and rinse it. Place the tripe back in the pot and cover with water again. Bring to a boil, reduce the heat and simmer, covered, for 2½ hours or until tender. Drain. Cool to room temperature. Cut into strips ¼ inch thick by 2 inches long.

In a bowl, marinate the liver strips in a mixture of the vinegar, salt and pepper for 10 minutes. Drain well and reserve the marinade liquid.

Sauté the garlic, onions and tomatoes in the oil for 2 minutes. Add the liver and sauté for another 3 minutes, pressing it with the back of a wooden spoon to extract some of the juice.

Add the marinade liquid, tripe slices and sugar, mix well, and simmer for 5 minutes. Add the radishes and optional red pepper flakes and continue to simmer until the radish is tender, another 8–10 minutes.

If possible, refrigerate for 1 or 2 days to let it age or mellow. Reheat to simmering before serving. Makes 4–6 servings.

1 pound tripe

½ pound beef liver, sliced into strips ¼-inch thick by 2 inches long

½ cup distilled white vinegar

1¼ teaspoons salt

¼ teaspoon black pepper

3 cloves garlic, minced

1 small onion, chopped

2 medium tomatoes, chopped

2 tablespoons vegetable oil

1 teaspoon sugar

1 pound daikon or red radishes, peeled and thinly sliced

⅛ teaspoon red pepper flakes (optional)

Pickled Pig's Ear
Kilawin Baboy

1 medium-sized pig's ear

2 cups vegetable oil

2 cakes tofu, 1 inch thick by 4 inches long by 3 inches wide

¼ cup soy sauce

¼ cup distilled white vinegar

2 cloves garlic, minced

This makes a good accompaniment to Rice Stick Noodles in Red Sauce (Pancit Luglug, page 82) or any rice dish.

Thoroughly scrape and wash the pig's ear to remove any dirt and hair. Place in a pan, cover with water and simmer for 30 minutes or until tender. Pour off the water and allow to cool. Cut into thin slices about 1 inch long. Discard the tough membranes and the inner ear section.

Heat the oil in a skillet and deep-fry the tofu. Do not touch the tofu with a utensil until it is golden brown. Drain on paper towels and cut into 1-inch cubes.

Place the pig's ear and tofu in a bowl, add the soy sauce, vinegar and garlic and mix well. Marinate for at least 20 minutes.

Makes about 8–10 one-tablespoon servings.

VARIATION:

Boiled and deboned pork hock may be used in place of the pig's ear.

Pickled Radish with Pork and Shrimp
Kilawin Labanos

Peel the daikon or radishes and slice paper thin. Sprinkle with 1½ teaspoons of the salt. Mix the radish slices and salt by hand, working the salt well into the radishes. Rinse with water and drain.

Remove the heads and shells and devein the shrimp. Put the heads and shells in a saucepan with the water and bring to a boil. Reduce the heat and simmer for 5 minutes. Remove the heads and shells from the broth and add the peeled shrimp. Cook for only 1 minute. Remove the shrimp and set aside. Reserve ½ cup of the shrimp broth.

Heat the oil in a skillet and fry the pork until light brown. Remove the pork and set aside. Sauté the garlic, onions and tomatoes in the same pan for a few minutes. Add the shrimp and ½ teaspoon of the salt. Sauté for 3 minutes.

Add the cooked pork and reserved shrimp broth. Cook over medium heat for 2 minutes, stirring constantly. Add the radishes, cover, and cook for about 10 minutes or until radishes just start to turn tender.

Add the vinegar and pepper, bring to a boil and immediately remove from heat.

Serve with rice. Makes 3–4 servings.

1 pound Japanese daikon or red radishes

2 teaspoons salt

12 whole shrimp

1 cup water

1 tablespoon vegetable oil

½ pound pork, cut into ½-inch cubes

1 clove garlic, crushed

½ cup onion, sliced

½ cup tomatoes, diced

¼ cup white distilled vinegar

½ teaspoon black pepper

Pickled Shrimp
Kilawin Hipon

1 cup water

1 teaspoon salt

12 large shrimp, peeled and deveined

½ cup distilled white vinegar

1 small onion, or 2 shallots, finely diced

2 cloves garlic, crushed

5 peppercorns, crushed

Put the water and salt in a small pan, bring to a boil, add the shrimp and cook for only 15–30 seconds. Immediately stop the cooking process by dropping the shrimp in ice water. Do not overcook the shrimp.

Put the drained shrimp in a bowl and add the vinegar, onions, garlic and peppercorns. Mix well. Cover the bowl with plastic wrap and marinate for at least 2 hours. Marinating for 2–3 days in the refrigerator will allow the flavor to mellow.

Serve cold. Makes 3–4 servings.

Pickled Oysters
Kilawin Talaba

½ cup white distilled vinegar

1 small onion, or 2 shallots, finely diced

2 cloves garlic, crushed

5 peppercorns, coarsely crushed

1 teaspoon salt

12 large oysters, shelled

In a bowl, mix together the vinegar, onion, garlic, peppercorns and salt. Add the oysters, mix well, and marinate for 2–3 hours in the refrigerator.

Place the oyster mixture in a saucepan and bring to a gentle simmering boil. When the edges of the oysters just start to curl, immediately remove them from the heat so they do not overcook. If the liquid is too sour, dilute with a little water.

Transfer the oysters and the marinade liquid to a ceramic bowl, cover, and refrigerate for at least 1 hour. The pickled oysters are best after 2–3 days in the refrigerator.

Serve cold. Makes 3–4 servings.

Pickled Radish and Vegetables
KILAWIN LABANOS

This is a delicious vegetable side dish. Its flavor improves if it is allowed to refrigerate for a day or two before serving.

Peel and slice the radishes paper-thin. Sprinkle with salt and work the salt in by hand. Rinse well and drain.

Mix the vinegar, sugar and black pepper together in a cup and pour over the radishes. Refrigerate for at least 1 hour.

Add the diced tomatoes and onions to the radishes just before serving, if desired.

Serve cold. Makes 3–4 servings.

1 pound red radishes or Japanese daikon

1½ teaspoons salt

¼ cup distilled white vinegar or native Philippine vinegar *(sukang paombong)*

2 teaspoons sugar

½ teaspoon black pepper

1 medium tomato, diced (optional)

1 medium onion, diced (optional)

Traditional Filipino DISHES

Lumpia
Filipino Egg Rolls or Springrolls

There are two versions: a fresh *Lumpia* in which a crepe-like wrapper is stuffed with cooked meats and vegetables, creating a tender yet crispy dish, and a fried *Lumpia*, definitely like a Chinese egg roll.

At most Filipino parties, the center of attention is the food. As many Filipino mothers and grandmothers show love to their family by cooking wonderful dishes, guests are honored at parties by the presence of an abundant amount of food.

When you are eight years old and less than three feet tall, everything looks large. I remember at these parties aircraft-carrier-sized tables laden down with different sizes and shapes of *lumpia* of every kind, with at least several different sauces to accompany them. It was a great experience, bordering on sensory overload. Visually, it was a wondrous eyeful that would have made Bacchus, the Roman god of food and wine, smile. Oh, and the smells that emanated from the tables and kitchen and wafted through the house and outdoors to the neighbors, alerting them to the impending party, were absolutely heavenly. If heaven were to have a smell, I would think it would smell like *lumpia*. But then came the tastes! Despite the *lumpia*, both fresh and fried, looking alike, the different fillings and sauces made each bite a surprise in flavor and texture. Somehow each bite was better than the last. Mind you, at Filipino parties there was more than just *lumpia* being served. There were always a few other tables overflowing with fish, meats, stews and desserts. It's just that *lumpia* has always occupied a special place in my memories of parties.

Not only was eating *lumpia* great fun, but I always enjoyed making them with older members of the family. There would always be a party before the party in which members of the immediate and extended family would gather together to wrap or roll *lumpia*. Mother, father, aunts, uncles, older cousins and close friends of the family, who would insist on your calling them "auntie" and "uncle," would gather on an evening a few days before the party. The coolness of the night would allow the *lumpia* wrappers to remain pliable, people were apt to be available in the evening, and the host of the party would have had the whole day to prepare the different *lumpia* fillings. The "family" would gather and the tedious task of wrapping the *lumpia* was lightened with conversation, gossip and an occasional song. *Lumpia* is so popular for parties because they can be made in advance, frozen and, while still frozen, fried just before being served. Most Filipinos keep *lumpia* in their freezer not only for parties but just in case guests unexpectedly drop by and they need something to serve them quickly.

Many people eat fried *lumpia* with their fingers or wrap them in a paper napkin and then dip them in a sauce. I've always preferred the Vietnamese way—wrap a fresh lettuce leaf around the *lumpia* before dipping it in the sauce. The lettuce not only adds an extra bit of texture, it keeps the oil off of one's fingers and cools the hot filling. Try them both ways. No matter which way you like *lumpia*, they're always a great treat to eat.

There are two versions of *lumpia*: a fresh *lumpia*, or springroll, that consists of a crepe-like wrapper stuffed with cooked meats or fish and vegetables, and the fried *lumpia*, or egg roll, also stuffed with meats, fish and vegetables. The fried *lumpia* can be made far in advance of cooking, frozen, and then fried without thawing.

There are a variety of excellent manufactured wrappers, dried or frozen, available at many Asian food stores. For the truly expert *lumpia* maker, there is a round wrapper, much more delicate in texture, that when fried, results in a crispier *lumpia*. The problem is that the wrapper is very delicate, and because it dries out and tears easily, one must work quickly and carefully. The advantage is that it makes a very superior *lumpia*.

There is nothing like homemade *lumpia* wrappers. The recipe and technique are similar to making crepes, except that the wrappers are not allowed to brown. Be patient, it takes practice to make them well, but once you get the knack, they are simple, and your friends and family will be delighted with the fruits of your efforts.

Fresh Springrolls #1
Lumpiang Sariwa #1

1 clove garlic, minced

1 medium onion, diced

2 tablespoons vegetable oil

½ pound pork, diced

½ cup water

1 teaspoon salt

1 tablespoon fish sauce

½ teaspoon black pepper

1 medium potato, peeled and diced

½ cup green beans, french cut

½ cup cabbage, shredded

½ cup jicama

½ cup peanuts, shelled, toasted and finely chopped

½ pound shrimp, peeled and diced

15–20 small lettuce leaves

15–20 egg wrappers for fresh *lumpia*

3–4 tablespoons minced garlic

In a skillet, sauté the garlic and onions in the oil. Add the pork and sauté until fat starts to render out. Add the water, bring to a boil, reduce the heat and cover. Simmer for 10 minutes, or until the pork is tender. Add the salt, fish sauce and pepper.

Add the potatoes and cook for 5–7 minutes. Add the green beans, cabbage, jicama, peanuts and shrimp. Stir-fry for 5–10 minutes or until the vegetables are tender. Add salt and pepper to taste if desired.

Remove from the heat and let cool to room temperature.

TO ASSEMBLE:

If wrappers are not available commercially, see the recipes for making your own egg wrappers (page 40–41). Also, you will need 3–4 tablespoons of fresh, minced garlic and the sauce for fresh springrolls (page 234).

Place a lettuce leaf at the center of an egg wrapper. On top, place 2 heaping tablespoons of the pork and vegetable filling. Fold the bottom part of the wrapper over the filling, wrap one side of the wrapper over the filling and roll to the other side to make a neat package with the top part of the lettuce protruding out the open end of the roll. Seal the edge with a few drops of water.

Cut waxed paper into pieces slightly larger than the springrolls and wrap each similar to the technique for assembling the *lumpia*. This prevents the springrolls from sticking to each other and drying out.

To eat the springroll, remove the wax paper or fold it back and use it like a napkin. Into the open end, drizzle some Sauce for Fresh Springrolls (page 234), along with a small sprinkling of the minced garlic. Makes 15–20 springrolls.

Fresh Springrolls #2
Lumpiang Sariwa #2

In a skillet, heat the ½ cup of oil. Add the tofu cubes, being careful not to disturb them until they are golden brown. Drain the tofu on paper towels.

In another large skillet or saucepan, heat the 2 tablespoons of oil and sauté the garlic and onion for 1–2 minutes. Add the pork and sauté until it is tender, about 5 minutes.

Add the chicken broth and bring to a boil. Add the potatoes and carrots, cover and cook for 5–7 minutes or until the potatoes are just tender.

Add the cabbage and sugar and simmer, covered, for 3–5 minutes. Add the garbanzo beans, shrimp, lima beans, Spanish sausage, ham and tofu. Let simmer for another 7–10 minutes. Season with the soy sauce, salt and pepper.

Let cool and wrap 2 tablespoons of the filling with lettuce and the fresh wrapper. (See directions for Fresh Springrolls #1, page 26). Wrap in wax paper. Serve with Vinegar and Garlic Dipping Sauce (page 234) spooned into the open end of the springroll. Makes 20–25 springrolls.

½ cup vegetable oil

1 cup tofu, cut into ¼-inch cubes

2 tablespoons vegetable oil

3 cloves garlic, crushed

1 cup onion, diced

½ pound pork, sliced into thin, short strips

1 cup chicken broth

1 cup potatoes, diced

½ cup carrots, julienned

2 cups cabbage, shredded

1 teaspoon sugar

1 8-ounce can garbanzo beans (chickpeas), drained

½ pound shrimp, peeled and diced

1 8-ounce can lima beans, drained

1 Spanish sausage (chorizo *de Bilbao*), diced

¼ cup ham, diced

1 tablespoon soy sauce

½ teaspoon salt

½ teaspoon black pepper

20–25 egg wrappers for fresh *lumpia*

20–25 fresh lettuce leaves

Fresh Springrolls with Bamboo Shoots
LUMPIA AT LABONG

5 cups tofu, cut into ½-inch cubes

2 cups + 2 tablespoons vegetable oil

6 cloves garlic, crushed

2 cups onions, diced

3 teaspoons pimientos, sliced or chopped

1 pound pork, sliced into short, thin strips

1 pound shrimp, peeled and chopped

½ cup chicken broth

1 16-ounce can shredded bamboo shoots, drained

Salt and pepper to taste

20–25 fresh lettuce leaves

20–25 egg wrappers for fresh *lumpia*

In a skillet, fry the tofu cubes in 2 cups of the hot oil, being careful not to disturb them until they are golden brown. Drain the tofu on paper towels.

In another skillet, heat the 2 tablespoons of oil and sauté the garlic, onions and pimientos until soft, about 2–3 minutes. Add the pork and cook for 5 minutes. Add the shrimp and chicken broth and cook for another 3–5 minutes.

Add the tofu and bamboo shoots to the pork and shrimp mixture and simmer for 5–10 minutes. Season to taste with salt and pepper. Remove from the heat and allow to cool.

Place a lettuce leaf in the middle of the egg wrapper, place 2 heaping tablespoons of the filling on the leaf and wrap, leaving one end open. (See directions for Fresh Springrolls #1, page 26.)

Serve with the Sauce for Fresh Springrolls (page 234). Makes 20–25 springrolls.

Fresh Springrolls with Green Papaya
LUMPIA AT PAPAYA

The papaya used here should be very green, and firm in texture, with no sign of yellow or softness. It is used like a vegetable, not a fruit. If green papayas are not available, chayote can be substituted. (In Louisiana, chayote is known as mirliton.)

Shred or grate the papaya or chayote, add the salt and mix thoroughly by hand. Let sit for a few minutes. Then rinse off the salt and squeeze the papaya dry in a towel. (This helps remove some of the bitterness.)

Sauté the garlic in hot oil for 1 minute, and add the onions, pork and shrimp. Continue sautéing until the pork is almost cooked, about 4–5 minutes.

Stir in the chicken broth and bring to a boil. Add the papaya, mix well and cover. Simmer for 10 minutes, or until the papaya is tender.

Add the soy sauce and annatto oil or water and mix well. Add salt to taste.

Let the mixture cool. Place a lettuce leaf on each wrapper, and put 2 heaping tablespoons of the filling on each leaf and wrap. (See directions for Fresh Springrolls #1, page 26.)

Serve with the Sauce for Fresh Springrolls (page 234). Makes 12 springrolls.

3 cups green papaya, or chayote, finely shredded

1 tablespoon salt

2 cloves garlic, finely chopped

2 tablespoons vegetable oil

½ cup onions, diced

½ pound pork, sliced into small, thin strips

½ pound shrimp, peeled and chopped

½ cup chicken broth

2 tablespoons soy sauce

2 tablespoons annatto oil or water

12 fresh lettuce leaves

12 wrappers for fresh springrolls

Fried Egg Rolls #1
Lumpiang Frito #1

2 cloves garlic, minced

1 cup onions, chopped

2 tablespoons vegetable oil

1 pound ground beef

1 teaspoon salt

½ teaspoon black pepper

1 tablespoon fish sauce

1 cup water

1 medium potato, peeled and diced

½ cup carrots, peeled and julienned

½ cup green beans, french cut

½ cup celery, diced

1 cup bean sprouts

20–25 frozen wrappers for Chinese egg rolls or springrolls, thawed

Because fried egg rolls freeze and store so well, it is best to make extra and store them in the freezer. They are great to have on hand when guests drop by unexpectedly.

In a skillet, sauté the garlic and onions in hot oil until the onions are translucent. Add the ground beef, salt, pepper and fish sauce and sauté until the beef is browned.

Drain the excess oil from the pan, add the water and bring to boil. Add the potatoes and carrots and simmer for 5–10 minutes. Add the green beans and celery and simmer for another 5 minutes. The vegetables should be slightly crisp.

Remove the pan from the heat and add the bean sprouts. Allow the mixture to cool to room temperature.

INSTRUCTIONS FOR ASSEMBLY:

Separate the individual sheets of wrappers, being careful not to tear them. Keep them moist and pliable during assembly by storing them in a plastic bag or under a moist towel. Do not allow them to dry out and become brittle.

Place 2 heaping tablespoons of the filling diagonally near one corner of the wrapper, leaving a 1½-inch edge of space at both ends. Fold the side along the length of the filling over the filling, tuck in both ends, and roll neatly. Moisten the other side of the wrapper with water or egg to seal the edge.

The egg rolls can be fried immediately or frozen for later use.

If frying them immediately, cover them with plastic wrap or a moist towel to keep the wrappers from drying out.

If freezing them, wrap them heavily with plastic wrap to prevent freezer burn, putting plastic wrap between layers. They can be stored in the freezer for up to 2 months. Do not thaw the frozen egg rolls before frying them. Just separate them and fry them while still frozen.

TO FRY EGG ROLLS:

Heat a skillet over medium heat, add oil to about ½-inch depth, and heat for 5–10 minutes. When the oil is hot, place 3–4 egg rolls in, gently, to prevent splashing the hot oil. Fry the rolls for 3–4 minutes on each side, or until all sides are golden brown. Place on paper towels to drain excess oil.

SUGGESTED DIPPING SAUCES TO SERVE WITH EGG ROLLS:

Catsup

Sweet and Sour Sauce (page 233)

Sauce for Egg Rolls (page 233)

Vinegar and Garlic Dipping Sauce (page 234)

Fried Egg Rolls #2
LUMPIANG FRITO #2

3 cloves garlic, crushed

2 medium onions, diced

2 medium tomatoes, diced

2 tablespoons vegetable oil

1 pound ground beef

½ pound ground pork

½ pound ham, diced

3 bay leaves

1 cup water

Salt

White pepper

1 12-ounce can garbanzo beans (chickpeas), drained

½ cup raisins

1 2-ounce can pimientos, drained and chopped, or ½ red bell pepper, finely diced

3 eggs, hard-boiled and chopped

20 egg roll wrappers

20 lettuce leaves (optional)

In a large skillet or saucepan, sauté the garlic, onions and tomatoes in hot oil. When the vegetables are tender add the beef, pork, ham, bay leaves and water. Simmer until the meat is almost cooked, about 30 minutes. Add salt and pepper to taste.

Add the garbanzos, raisins and pimientos, and cook for another 5 minutes. Remove the bay leaves and remove the excess fat with a spoon. Set the filling aside and allow to cool to room temperature.

Just before assembling the egg rolls, mix in the chopped eggs.

Wrap and fry the egg rolls as instructed in Fried Egg Rolls #1 (page 30). Serve with the Vinegar and Garlic Dipping Sauce (page 234), catsup, or Sweet and Sour Sauce (page 233).

If desired, serve the lettuce leaves so that guests can wrap their egg rolls in a fresh lettuce leaf for extra crunch and freshness. Makes 20 egg rolls.

Fried Egg Rolls #3
LUMPIANG FRITO #3

If using dried mushrooms, soak them in water for 30 minutes. Drain and finely chop them.

Heat the oil in a skillet and sauté the onions until they are soft. Add the ground beef and sauté until brown. Drain off the excess fat.

Add the shrimp or crab meat and sauté for 5 minutes. Add the green beans and sauté for another 5 minutes. Add the garbanzo beans, mushrooms, and salt and pepper to taste. Mix well. Remove from the heat and allow the filling to cool to room temperature.

Wrap and fry the egg rolls as described in Fried Egg Rolls #1 (page 30). Drain them on paper towels.

Serve with catsup or Sweet and Sour Sauce (page 233). Makes 20 egg rolls.

½ cup fresh or dried shiitake mushrooms, finely chopped

2 tablespoons vegetable oil

1 small onion, diced

1 pound lean ground beef

¼ pound shrimp, peeled and diced, or crabmeat, flaked, or imitation crabmeat, finely chopped

½ cup green beans, thinly sliced lengthwise

1 12-ounce can garbanzo beans (chickpeas), drained

Salt

White pepper

20 egg roll wrappers

Fried Egg Rolls with Pork
Lumpiang Shanghai

1 pound ground pork

½ pound shrimp, peeled and chopped

¼ cup dried shiitake mushrooms, soaked in water for 30 minutes and chopped

½ cup jicama, peeled and julienned, or 1 12-ounce can water chestnuts, drained and finely chopped

¼ cup green onions, chopped

2 egg yolks

3 tablespoons soy sauce

1 teaspoon sesame oil

Salt and pepper to taste

12 egg roll wrappers

The open ends of this lumpia *are its hallmark.*

Combine all the ingredients except the wrappers in a bowl and mix well with your hands. NOTE: The filling is not cooked before it is placed in the wrapper.

TO WRAP: Cut a square egg roll wrapper in half to form a rectangle. Along the long end of the wrapper, place a thin line of filling. Then roll lengthwise like a cigar and seal with water. The ends of the wrapper are left open.

Fry in hot oil until golden brown on all sides, about 3–5 minutes. Drain on paper towels and cut into 1½-inch pieces.

Serve with Sweet and Sour Sauce (page 233). Makes 12 egg rolls.

Steamed Pork Dumplings
LUMPIANG MACAO

Combine all the ingredients except the wonton wrappers in a bowl and mix well.

To assemble, place 1 heaping tablespoon of the filling on the center of each wrapper. Lift the edges up and around the filling, leaving an opening at the top.

Put the dumplings on a plate in a steamer. Be sure to leave space around each to prevent them from sticking to each other. Steam for 15 minutes.

Serve with a dipping sauce of 3 tablespoons of soy sauce and the juice of half a lemon; if available, use *kalamansi* and dark Filipino soy sauce. Add bits of finely chopped jalapeño pepper or a few dashes of hot chili oil to the sauce for extra spice. Makes 20–25 dumplings.

1 pound ground pork

½ pound shrimp, peeled and chopped

1 pound crab meat, chopped, or imitation crab meat, finely diced

3 tablespoons cornstarch

2 tablespoons soy sauce

2 eggs

1 teaspoon sesame oil

3 tablespoons chopped green onions

6 shiitake mushrooms, soaked in water for 30 minutes, the stems removed, and chopped fine

1 8–ounce can water chestnuts, drained and chopped, or 1 cup jicama, peeled and finely shredded

30 round wonton wrappers (do not use *lumpia* wrappers)

Fried Egg Rolls with Milkfish
LUMPIANG BANGUS

2 2-pound milkfish *(bangus)*, or 3 pounds cod, or any fleshy white fish such as bass

2 tablespoons salt

3 cloves garlic, crushed

1 cup onion, diced

2 tablespoons vegetable oil

3 small tomatoes, diced

¼ cup raisins

Salt

White pepper

20–25 egg roll wrappers

Vegetable oil

Clean and gut the fish, discarding the heads and tails. Cut each into 3 or 4 pieces. Put the fish into a pot, cover them with water, add the 2 tablespoons of salt, and bring to a boil. Cook for 15–20 minutes. Remove the fish from the water and allow to cool. When cool enough to handle, separate the flesh from the bones and set aside. NOTE: Milkfish are very bony.

In a skillet, sauté the garlic and onions in hot oil until the onions are translucent. Add the tomatoes and cook for 5 minutes.

Add the fish and raisins, season with salt and pepper to taste, set aside and allow to cool.

Wrap and fry the eggrolls as directed in Fried Egg Rolls #1, (page 30).

These can be frozen for later use. Simply wrap them thoroughly in plastic wrap to prevent freezer burn. Do not thaw frozen egg rolls before frying them. Makes 20–25 egg rolls.

Stuffed Shrimp #1
RELLENONG CAMARONES #1

Peel and devein the shrimp, keeping the tails attached. Sprinkle with the salt and set aside.

In a bowl, combine all the rest of the filling ingredients and mix well.

In another bowl, mix the batter of water, egg whites, cornstarch and salt.

To assemble, surround each shrimp with 2–3 tablespoons of the filling and dip each into the batter, holding it by the tail.

Heat the vegetable oil in a skillet until hot. Fry the shrimp until they are golden brown, about 3–5 minutes. Drain on paper towels.

Serve hot with catsup or Sweet and Sour Sauce (page 233). Makes 6–8 servings.

2 pounds large, headless shrimp (about 32–35 pieces)

1 teaspoon salt

2 cups water chestnuts, chopped, or jicama, peeled and julienned

6 dried shiitake mushrooms, soaked in water for 30 minutes, and cut into thin strips

½ pound ground pork

1 cup carrots, julienned

1 cup green onions, cut in half lengthwise and into 1-inch lengths

1 cup ham, julienned

1 teaspoon white pepper

3 tablespoons soy sauce

2 teaspoons sugar

2 egg yolks

2 tablespoons cornstarch

1 teaspoon sesame oil

BATTER:

¼ cup water

3 egg whites

¾ cup cornstarch

½ teaspoon salt

2 cups vegetable oil

Stuffed Shrimp #2
RELLENONG CAMARONES #2

12 large headless shrimp

½ pound ground pork

¼ cup green onions, finely chopped

1 teaspoon salt

1 teaspoon black pepper

12 wonton wrappers

1 egg, slightly beaten

2 cups vegetable oil

Peel and devein the shrimp, leaving the tails attached.

Mix the ground pork, green onions, salt and pepper together.

Surround each shrimp with 1 tablespoon of the filling.

Wrap in wonton wrappers. Seal with the beaten egg. Allow the tail to show through an open end.

Heat the oil and fry until they are golden brown, or 3–5 minutes.

Serve with catsup or Sweet and Sour Sauce (page 233). Makes 3–4 servings.

Traditional Filipino DISHES

Egg Wrappers

There are a variety of excellent manufactured wrappers for fried egg rolls available dried or frozen at many Asian food stores. But, when making fresh springrolls there is no substitute for making one's own egg wrappers. The recipes and technique are similar to making crepes, except that the egg wrappers aren't allowed to brown. It takes a lot of practice to make a proper egg wrapper, but once you get going, they are simple and your friends and family will hopefully appreciate the fruits of your efforts.

Egg Wrapper #1

3 eggs
¼ teaspoon salt
2 cups flour
2 cups milk
¼ cup vegetable oil

In a medium-sized mixing bowl, combine the eggs and salt. Gradually add the flour, alternating with the milk, beating with a whisk until smooth.

Beat in the oil gradually.

Refrigerate the batter for at least 1 hour.

Brush a warm non-stick crepe pan with oil and place over low to medium heat. Ladle 2 tablespoons of the batter into the pan. Swirl the pan to evenly and thinly coat the bottom. Pour any excess back into the bowl. Cook until the wrapper can be easily lifted from the pan, about 1 minute. (If bubbles form, the pan is too hot.) Turn over just long enough to warm the other side. The cooking time will vary according to the weather and the skill of the cook. Note: One needs to practice with this or any other crepe recipe.

Place the cooked wrapper on a plate and cover with a moist towel. Repeat as before until all batter is cooked. Makes 20 wrappers.

Egg Wrapper #2
FOR MAKING FRESH SPRINGROLLS

This wrapper is slightly crisper and thinner than the previous one, and takes more practice to get just right. The secret is to take it off the heat before it is so crisp it won't fold.

In a bowl, separate the egg yolks from the whites. Beat the whites until they are frothy. Add the yolks and beat until just blended together.

In another bowl, add the cornstarch to the water and mix well. Add this mixture to the beaten eggs and mix well. Let stand for 5–10 minutes to allow the bubbles to settle.

Brush a hot, non-stick crepe pan with the oil. Place over low to medium heat.

Give the batter a quick stir, pour 2 tablespoons of the batter into the pan and quickly tip the pan from side to side to spread the batter into a thin 7–8" wrapper. Cook until the wrapper can be lifted easily from the pan, about 1 minute. Too hot a skillet will cause bubbles. Adjust the temperature as needed.

Proceed with the rest of the batter, adding oil to the pan as needed and stacking wrappers on a plate and covering with a moist towel until ready to use. Makes about 20 wrappers.

3 large eggs
¾ cup cornstarch
½ cup water
½ cup vegetable oil

Traditional Filipino DISHES

Merienda

Of all the customs Filipinos have adopted from the Spanish, two daily practices stand out: the siesta and the *merienda.* The siesta is the afternoon nap taken to preserve one's energies in the tropical heat when the afternoon sun is at its hottest. Unfortunately, in today's busy world, the siesta has become impractical. The *merienda,* a light meal taken at mid-morning or mid-afternoon, is used to restore one's energies through nourishment. The *merienda* is still a must for many Filipinos.

Anything can be served for the *merienda:* a plate of sautéed noodles *(pancit)*, a bowl of chocolate rice porridge *(champorado)*, a fire-roasted banana on a stick (a banana-cue), a sandwich, a slice of cake and cup of coffee, a glass of *Halo-halo,* or a handful of cookies, and soft drinks. Any of the following dishes might be found in a typical *merienda*.

Wheat Flour Tea Cake
BIBINGKANG ESPECIAL

Preheat oven to 350° F.

Grease two 8-inch layer cake pans with the butter or margarine. Line bottoms with wax paper or banana leaves. If using banana leaves, pass them over a flame to make the leaves soft and pliable.

Sift the flour, baking powder and salt together and set aside.

In a large mixing bowl, beat the eggs until light and creamy. Gradually add the cup of sugar, about ¼ cup at a time, beating well after each addition. Add the sifted flour mixture slowly, alternating additions of flour with the coconut milk. Beat well to blend thoroughly. Add 2 tablespoons of the melted butter or margarine and mix well.

Pour the batter into the lined pans, spreading it thin and evenly. Bake for 15 minutes in the oven. Then sprinkle the grated cheese over the top of each cake and bake for 10 minutes more.

Remove the cakes from the oven and immediately brush each with the remaining 2 tablespoons of melted butter or margarine. Mix the 1 tablespoon of sugar with the grated coconut and sprinkle the top of each cake with the mixture.

Serve warm. Makes 6–8 servings.

2 tablespoons butter or margarine

2 cups white flour

2 teaspoons baking powder

1 teaspoon salt

3 eggs

1 cup + 1 tablespoon sugar

1¼ cups coconut milk

4 tablespoons butter or margarine, melted

¼ cup mild cheddar cheese, grated

4 tablespoons grated fresh coconut

2 sheets of wax paper or banana leaves, cut into 10-inch squares

Rice Flour Tea Cake
BIBINGKANG GALAPONG

BATTER:

16 ounces sweet rice flour

½ cup butter, melted

2 cups sugar

4 eggs, slightly beaten

12 ounces coconut milk

2½ cups milk

14 ounces evaporated milk

1 tablespoon vanilla extract

TOPPING:

3 tablespoons butter or margarine, melted

4 tablespoons sugar

4 tablespoons mild cheddar cheese, grated

4 tablespoons grated fresh coconut

2 banana leaves, cut into 10-inch by 14-inch rectangles

2 9-inch by 13-inch shallow layer cake pans

Preheat oven to 250° F.

Pass the banana leaves over a flame to make them pliable. Line the cake pans with the softened leaves.

In a large bowl, combine all the ingredients for the batter and stir well until thoroughly blended.

Pour the batter equally into the two lined pans and bake for 3 hours at 250° F or until the top is a light golden brown and a toothpick inserted in the center comes out clean.

Remove the cakes from the oven and brush the tops with the melted butter. Raise the oven temperature to 325° F. Sprinkle each cake equally with sugar and grated cheese and return to the oven for 15–20 minutes to melt the cheese.

Remove from the oven and sprinkle with the grated fresh coconut. Place on racks and allow to cool slightly.

To serve, cut into 2-inch squares. Makes approximately 48 squares.

Cassava Tea Cake
Bibingkang Kamoteng-Kahoy

Preheat oven to 350° F.

Combine all the ingredients for the batter and mix thoroughly. Pour the batter into a foil-lined 8-inch layer pan.

Bake for 35–40 minutes or until a toothpick inserted in the center comes out clean. Remove from the oven and allow to cool slightly.

To prepare the topping, blend the flour and condensed milk in a saucepan. Cook over medium heat, stirring until thickened, about 5 minutes. Mix 2 tablespoons of the thickened milk with the beaten egg yolk, and add the mixture back to the simmering condensed milk. (This prevents the egg from curdling when adding it to the hot milk.) Stir in the *macapuno* and cook for 2 minutes more.

Spread the topping on the cake. Set the oven to broil and brown the topping for 2–3 minutes, about 4 inches from the heat. Watch carefully, as the topping can be easily scorched.

Serve warm. Makes 6–8 servings.

BATTER:

2 cups cassava, coarsely grated

1 egg, slightly beaten

½ cup sugar

2 tablespoons butter or margarine, melted

1 cup coconut milk

3 heaping tablespoons *macapuno* (preserved shredded young coconut)

TOPPING:

1 tablespoon flour

15 ounces condensed milk

1 egg yolk, beaten

3 heaping tablespoons *macapuno* (preserved shredded young coconut)

Sweet Rice Tea Cake
Bibingkang Malagkit

2 cups coconut milk

2 cups water

2 cups glutinous rice
(malagkit)

1 teaspoon salt

1¼ cups brown sugar

2 tablespoons butter or
margarine

¾ cup coconut milk

¼ teaspoon ground anise
seed

10-inch square of banana
leaf or foil

Mix the coconut milk and water in a large skillet and bring to a boil. Add the rice and salt and cook over medium heat, stirring, until the rice is tender and almost dry, about 15–20 minutes.

Stir in ¾ cup of the brown sugar, lower the heat and cook, covered, for 5 minutes.

Line an 8-inch-square pan with the banana leaf that has been softened by passing it over a flame, or with the foil, and grease the surface with 2 tablespoons of butter. Spread the cooked rice in the lined pan.

In a bowl, mix together the remaining ¾ cup of sugar and the coconut milk. Pour this over the rice, spreading it to cover the top evenly. Sprinkle with the ground anise seed.

Broil in the oven for 4–5 minutes or until the top is brown.

Serve warm. Makes 6–8 servings.

Green Rice Tea Cake
BIBINGKANG PINIPIG

Preheat oven to 350° F.

In a saucepan, mix 1 cup of the coconut milk with the water. Add the *pinipig* and salt. Bring to a boil, lower the heat and add 1 cup of the sugar. Mix well and simmer for 10–15 minutes, stirring constantly, until the mixture is very dry.

Line an 8-inch square pan with the banana leaf that has been softened by passing it over a flame, or with the foil and grease the surface with 2 tablespoons of butter.

Transfer the cooked *pinipig* to the lined pan and spread evenly.

Pour the remaining coconut milk over the *pinipig* and spread evenly. Sprinkle the remaining sugar and the ground anise seed over the coconut milk.

Bake for 10–15 minutes at 350° F. Or set the oven to broil and broil for 3–5 minutes, about 4 inches from the heat, until brown. Watch carefully, as the topping can easily be burned.

Serve warm. Makes 6–8 servings.

1¾ cups coconut milk

1 cup water

3 cups *pinipig* (pounded green rice)

1 teaspoon salt

1½ cups brown sugar

2 tablespoons butter or margarine

¼ teaspoon ground anise seed

10-inch square of banana leaf or foil

Sweet Rice Cake
with Caramel Topping
BIKO

2 cups coconut milk

2 cups water

2 cups glutinous rice
  (*malagkit*)

¾ cup sugar

½ stick butter or margarine,
  softened

1 egg, beaten

TOPPING:

6 ounces cocojam*

or

15 ounces condensed milk

¾ cup coconut milk

2 tablespoons flour

Preheat oven to 300° F.

Mix 2 cups of coconut milk with the water in a large, heavy pot. Add the rice and bring the mixture to a boil. Simmer for 15–20 minutes, stirring constantly to keep from burning.

When the rice is almost dry, lower the heat and add the sugar and butter. Mix well and set aside. When cool, stir in the beaten egg.

Using butter or margarine, grease well an 11¾-inch by 7½-inch baking pan. Pour the rice mixture into the dish and spread out evenly. Bake for 20 minutes.

If not using cocojam, mix all the topping ingredients in a heavy saucepan and cook over low heat, stirring constantly, for 15 minutes.

Spread the topping over the cooked rice. Increase the oven temperature to 350° F and bake for another 15 minutes, or until the top is brown.

Serve warm. Makes 12 servings.

*Cocojam or cocojelly is thick, heavily sweetened coconut milk, available at many Asian food stores.

Bread Pudding
BUDIN

Preheat oven to 350° F.

In a medium saucepan, heat the milk over low heat until tiny bubbles appear around the edges. Remove from the heat and add the diced bread. Allow the bread to soak for an hour.

Grease a 1½-quart casserole dish with butter or margarine.

Add the eggs, sugar, salt, vanilla and melted butter to the bread mixture. Stir thoroughly. Stir in the *macapuno* or jackfruit, and mix well. Pour the mixture into the greased casserole dish.

Set the casserole in a baking pan; add warm water to 1 inch from the top of the casserole. Bake for 1¼ hours, or until a toothpick inserted in the center comes out clean.

Serve hot or warm, topped with whipped cream or ice cream if desired.

Makes 6–8 servings.

4 cups milk

2 cups (6–8 slices) stale bread, diced and crusts removed

2 eggs, slightly beaten

⅓ cup sugar

½ teaspoon salt

2 teaspoons vanilla extract

4 tablespoons melted butter or margarine

1 cup *macapuno* (preserved, shredded young coconut) or 1 cup jackfruit *(langka),* drained and sliced into thin strips

Fried Dumplings with Rice
Bombones de Arroz

1 cup white rice, washed and drained

2¼ cups water

1 cup flour

2 tablespoons baking powder

½ teaspoon salt

2 eggs, well beaten

¼ cup coconut milk

1 teaspoon vanilla extract

2 cups vegetable oil

½ cup maple syrup

Place washed rice in the water in a saucepan. Bring to a boil, reduce heat, cover, and simmer for 30 minutes, or until the rice is cooked a little on the soft side. Set aside to cool.

Sift together the flour, baking powder and salt. Add the eggs, coconut milk, soft-boiled rice and vanilla. Mix thoroughly.

Heat the oil in a deep, large pot. Drop the batter by the spoonful into the hot oil, a few at a time. Fry to a golden brown, about 10–15 minutes.

Remove the dumplings with a slotted spoon and drain on paper towels. Transfer to a plate and drizzle with maple syrup.

Serve hot. Makes approximately 20–24 dumplings.

Chocolate Rice Porridge
Champorado

1 cup glutinous rice (*malagkit*), washed and drained

2 cups coconut milk mixed in 2 cups water

¼ teaspoon salt

1 cup sugar

6 tablespoons unsweetened powdered cocoa or 2 squares unsweetened chocolate, grated

1 cup coconut milk

Put the rice in a pot with the coconut milk diluted in water. Cover and bring to a boil. Reduce the heat and simmer for 15–20 minutes. Stir occasionally to prevent scorching.

In a bowl, combine the salt, sugar and powdered cocoa or grated chocolate. Add to the rice and stir until well blended. Cover and simmer for 15 minutes more, or until the rice is fully cooked, stirring occasionally.

Mix in the undiluted coconut milk and remove from the heat.

Serve hot or cold. This is usually eaten with fried smoked or dried fish or crispy fried dried beef. Makes 6 servings.

Fried Dumplings with Mung Beans
BUCHI-BUCHI

Soak the rice in 1 cup of the water overnight. The next day, drain off any excess water and grind the rice in a mortar and pestle or food processor to make a dough. Form it into a ball and wrap it in cheesecloth. Hang it to drip dry for 6–8 hours.

Put the mung beans in a small pan with 1 cup of water and bring to a boil. Reduce the heat and simmer, covered, for 1 hour, or until the beans are very soft. Mash the beans with the back of a wooden spoon against the side of the pan.

Dissolve ⅓ cup of the sugar in 2 tablespoons of water. Add to the mashed beans and cook over moderate heat until dry, 15–20 minutes. Stir constantly.

Remove the beans from the heat and allow to cool. Form into balls about 1 inch in diameter. Set aside.

When the ground rice is dry, mash it with the 2 tablespoons of sugar dissolved in water. Form into balls slightly larger than the mung bean balls, then flatten each ball of rice dough in the palm. Press it thin enough to wrap around a ball of mung beans.

Roll the dumplings in the sesame seeds, lightly pressing the seeds into the dough.

Deep fry in the hot oil, a few at a time, for 10–12 minutes, or until a deep golden brown.

Serve immediately, sprinkled with powdered sugar or dipped in fresh grated coconut, if desired. Makes approximately 16–20 dumplings.

1 cup white rice

2 cups plus 2 tablespoons water

½ cup mung beans

⅓ cup sugar

2 tablespoons sugar dissolved in 2 teaspoons water

1 cup vegetable oil

¼ cup sesame seeds

Spanish Bread Sticks
CHURROS

1 cup water
¼ teaspoon salt
1 cup flour, sifted
2 cups vegetable oil
¼ cup sugar

A cooking utensil called a churrera, *designed specifically to make* churros, *is available in Filipino or Latin American food stores. Or one can use a pastry bag with a large, star-shaped tip.*

Preheat oven to 250° F.

In a saucepan, bring the water and salt to a brisk boil.

Put the sifted flour in a bowl and add the boiling water. Mix well to form a thin dough.

Place the dough in a *churrera* and press out 6-inch lengths.

Deep fry the dough in hot oil until the bread sticks are golden brown, 3–5 minutes. Drain on paper towels. Keep warm in a 250° F oven.

Sprinkle with sugar just before serving. Serve warm. Makes about 6–8 *churros*. Recipe can be easily multiplied.

Steamed Cakes #1
CUCHINTA

In a bowl, mix together the water, sugars, flour and lye water. If you want to give the cakes the typical reddish tinge, soak 2 tablespoons of annatto seeds in ¼ cup of hot water for 20 minutes. Add 4 tablespoons of this red water to the batter.

Fill lightly oiled muffin pans or *cuchinta* molds ⅔ to ¾ full with the batter.

Place in a steamer, cover, and steam for 15–20 minutes.

Remove the pans from steamer and allow to cool before removing the cakes, by running the tip of a knife between the cakes and the sides of the pan. Sprinkle with the grated coconut.

Serve at room temperature. Using muffin pans, makes about 10–12; using the *cuchinta* molds, makes 24–30.

2 cups water

1 cup golden brown sugar

1 cup white sugar

1 cup flour

1 teaspoon lye water *(ligia)* (see Author's Notes, page 265)

4 tablespoons annatto water (optional)

Grated fresh coconut

Thick Rice Cakes
ESPASOL

In a large skillet, brown the rice flour over medium-high heat until it is a golden brown. Stir occasionally for an even color.

In a large pot, mix together the sugar, coconut milk, vanilla and salt and bring to a boil.

Add 3 cups of the pan-roasted flour to the liquid, stir, and cook until it is thick and dry, stirring frequently, for 30–40 minutes.

Turn out the dough onto a board or surface that has been well dusted with some of the remaining 1 cup of flour. Flatten with a rolling pin to ¼–½ inch in thickness.

With a sharp knife, cut the dough into rectangles ¼–½ inch wide by 3–4 inches long. Roll each in the remaining pan-roasted rice flour. Wrap each *espasol* in wax paper to keep them from sticking.

Serve at room temperature. Makes 24–30 rice cakes.

4 cups sweet rice flour

1½ cups sugar

3 cups coconut milk

1 tablespoon vanilla extract

½ teaspoon salt

Spanish Meat Pies
Empanada

FILLING:

1 tablespoon vegetable oil

2 cloves garlic, crushed

1 large onion, diced

1 cup carrots, diced

1 cup potatoes, diced

1 teaspoon sugar

1 tomato, chopped

½ pound ground beef

½ pound ground pork

½ pound ground chicken

3 tablespoons raisins

1 teaspoon salt

½ teaspoon black pepper

5–6 eggs, hard-boiled and
    quartered

20–24 slices sweet pickle

PASTRY:

2 egg yolks, slightly beaten

¾ cup water

⅓ cup sugar

1 teaspoon salt

4 cups flour, sifted

¼ cup melted butter or
    margarine

2 cups vegetable oil for frying

Heat the oil in a large skillet and sauté the garlic and onions for 1 minute. Add the carrots, potatoes and sugar, and sauté for 3 more minutes. Add the tomatoes and sauté for 3 minutes.

Add the ground beef, pork, chicken, raisins, salt and pepper and mix well. Cook for 15–20 minutes, stirring occasionally.

Allow to cool before using.

To make the pastry, mix together the egg yolks, water, sugar and salt in a bowl.

Sift the flour into another bowl, and add the liquid ingredients. Mix to a stiff dough. Knead until a fine texture is obtained.

On a floured board, roll out the dough until it is *very* thin. Sprinkle it with more flour if necessary to keep from sticking.

Lift one end of the dough, and brush the outer surface with melted butter. From this end, roll the dough like a jelly roll, brushing the surface with more butter until the whole roll is about ½ inch thick.

Cut into 1-inch-thick slices.

Flatten each into thin rounds about 3–4 inches in diameter. Cover with plastic wrap or a moist towel to keep the dough from drying out.

TO ASSEMBLE:

Place a heaping tablespoon of the meat filling onto each circle. Add a piece of hard-boiled egg and a slice of sweet pickle. Brush the inside edges of the dough, halfway around, with cold water. Fold the pastry over the filling like a turnover and press the edges together. Decorate the edges by fluting using the tines of a fork, or your fingers.

TO DEEP FRY:

Heat 2 cups of vegetable oil in a deep pan or wok. Fry 2–3 *empanadas* at a time for 15 minutes, until they are a golden brown. Drain on paper towels.

TO BAKE:

Place a 3-4-inch square of parchment paper beneath each *empanada*. Arrange on a cookie sheet. Brush each with an egg wash. Bake in a preheated 400° F oven for 15–20 minutes or until golden brown.

Serve warm or at room temperature. Makes about 20–24 *empanadas*.

The uncooked *empanadas* can be frozen for up to 2–3 months.

Cheese Rolls
Ensaymada

½ cup + 1 tablespoon sugar

¾ cup warm water

2 packages active dry yeast

1 teaspoon salt

1 cup butter or margarine, softened

6 egg yolks

4 cups flour, sifted

TOPPING:

⅓ cup butter or margarine, softened

½ cup Edam cheese or mild cheddar cheese, grated

½ cup sugar

Preheat oven to 350° F.

In a large bowl, dissolve 1 tablespoon of the sugar in the warm water. Sprinkle the yeast over the water and let stand for 3 minutes. Then stir to dissolve the yeast completely. Add the remaining ½ cup of sugar and the salt, stirring until fully dissolved.

Add ½ cup of the butter, the egg yolks and 3 cups of the flour. Beat with a wooden spoon or spatula until smooth.

Gradually add the remaining 1 cup of flour, mixing first with the spoon or spatula and then with the hands until the dough is smooth and stiff enough to leave the sides of the bowl.

Place the dough on a lightly floured surface and knead until it is smooth, about 5–6 minutes.

Place the dough in a lightly greased, large bowl. Coat the dough with the oil from the surface of the bowl. Cover with a towel and allow to rise in a warm place for about 1½ to 2 hours, or until the dough has doubled in bulk.

Punch the dough down and turn it out onto a lightly floured surface. Divide into two even portions. Roll each portion into ⅛-inch thin sheets about 6 inches x 24 inches. Spread the remaining ½ cup of softened butter or margarine on top. Roll the long edge of the dough like a jelly roll.

Generously butter the sides and bottoms of two 8-inch layer baking pans.

In the buttered pans, coil the rolled dough, starting at the edge of the pan, twisting the dough gently as it fills the pan. This will create a coiled spiral of dough in both pans.

Cover the pans with a towel and let the dough rise in a warm place until doubled in bulk, about 1 to 1½ hours.

Bake for 25–30 minutes, or until the rolls are golden brown.

Remove from oven and allow to cool slightly, about 5–7 minutes.

Brush the tops with the ⅓ cup of softened butter and sprinkle with the grated cheese and sugar. The warm *ensaymada* will melt the sugar and cheese.

Serve warm. Makes 8 servings.

Rice Balls in Coconut Milk
GUINATAAN AT BILO-BILO

1 cup water

1 cup sweet rice flour

3 cups coconut milk diluted with 2 cups water

2 cups sweet potatoes, peeled and cut into ½-inch cubes

2 cups taro root, peeled and cut into ½-inch cubes

2 cups purple yam, peeled and cut into ½-inch cubes

3 cups plantain bananas, peeled and cut into thin slices crosswise

1 cup jackfruit, cut into strips

3 tablespoons tapioca, small pearl size

2 teaspoons ground anise seed

½ cup sugar

1 cup coconut milk

In the context of the merienda, guinataan *refers to a thick coconut milk-based dessert soup. Traditionally in the Philippines, this dish is made by soaking sweet rice in water overnight, then grinding it to a stiff dough and forming it into small balls. Here is a less time-consuming approach.*

Add approximately 1 cup of water to the flour and mix to form a stiff dough. Form into balls about ½ inch in diameter. Place on a plate and cover with a moist towel. Set aside until ready to use.

In a large pot, bring the 5 cups of diluted coconut milk to a boil over medium-high heat.

Add the sweet potatoes, taro root and purple yam and boil for 5–7 minutes.

Add the rice balls, plantains, jackfruit, tapioca, anise and sugar. Simmer for 35–45 minutes, or until the rice balls are cooked all the way through. Stir occasionally to keep everything from sticking to the bottom of the pot.

Serve the *guinataan* in bowls and top each with a few tablespoons of the undiluted coconut milk. Serve with Steamed Rice Cakes (*Puto Maya,* page 70). Makes 8–10 servings.

Corn in Coconut Milk
GUINATAAN AT MAIZ

Put the 3 cups of coconut milk diluted with 2 cups of water into a large pot. Add the rice and bring to a boil. Boil for 7–10 minutes, or until the rice is half done.

Stir in the whole corn, creamed corn, sugar and salt, and simmer, stirring occasionally, for 10 minutes more, or until the rice and corn are fully cooked.

Mix in the undiluted coconut milk and simmer, while stirring, for 1–2 minutes more.

Serve hot. Makes 6–8 servings.

3 cups coconut milk diluted with 2 cups water

½ cup sweet rice (*malagkit*), washed and drained

1 cup whole corn, canned or freshly scraped off the cob

¼ cup canned creamed corn

½–¾ cup sugar, to taste

1 teaspoon salt

1 cup coconut milk, undiluted

Mung Beans in Coconut Milk
GUINATAAN AT MUNGO

In a dry skillet, roast the beans over high heat until a dark brown. Break the grains, using a rolling pin. Separate the beans from the hulls, discarding the hulls. This makes the *guinataan* smooth and toasty.

Place the 3 cups of coconut milk diluted with 2 cups of water into a large pot. Add the rice and roasted beans and bring to a boil. Boil for 15–20 minutes, or until the rice is cooked, stirring occasionally to keep the mixture from burning.

Add the sugar and salt.

Serve hot or cold, topping each portion with a few tablespoons of the undiluted coconut milk. Makes 8 servings.

½ cup whole mung beans

3 cups coconut milk diluted with 2 cups water

1 cup sweet rice (*malagkit*), washed and drained

¾ cup sugar

½ teaspoon salt

1 cup coconut milk, undiluted

Thick Rice Pudding
Maja Blanca

2 cups white rice

3 14-ounce cans coconut milk (to make coconut oil)

1 teaspoon ground anise

10 cups milk

1 cup sugar

The night before, wash the rice and soak it in 2 cups of water overnight. In the morning, grind the rice with a mortar and pestle or a food processor. Form the resulting dough into a ball and wrap it with a few layers of cheesecloth. Hang this for 4–6 hours to drain off any excess moisture. This makes the rice dough or *galapong.*

To make coconut oil, bring the coconut milk to a boil in a saucepan, reduce the heat, and let it simmer for 45–60 minutes. The oil will rise to the top, and can be scooped off. Reserve ½ cup of the oil. (The reduced milk, called *latik,* can be used in other recipes.)

Toast the anise for 3–5 minutes in a hot skillet. Allow to cool and set it aside.

Grease a platter or small individual plates with 3 teaspoons of the coconut oil.

In a large pot, mix the well-drained rice dough with the milk and sugar. Cook over medium heat, stirring constantly, adding the rest of the fresh coconut oil 1 teaspoon at a time, to avoid burning, for 15–20 minutes.

When thick, add the toasted ground anise and mix very well. Pour the pudding onto the greased platter or plates, tipping it slightly to make it even and smooth. Allow to cool slightly and sprinkle with *latik.*

Serve warm or at room temperature. Makes 6–8 servings.

Rice and Corn Pudding
Maja Blanca Maiz

Scrape the corn from the cobs and wrap it in coarse cheese-cloth to strain. Place the strained corn in a large pot and discard the hulls left in the cheesecloth.

Add 1 cup of the sugar, the coconut milk and rice flour and mix well. Add 4 tablespoons of the fresh coconut oil ½ tablespoon at a time. Cook for 20–30 minutes over moderate heat, stirring constantly.

When the pudding is thick, pour it onto a serving platter greased with 1 or 2 tablespoons of coconut oil. Tip and swirl the platter until the pudding is smooth and even.

Sprinkle with the *latik,* toasted coconut and the remaining 1½ tablespoons of sugar.

Serve warm or at room temperature. Makes 6–8 servings.

3 cups fresh whole corn kernels (approximately 12 ears of corn)

1 cup + 1½ tablespoons sugar

4 cups coconut milk

1 cup rice flour

5 tablespoons fresh coconut oil (see page 11)

3 tablespoons *latik* (see page 228)

3 tablespoons toasted shredded coconut

Sweet Potato Fritters
Maruyang Kamote

1 cup flour

2 tablespoons baking powder

1 tablespoon sugar

¼ teaspoon salt

1 cup sweet potato, grated

1 egg, beaten

¼ cup milk

2 cups vegetable oil for frying

Powdered sugar

Sift together the flour, baking powder, sugar and salt. Mix in the grated sweet potato thoroughly. Add the egg and milk and beat together until the batter is thick and a little lumpy.

In a large skillet, heat the oil. Drop the batter by spoonfuls into the hot oil and fry until golden brown, 3–5 minutes. Drain on paper towels. Sprinkle with powdered sugar before serving.

Serve hot. Makes 6–8 servings.

Banana Fritters
Maruyang Saba

3 ripe plantain bananas or 6 ripe saba bananas

1½ cups flour

1½ teaspoons baking powder

½ teaspoon salt

⅔ cup milk

1 egg, beaten

2 cups vegetable oil for frying

½ cup sugar

If using plantain bananas, peel and slice in half lengthwise and again crosswise. If using saba bananas, peel and slice in half lengthwise only.

Sift 1 cup of the flour, the baking powder and salt together in a bowl. Add the milk and eggs and stir together until the batter is smooth.

In a skillet, heat the oil.

Roll the bananas in the remaining ½ cup of flour, dip in the batter and fry in the hot oil for 1–2 minutes if the bananas are very ripe, or 2–3 minutes if just ripe, until golden brown. Drain thoroughly on paper towels. Before serving, roll each in the sugar.

Serve hot. Makes 6 servings.

Dumplings in Coconut and Sesame Seeds
PALITAO

Mix the grated coconut, sesame seeds and sugar together in a bowl. Set aside.

Place the sweet rice flour in a large mixing bowl and add the water, mixing by hand, until able to form a stiff ball of dough.

Pinch off balls 1 inch in diameter. Flatten each to rectangles ¼-inch thick and 1 inch by 3 inches, about the size of 2 fingers.

Bring 8 cups of water to a boil in a large pot. Drop the dumplings in the boiling water and boil for 6–8 minutes, or until they start to float to the surface. Remove with a slotted spoon and drain.

While still warm, roll the dumplings in the coconut, sugar and sesame seed mixture.

Serve warm or at room temperature. Makes 24–36 dumplings.

½ cup grated coconut

4 tablespoons toasted sesame seeds

2 tablespoons sugar

2 cups sweet rice flour

1 to 1½ cups water

Bite-Size Fried Meat Pies
PANARA

These pies make a wonderful breakfast when they are served with Steamed Rice Flour Cakes (page 70).

2 cups green papaya, grated

3 tablespoons salt

2 tablespoons vegetable oil

2 cloves garlic, crushed and chopped

1 small onion, diced

½ pound pork, sliced into thin strips

¼ pound shrimp, peeled and chopped

½ cup chicken broth

1 tablespoon shrimp paste (*bagoong alamang*)

½ teaspoon black pepper

PASTRY:

2 cups sweet rice flour

2 cups water

2 eggs, beaten

3 tablespoons anise extract

1 teaspoon salt

3 tablespoons annato water

½ cup vegetable oil

2 cups vegetable oil for frying

Sprinkle the grated papaya with the salt and mix together by hand. Rinse well with water to remove the salt. Squeeze dry and set aside.

Heat the vegetable oil in a large skillet and sauté the garlic until lightly browned. Add the onions and sauté until translucent.

Add the pork and sauté for 3 minutes. Add the shrimp and sauté for 1 minute. Add the chicken broth, shrimp paste and black pepper and simmer for 2 minutes. Stir in the grated papaya and cook until it is slightly tender and the mixture is quite dry, about 7–10 minutes. Remove from the heat and allow to cool. Set aside until ready to use.

In a bowl, mix together all the ingredients for the pastry.

Cook over medium-high heat in a deep pan or wok, stirring constantly. Add more vegetable oil if necessary to prevent sticking. When the mixture is thick enough to shape into balls, remove from the heat and cool.

Pinch off balls 1 inch in diameter and roll into rounds with your hands. With a rolling pin, roll each into a thin sheet of dough 2½ inches to 3 inches wide.

To assemble, place a tablespoon or less of filling on each piece of pastry and brush the edges with water. Fold the pastry like a turnover and press the edges together tightly.

In a large skillet, heat the 2 cups of oil. Fry a few pies at a time in the hot oil for 3–5 minutes until they are golden brown. Drain well on paper towels.

Serve hot. Makes 16–20 meat pies.

Coconut Sweet Rolls
Pan de Coco

Preheat oven to 375° F.

In a bowl, combine the milk, yeast and 2 cups of the flour and mix into a soft dough. Place in a large greased bowl, cover with a towel, and set aside in a warm place. Allow the dough to double in size, 30–40 minutes. This forms the sponge.

While the dough is rising, prepare the filling: Place the cocojam in a pan and soften over medium heat. Mix in the shredded coconut thoroughly. Add a few tablespoons of water if the cocojam is too thick to mix with the coconut. Remove from the heat and allow to cool slightly. Set aside until ready to use. Keep warm.

In a mixer, cream the butter, sugar and salt until well blended. Mix in the eggs, vanilla and cinnamon.

When the sponge has risen, add it to the butter and egg mixture and mix well to break up the sponge.

Add the remaining 2 cups of flour. The dough should be smooth and elastic. Add more flour or milk to achieve this consistency.

Pinch off balls about 2 inches in diameter and flatten slightly with thumb and fingertips. In the center of each patty of dough, place 1 heaping tablespoon of the coconut filling. Fold the dough over the filling and seal the edges with water. Roll the filled dough back into a ball. Put on a greased cookie sheet, leaving at least 1 inch between each ball. Set aside and allow to double in size, about 30–40 minutes.

In a bowl, mix the 2 eggs and the water.

Just before baking, brush each roll with the egg wash. Bake for 35–40 minutes or until golden brown. While still warm, sprinkle them lightly with powdered sugar, so the sugar will melt. Makes about 24 coconut-filled sweet rolls.

1 cup milk, scalded and cooled

1 ounce active yeast

4 cups white flour

15 ounces cocojam

8 ounces shredded coconut

½ pound butter or margarine

½ cup sugar

½ tablespoon salt

4 eggs, beaten

2 teaspoons vanilla extract

1 teaspoon cinnamon

EGG WASH:

2 eggs, well beaten

2 tablespoons water

Powdered sugar

Sweet Bread
Pan de Leche

1 cup milk, scalded and cooled

1 ounce active yeast

4 cups white flour

½ pound butter or margarine

½ cup sugar

½ tablespoon salt

4 eggs, beaten

1 teaspoon vanilla extract

EGG WASH:

2 eggs

¼ cup water

4 tablespoons sugar

Preheat oven to 375° F.

In a bowl, combine the milk, yeast and 2 cups of the flour and mix into a soft dough. Place in a large greased bowl, cover with a towel and set aside in a warm place. Allow to double in size, about 30–40 minutes. This forms the sponge.

In a mixer, cream the butter, the ½ cup of sugar and the salt until well blended. Mix in the 4 eggs and vanilla extract.

When the sponge has risen, add it to the butter and egg mixture and mix well to break it up.

Add the remaining 2 cups of flour. The dough should feel smooth and elastic. Add more flour or milk to achieve this consistency.

Place the dough on a greased cookie sheet. Using a rolling pin, shape and flatten the dough into a rectangle 1 inch thick. Allow to rise again for 30–40 minutes.

In a bowl, combine the ingredients for the egg wash.

Just before baking, score the dough lightly with a knife to make a checkerboard pattern of rectangles 1½ inches by 3 inches. Brush the top of the dough with the egg wash.

Bake for 35–40 minutes or until golden brown.

Allow to cool. Cut in half to make 2 approximately 1-pound loaves.

Dinner Rolls
PAN DE SAL

Preheat oven to 375° F.

Dissolve the yeast in ¼ cup of the lukewarm water. Let sit for 10 minutes.

In a bowl, combine the remaining 1¼ cups of water, sugar, salt and shortening. Add the yeast and flour and mix well. The dough should just hold together. Add more flour or water if needed to get the correct consistency.

Transfer the dough to a floured surface and knead until it is smooth and elastic. Place the dough in a greased bowl, cover with a damp cloth, and let it rise for 1 to 1½ hours or until doubled in bulk.

Punch down the dough and divide it into 20–24 balls. Form into ovals and roll in the bread crumbs. Place on baking sheets and let rise until doubled in size again, about 1 to 1½ hours.

Bake for 15–20 minutes or until golden brown.

Serve warm. Makes 20–24 rolls.

2 teaspoons active yeast
1½ cups lukewarm water
2 tablespoons sugar
1 teaspoon salt
2 teaspoons vegetable
 shortening
4 to 4½ cups white flour
bread crumbs

Steamed Cakes #2
PUTO

2 cups Bisquick mix

2 eggs

1 cup sugar

1½ cups milk

½ teaspoon baking powder

2 tablespoons melted butter
  or margarine

½ cup grated coconut

Thoroughly blend together the Bisquick, eggs, sugar, milk, baking powder, and melted butter or margarine. Stir until smooth.

Fill greased muffin pans or *puto* molds ⅔–¾ full with the batter.

Place the pans or molds in a steamer and steam for 20 minutes or until a toothpick inserted into the center of the cake comes out clean. Unmold by slipping the tip of a knife between the cakes and the sides of the pan.

Serve hot or warm with a bowl of grated coconut for dipping. Makes 16–20 cakes.

VARIATIONS:

White Cakes — *Putong Puti*: Replace the butter or margarine with 2 tablespoons of mayonnaise. Proceed as above.

Purple Yam Cakes — *Putong Ube*: Reduce the amount of Bisquick to 1½ cups and add ½ cup of powdered purple yam. Proceed as above.

Steamed Purple Rice Cakes
Puto Bumbong

Traditionally, these cakes are served after Sunday Mass and at Christmas season. A puto bumbong steamer and bamboo puto tubes are a must for making them. They are available at some large Asian markets, as is the purple rice.

Grind the purple rice in a mortar and pestle or food processor to a coarse powder.

In a bowl, mix the purple rice powder with the rice flour and add enough of the water to form a dry dough.

Lightly fill the bamboo *puto* tubes ¾ full with the dough. Do not pack.

Steam in the *puto bumbong* steamer for 10 minutes.

Remove the cakes from the tubes by shaking them out.

In a bowl, mix together the grated coconut and the sugar. Roll the cakes in the mixture.

Serve hot. 4–6 cakes per serving. Makes 24 cakes.

½ cup purple rice
 (*pirurutong*)

2 cups sweet rice flour

1 to 1½ cups water

½ cup grated coconut

½ cup sugar

Steamed Sweet Rice Cakes
Puto Maya

3 cups sweet rice *(malagkit)*
5 cups coconut milk
1 cup sugar
1 cup grated coconut

Wash and drain the rice, place in a 2-quart saucepan, and add the coconut milk. Cover and cook over high heat until the steam starts to escape under the lid.

Lower the heat and simmer for 15–20 minutes.

Using a coffee cup, mold each serving and unmold it onto a saucer.

Mix the sugar and coconut, and sprinkle each serving with a few tablespoons of the mixture.

Serve warm. Makes 10–12 servings.

Steamed Rice Flour Cakes
Putong Puti

2 cups sweet rice flour
1½ cups water
3 teaspoons baking powder
1½ cups sugar
½ teaspoon salt
½ cup grated coconut

In a bowl, mix the flour and just enough of the water to make a thick batter. Add the baking powder, sugar and salt and mix thoroughly.

Pour into greased muffin pans or *puto* molds until each is ⅔ full.

Place in a steamer and steam for 30 minutes or until a toothpick inserted into the center comes out clean.

Sprinkle the top with the grated coconut.

Serve hot or warm. Makes 3 dozen cakes using the *puto* molds or 18–20 with the muffin pans.

Steamed Purple Yam Cakes
PUTONG UBE

Wash and peel the purple yam and cut into 1-inch cubes. Place in a large pot, cover with water, and boil for 30–45 minutes or until soft. Drain off the water. Mash the yams until smooth.

In a large bowl, mix the flour with the water to make a thick batter. Add the sugar and mashed purple yams and blend well. Pass the mixture through a strainer to remove any lumps.

Add the coconut milk and the baking powder and mix well.

Pour the mixture into greased muffin pans or *puto* molds, filling each ⅔ full.

Set in a steamer over boiling water, cover, and steam for 30 minutes or until a toothpick inserted in the center comes out clean. Remove from the molds or pans by inserting the tip of a knife between the cakes and side of the pan and sprinkle with the coconut.

Serve hot or warm. Makes 3 dozen cakes if using the *puto* molds or 18–20 if using the muffin pans.

2 cups purple yam, mashed (approximately 3 pounds purple yam)

2 cups sweet rice flour

1½ cups water

1 cup sugar

1¼ cups coconut milk

4 tablespoons baking powder

½ cup grated coconut

Meringue Cookies
PACIENCIA

Preheat oven to 275° F.

In a bowl, beat the egg whites with the cream of tartar, or in a copper mixing bowl, until the egg whites are stiff. Add the sugar gradually, beating until the egg whites are stiff again.

In another bowl, sift the flour and baking powder together. Gently fold the flour into the egg whites. Add the lemon juice and grated rind and stir in gently.

Place in a pastry bag and pipe out the meringue onto a greased or parchment-paper-lined cookie sheet. The cookies should be 1 to 1½ inches in diameter.

Bake for 5–10 minutes or until light brown.

Allow to cool. Store in an airtight container. Makes 24–36 cookies.

4 egg whites

½ teaspoon cream of tartar

1 cup sugar

½ cup flour

¼ teaspoon baking powder

1 teaspoon lemon juice

1 teaspoon grated lemon rind

Steamed Layered Rice Cake
Sapin-Sapin

INGREDIENTS FOR THE WHITE LAYER:

1½ cups coconut milk

½ cup sweet rice flour

⅔ cup sugar

INGREDIENTS FOR THE PURPLE LAYER:

1½ cups coconut milk

½ cup sweet rice flour

1 cup mashed purple yam
(1½ pounds purple yam)

⅔ cup sugar

¼ teaspoon ground anise

INGREDIENTS FOR THE BROWN LAYER:

1½ cups coconut milk

½ cup sweet rice flour

⅔ cup golden brown sugar

1 tablespoon annatto water

¼ teaspoon ground anise

This is a colorful cake to serve at parties, so several are usually made at a time. The top layer is white, the middle layer purple, and the bottom layer is brown.

Wash the purple yam well, peel it and cut into 1-inch cubes. Place in a large pot, cover with water, and boil for 30–45 minutes or until soft. Drain off the water. Mash the yam to a smooth consistency, and set aside. (You can use purple food coloring to intensify the color of the yam.)

In a small bowl, soak 3 tablespoons of annatto seeds in ¼ cup of hot water for 20–30 minutes, until the water is red. Remove the seeds and save the water. Annatto water can be purchased at Asian or Latin American markets.

Mix the ingredients for each layer in individual bowls. Each batter should be smooth and thin in consistency.

Bring water to boil in a steamer. Have hot water available in case the water evaporates while cooking.

Pour about ¾ cup of the brown batter into an 8-inch pie pan. Place in the steamer and cover. Steam for 20–25 minutes or until this layer is firm.

Over this bottom layer, pour ¾ cup of the purple batter. Steam for 20–25 minutes again, until also firm.

Over this layer, pour ¾ cup of the white batter. Steam also until this layer is firm.

Remove the cake from the steamer and allow to cool to room temperature. Slice into 8 wedges with a wet, sharp knife. Arrange on a serving platter. Makes 3 cakes.

Tapioca in Syrup
SAGO COOLER

Sago, *or tapioca pearls, is available in stores that carry Asian or Filipino food and comes in a variety of sizes. For this recipe, use sago ¼ inch in diameter or about the size of large peas. It also comes already cooked and frozen. Once it is defrosted, it is ready to use.*

In a large saucepan, bring the 6 cups of water to a boil, add the tapioca pearls, and lower heat to moderate. Cook the tapioca until it becomes clear all the way through, about 3–4 hours. Stir frequently to prevent sticking. Pour the tapioca into a colander and drain.

To make the syrup, combine the water and sugar in a saucepan, bring to a gentle boil and add the vanilla or banana extract. Simmer for 5–7 minutes. Remove from the heat and allow to cool.

To assemble, put 3–4 heaping tablespoons of the tapioca into a 12-ounce glass. Add 3–4 heaping tablespoons of crushed ice and fill the glass ⅔ full with ice water. Stir in 1–2 tablespoons of the cooled syrup, and serve. Guests will want to eat the tapioca, so give each a dessert spoon. Makes 6–8 servings.

VARIATION: Omit making the syrup. Add to each glass 2 tablespoons of light corn syrup, 1 heaping tablespoon of brown sugar and ½ teaspoon of vanilla or banana extract. Add a few tablespoons of the cooked tapioca pearls and crushed ice. Mix well and serve.

6 cups water

1 cup tapioca pearls *(sago)*

SYRUP:

1½ cups water

1 cup brown sugar

3 teaspoons vanilla or
  banana extract

Chinese Steamed Buns with Pork Filling
SIOPAO

FILLING:

2 tablespoons vegetable oil

6 cloves garlic, diced

2 pounds pork shoulder, diced

2 medium onions, sliced

4 tablespoons soy sauce

3 tablespoons sugar

2 tablespoons oyster sauce

3 eggs, hard-boiled and finely chopped

PASTRY:

1 teaspoon or package active yeast

½ cup + 1 tablespoon sugar

½ cup lukewarm water

4½ cups flour

1 cup lukewarm milk

1 tablespoon baking powder

2 tablespoons vegetable shortening

24 pieces of waxed paper cut into 3-inch squares

Heat the oil in a large skillet and sauté the garlic for 2 minutes. Add the pork and lightly brown. Add the onions, soy sauce, sugar and oyster sauce, mix well and cook until tender, about 15 minutes. Remove from the heat and allow to cool.

To make the pastry, mix the yeast and 1 tablespoon of the sugar into the lukewarm water. Stir until they are dissolved completely. Let stand for 10 minutes. (If foam does not form on top, the yeast is not active. Discard and start with a new package of yeast.)

Sift the flour into a large bowl. Slowly pour in the yeast mixture, lukewarm milk, baking powder, sugar and vegetable shortening. Stir with a wooden spoon or rubber spatula, then mix with hands until the ingredients are thoroughly combined.

Place the dough on a lightly floured surface and knead for 5 minutes. Put it in a lightly oiled, large bowl, cover with a damp towel, and let it rise in a warm place for 2 hours, or until the volume of the dough doubles in size.

Punch down the dough, cover with a damp towel again, and let it rise another 30 minutes, or until it doubles in volume again.

Turn the dough out onto a lightly floured surface and knead until it is smooth and satiny in texture, about 5–7 minutes. Roll the dough into a cylinder 2 inches in diameter and 24–26 inches in length. Cut into 1-inch rounds. Flatten each into 5-inch rounds.

To assemble, place 1 heaping tablespoon of the filling and a few pieces of chopped egg in the center of each pastry round. Gather the edges of the dough to form a pouch. Press edges together. Place each bun, with the folded edge down, on a 3-inch-square piece of waxed paper. Cover with a dry kitchen towel and let rise in a warm place for 30 minutes. The buns will almost double in volume.

Arrange the buns in a steamer at least 1 inch apart. Cover and steam for 10–15 minutes.

Serve hot with oyster sauce. Makes 24 siopao. Serve 2 per person.

Fried Egg Rolls with Bananas
TORRONES

Take an egg roll wrapper and put a slice of banana on top, near one edge.

Put a few pieces of jackfruit on top of the banana.

Wrap the egg roll by rolling it once, folding in the edges toward the middle and continuing the roll. Seal the edges with water or egg.

Deep fry the egg rolls in hot oil until they are golden brown, 3–4 minutes on each side. Drain on paper towels. Sprinkle with sugar. Makes 12 *torrones*.

12 egg roll wrappers, square or round

6 ripe saba bananas, peeled and halved, or 3 plantains, peeled, cut in half length-wise and again crosswise

½ cup jackfruit, sliced

2 cups vegetable oil for frying

1 tablespoon sugar

Shrimp Fritters
UKOY

Preheat oven to 250° F.

Trim off the whiskers and sharp points of the heads of the shrimp. Wash well in a colander and drain thoroughly.

Sift together the cornstarch, baking soda, baking powder and salt in a bowl. Add the water and stir. The batter should be lumpy.

Mix in the shrimp and bean sprouts gently, being careful not to damage the bean sprouts or the heads of the shrimp.

Heat the oil in a skillet or wok. Drop the batter into the hot oil a few heaping tablespoons at a time. Form into patties 2–3 inches in diameter. Fry only a few at a time, until a golden brown. Remove with a slotted spoon and drain on paper towels. Keep the cooked fritters warm in a 250° oven.

Serve warm with Vinegar and Garlic Dipping Sauce *(Suka't Bawang Sawsawan*, page 234). Makes 2 servings. Multiply the recipe as needed to serve family or guests.

½ pound small shrimp with heads on, 100–200 count

1 cup cornstarch

½ teaspoon baking soda

½ teaspoon baking powder

½ teaspoon salt

1 cup water

1 cup bean sprouts

2 cups vegetable oil for frying

Filipino Tamales in Banana Leaves

1 pound peanuts, raw

3 cups white rice

¼ cup annatto (atsuete) water

½ pound chicken breast

½ pound shrimp, peeled and deveined

1 Chinese sausage or Spanish sausage, sliced thin

¼ pound ham, diced

3 eggs, hard-boiled and diced

1½ cups unsalted peanuts, roasted

7 cups coconut milk

1 cup brown sugar

2 teaspoons salt

1 teaspoon black pepper

18–24 banana leaves, cut into 6-inch by 9-inch rectangles

In the United States, we are used to Mexican tamales, made with corn meal and spiced beef wrapped in corn husks. Filipinos have also adapted this once-Spanish dish, based on what is readily available. This recipe is also influenced by the Chinese use of lotus leaves for wrapping ingredients.

Wash the raw, unshelled peanuts thoroughly, place them in a large pot, cover with water, and boil for 45–60 minutes, or until the peanuts are soft. Drain in a colander and let cool. Shell the boiled peanuts and set aside.

Wash and drain the rice. Heat a large, non-stick skillet and toast the rice to a golden brown, stirring frequently, for 25–35 minutes. Remove from the heat and cool slightly. In a food processor, grind to a fine powder. Set aside.

Make the annatto (atsuete) water by putting 3 tablespoons of annatto seeds in ⅓ cup of hot water. Set aside for 25–30 minutes, until the water is red. Reserve ¼ cup of the red water for later use. Discard the seeds and excess water.

Skin the chicken breast and cook it in boiling water for 10–15 minutes. Remove from water and allow to cool slightly. Debone, and dice the meat. Set aside.

In the same water, boil the shrimp for 1 minute. Remove with a slotted spoon and dice.

Set the sausage, ham and hard-boiled eggs on individual plates and cover with plastic wrap until ready for final assembly of tamales.

In a food processor or stone grinder, coarsely grind the roasted peanuts. Leave some small chunks of peanut to give the tamale extra texture.

In a large pan or wok, combine the rice flour, coconut milk, brown sugar, salt and pepper and mix well. Cook over low heat for 25–30 minutes, stirring constantly to prevent sticking and burning.

Add the ground peanuts and mix in well. Cook for 5 minutes more.

Divide the mixture into two halves, leaving one half in the pan and putting the other in a bowl. To the mixture in the pan add the annatto water, mix well and cook for 2 minutes more.

To assemble, take 3 sheets of banana leaves that have each been softened by passing them over a flame or blanched in hot water for a few seconds, and place one on top of another. Along the long side of the leaves, put 3 tablespoons each of the red mixture and the uncolored mixture. Pat lightly with fingers to flatten. Leave at least 1 inch of banana leaf on either side of the filling. Add a few pieces each of the chicken, shrimp, sausage and ham. On top, sprinkle some boiled peanuts and diced hard-boiled eggs. Roll the mixture once, fold in the sides and complete the rest of the roll. Tie securely with string.

Put the wrapped tamales in a steamer and cook, covered, for 2 hours. Or put them in a large pot, covered halfway with hot water. Cover and bring to a boil. Reduce the heat and simmer for 1½ hours. The disadvantage with boiling the tamales is that if the banana leaves are not tied securely, the water will penetrate and ruin the filling.

Allow to cool. These will stay fresh in a cool, dry place for 24 hours. Makes 6–8 tamales.

Traditional Filipino DISHES

Pancit

Pancit are Filipino noodle dishes using wheat, rice or mung bean noodles to which meats and vegetables are added. They are probably Chinese in origin but have been adapted to the Filipino taste.

Sautéed Rice Noodles
PANCIT BIHON GUISADO

Place the chicken in a pot, cover with water and add 1 teaspoon of the salt and the bay leaves. Coarsely cut and crush 2 of the green onions and add to the water. Bring to a boil and simmer for 30 minutes. Remove the chicken, allow it to cool, remove the meat from the bones and cut into small pieces. Set the chicken meat aside.

In the same broth, simmer the pork for 10 minutes. Remove the pork and set it aside. To the broth, add the shrimp and 1 tablespoon of the fish sauce and simmer for 3 minutes.

Remove and drain the shrimp and set them aside. Discard the bay leaves and green onions, and save the broth.

In a large skillet, sauté the garlic and onion in hot oil. Add the chicken, pork and 1 tablespoon of fish sauce, and sauté for 3 minutes. Add 2 cups of the broth and simmer for 10 minutes.

Add the carrots and cabbage, return to a boil, reduce heat, and add the rice vermicelli or rice sticks, salt and pepper. Add more broth if mixture becomes too dry before noodles are done in 3–4 minutes.

Finely chop the 2 remaining green onions. Put the noodles and vegetables on a platter and garnish with the quartered eggs, green onions, lemon wedges and shrimp. Drizzle with the lemon juice. Makes 8–10 servings.

2-pound chicken, whole

2 teaspoons salt

2 bay leaves

4 green onions

½ pound pork, sliced into short, thin strips

½ pound shrimp, peeled, deveined and halved

2 tablespoons fish sauce

2 cloves garlic, minced

1 cup onion, thinly sliced

3 tablespoons vegetable oil

1 cup carrots, julienned

1½ cups cabbage, finely shredded

1 pound rice vermicelli or rice stick noodles, soaked in warm water for 15 minutes and drained

½ teaspoon black pepper

3 eggs, hard-boiled and quartered

1 lemon, cut into 8 wedges

Juice of 1 lemon

Sautéed Chinese Noodles
PANCIT CANTON

1 egg, slightly beaten

3 tablespoons cornstarch

½ pound medium shrimp, peeled, deveined, and tails left attached

5 tablespoons vegetable oil

1 chicken breast, deboned and sliced in strips

1 teaspoon salt

3 dried shiitake mushrooms, soaked in warm water for 30 minutes

2 cloves garlic, minced

1 cup onion, sliced

1 tablespoon soy sauce

¼ teaspoon black pepper

2 cups chicken broth

20 Chinese snowpeas, tips and fiber removed

1 cup carrots, julienned

1 cup cabbage, shredded

1 8-ounce package Chinese wheat noodles

2 Chinese pork sausages, thinly sliced diagonally

In a bowl, stir together the egg and 2 tablespoons of the cornstarch. Coat the shrimp with this mixture.

In a skillet, heat 2 tablespoons of the oil and lightly brown the shrimp on both sides. Drain on paper towels and set aside.

In another bowl, toss the chicken slices with the remaining 1 tablespoon of cornstarch and the salt. Coat the chicken evenly and set aside.

Drain the mushrooms, discard the tough stems, and slice thinly.

Heat the remaining 3 tablespoons of oil and sauté the garlic and onions. Add the chicken and cook on high for 3–4 minutes until the chicken is slightly firm. Add the soy sauce, pepper and broth and bring to a boil. Add the snowpeas and mushrooms. Cook for 3 minutes and add the carrots and cabbage. Correct the seasonings with more salt and pepper, if desired.

Lower the heat to medium, add the noodles and cook, stirring, until they are done and most of the broth is absorbed. Add more broth if needed.

Lightly sauté the Chinese sausages in a skillet for 5–7 minutes. Drain the sausages on a paper towel.

Serve the noodles and vegetables in a bowl, garnished with the shrimp and Chinese sausages. Makes 3–4 servings.

Noodles in Broth
PANCIT CON CALDO

Cook the noodles in boiling water for 5 minutes if using dried noodles, 2 minutes for fresh. Drain in a colander and stir in 1 tablespoon of the oil to keep noodles from sticking together. Set aside.

Sauté the garlic and onion in the remaining 1 tablespoon of oil in a large pot for 1 minute. Add the pork, salt, fish sauce and pepper and sauté for another 2 minutes.

Add the water and bring it to a boil. Add the noodles. Heat, stirring occasionally, for 6–8 minutes.

Add the zucchini and shrimp and cook for 3 minutes. Add the 2 whole eggs, being careful not to break the yolks. Bring the broth to a boil again and poach the eggs for 1–2 minutes, or until they are cooked.

Garnish with the chopped green onions and serve. Makes 4–6 servings.

½ pound Chinese egg noodles (*miki*), dried or fresh

2 tablespoons vegetable oil

2 cloves garlic, minced

1 small onion, sliced

½ pound lean pork, sliced into thin strips

2 teaspoons salt

1 tablespoon fish sauce

½ teaspoon black pepper

6 cups water

1 small zucchini, cut into ¼-inch slices

¼ pound shrimp, peeled and deveined

2 eggs

1 tablespoon green onions, finely chopped

Rice Stick Noodles in Red Sauce
PANCIT LUGLUG

NOODLES:

1 pound rice sticks *(bihon)*

3 cloves garlic, minced

2 cups + 2 tablespoons
 vegetable oil

½ pound pork, diced

½ pound small shrimp, peeled

½ cup chicken broth

2 tablespoons fish sauce

1 teaspoon salt

⅛ teaspoon black pepper

½ cup pork rind cracklings,
 finely crushed

¼ pound smoked fish *(tinapa)*,
 finely shredded and deboned

1 cup tofu, diced

3 hard-boiled eggs, chopped
 coarsely

4 tablespoons green onions,
 finely chopped

ANNATTO SAUCE:

2½ cups chicken broth

½ cup white flour

1 8-ounce can cream of
 mushroom soup

¼ cup annatto water or 2
 tablespoons annatto oil

½ cup water

2 tablespoons soy sauce

Soak the rice sticks in water for 30 minutes and drain.

In a skillet over medium heat, sauté the garlic in 2 tablespoons of the oil for 1 minute or until brown. Remove the garlic from the oil and set aside to use for garnishing.

Sauté the pork in the garlic-flavored oil for 10 minutes. Add the shrimp, chicken broth, fish sauce, salt and pepper and simmer for 5 minutes. Strain the mixture, reserving the liquid, and set the meat aside. The liquid can be added to the annatto sauce later for more flavor, if desired.

In a skillet, heat the 2 cups of oil. When it is hot, carefully add the diced tofu. Let it cook for 3–4 minutes without touching it with a utensil. When it is golden brown, separate it with a spatula, remove it from the oil, and drain it on paper towels.

In a large pan, bring 2 quarts of water to a boil. Place a handful of the drained noodles in a strainer and submerge in the boiling water. Boil for 2–4 minutes, until tender. Lift strainer out of water, drain the noodles thoroughly and transfer to a large platter. Cook all the noodles in the same manner.

Pour the annatto sauce (below) over the noodles and sprinkle the crushed pork rinds and *tinapa* over the sauce. Top with the fried garlic, the pork and shrimp, fried tofu, green onions and hard-boiled eggs.

Serve warm. Makes 6–8 servings.

ANNATTO SAUCE: In a saucepan, add ¼ cup of the chicken broth to the flour to make a thin paste. Stir in the rest of the broth, place over medium heat and bring to a boil.

Mix in the cream of mushroom soup, ½ cup of water, the annatto water and soy sauce and simmer for 5 minutes. Correct the seasonings with salt and pepper, if desired. Keep warm over low heat until ready to use. Makes 3–4 cups of annatto sauce.

Sautéed Egg Noodles
PANCIT MAMI

Heat the oil in a skillet and sauté the garlic and green onions for 1 minute.

Add the pork and sauté for 3 minutes. Add the chicken and sauté for 3 minutes more.

Add the fresh noodles and mix well with the vegetables and meat. Sauté for 2 minutes.

Add the chicken broth, salt and pepper and bring to a boil. Lower the heat, cover and simmer for 4–5 minutes, stirring occasionally. The noodles will absorb most of the broth.

Serve hot. Makes 3–4 servings.

2 tablespoons vegetable oil

2 cloves garlic, minced

2 tablespoons green onion, finely chopped

½ pound lean pork, sliced into thin strips

½ pound chicken, diced

1 pound fresh Chinese wide egg noodles *(mami)*

1 cup chicken broth

1 teaspoon salt

½ teaspoon white pepper

Sautéed Chinese Noodles with Mushrooms
PANCIT MIKI

½ pound Chinese egg noodles *(miki)* or 3 packages of ramen noodles

1 cup vegetable oil

2 eggs, beaten

½ pound lean pork, cut into thin strips

1 tablespoon fish sauce

2 tablespoons cornstarch

4 pieces dried shiitake mushrooms, soaked in water for 30 minutes

½ pound bean sprouts

1 tablespoon soy sauce

½ cup chicken broth

Cook the noodles according to package directions and drain in a colander. Stir in 1 tablespoon of vegetable oil to keep the noodles from sticking together.

In a skillet, heat 2 tablespoons of the oil, and pour in the eggs. Let them cook for 2 minutes, then turn them and let them cook 2 minutes more. Remove from pan. Allow the omelet to cool. Roll it like a cigar and cut into thin strips. Set aside.

Combine the pork, fish sauce and cornstarch. Heat 2 tablespoons of the oil in a skillet and stir-fry the coated pork over medium heat for 5–10 minutes.

Discard the tough stems of the mushrooms and dice the caps.

Add the bean sprouts, mushrooms, soy sauce and chicken broth to the pork. Cook, stirring, for 3–5 minutes or until bean sprouts are done. Set aside.

Heat the remaining oil in a large skillet. Add the noodles and fry, without stirring, until they are golden brown on one side. Turn over and brown the other side. Transfer to layers of paper towels to drain excess oil.

Place the noodles on a serving platter, add the vegetables and pork, and garnish with the egg strips. Makes 3–4 servings.

Sautéed Mung Bean Thread Noodles
PANCIT SOTANGHON

In a skillet, sauté the onions in the hot oil until they are soft and translucent. Add the chicken and sauté for 3–4 minutes, until the meat becomes slightly firm and white. Season with the salt, white pepper and fish sauce.

Add the chicken broth, bring to a boil, lower the heat and simmer for 10 minutes. Add the snow peas, green onions and mushrooms and cook for 4–5 minutes. Add the noodles and cook for 5 minutes more, stirring well.

Serve hot. Makes 4 servings.

1 medium onion, thinly sliced

1 tablespoon vegetable oil

1 pound chicken breast meat, cut into thin slices

1 tablespoon fish sauce

1 teaspoon salt

¼ teaspoon white pepper

2 cups chicken broth

2 cups snow peas

3 green onions, cut into 1-inch lengths

3 pieces dried shiitake mushrooms, soaked in water for 30 minutes and sliced into thin strips

¼ pound mung bean thread noodles *(sotanghon)*, soaked in water for 30 minutes and cut into 3-inch to 4-inch strands

Traditional Filipino
DISHES

Relleno

From the central plains of the Philippine island of Luzon comes the epitome of sophisticated Philippine cuisine—the *relleno* or *rellenong*. In these dishes, chicken, fish or a vegetable is further enhanced by a delicious stuffing. What makes this so sophisticated is that Filipino cooks have taken what originally was a Spanish recipe, then using food native to the Philippines and combining them with cooking techniques familiar to the Chinese, have developed truly wonderful food creations. *Rellenos* not only satisfy one's desire for good tastes and textures, but they envelop the senses of sight and smell as well.

Stuffed Pork Hocks
RELLENONG PATA

Preheat oven to 350° F.

Debone the hocks by running a small paring knife just inside the skin, separating the bone and meat from the skin.

Slice the meat from the bone and cut into ½-inch cubes. Put the skin and meat in a ceramic or plastic dish with a lid.

In a bowl, combine the soy sauce, lemon juice, sugar, sherry and salt. Pour this over the hock skin and meat, cover, and refrigerate for 1 or 2 days.

Stuff the meat into the hock skin. Put in a ceramic or glass baking dish.

Mix the water and pineapple juice and pour it over the stuffed hocks. Cover and bake for 1½ to 2 hours, or until the hocks are tender.

Remove the hocks to a platter. Pour the pan drippings into a saucepan over medium heat and stir in the cornstarch and water mixture. Spoon the thickened sauce over the stuffed pork hocks. Makes 6 servings.

6 pork hocks, about 2 pounds
2 tablespoons soy sauce
1 teaspoon lemon juice
2 tablespoons sugar
2 tablespoons sherry
1 teaspoon salt
1 cup water
1 tablespoon cornstarch dissolved in 2 tablespoons water
½ cup pineapple juice

Stuffed Pork Roll with Sauce
RELLENONG CARNE

PORK WRAPPING:

2 pounds pork leg or shoulder, butterfly cut into ¼-inch thickness

6 cloves garlic, crushed

1 tablespoon salt

1 tablespoon black pepper

STUFFING:

1 8-ounce can Vienna sausage

1 pound ground pork

1 Spanish sausage (chorizo de Bilbao), finely chopped

½ cup sweet pickle relish, drained

½ cup Edam or sharp cheddar cheese, grated

1 teaspoon salt

1 teaspoon black pepper

2 cups carrot, cubed

2 eggs

2 tablespoons flour

2 eggs, hard-boiled and quartered

2 sweet pickle slices, quartered

Preheat oven to 350° F.

To prepare the pork wrapping, spread the pork meat open. Rub it well with the garlic, salt and pepper. Set it aside.

Drain the Vienna sausages. Cut 2 in half lengthwise and chop the rest.

To make the stuffing, mix together the ground pork, chopped Vienna sausages, Spanish sausage, pickle relish, cheese, salt, pepper, carrots, raw eggs and flour.

Spread half the filling in the middle of the pork wrapping. Arrange the Vienna sausage halves, the hard-boiled egg quarters and pickle slices in the middle of the filling. Spread the rest of the filling evenly over the wrapping. Roll and tie up with string.

Place in a ceramic or glass baking dish. Set aside.

To prepare the sauce, mix the chicken broth and tomato sauce in a bowl. Add the rest of the sauce ingredients and stir well.

Pour the sauce over the rolled pork and cover the dish. Bake for 1 hour. Uncover and bake for 15–20 minutes longer.

Allow to cool for 20 minutes.

To serve, slice and arrange on a platter. Pour the sauce left in the pan over the sliced meat. Makes 8–10 servings.

SAUCE:

1½ cups chicken broth

1 8-ounce can tomato sauce

1 cup onion, chopped

1 cup tomato, chopped

4 cloves garlic, minced

3 bay leaves

2 tablespoons black peppercorns, coarsely crushed

3 tablespoons white wine or sherry

Stuffed Milkfish #1
Rellenong Bangus #1

1 whole milkfish *(bangus),*
  1½ to 2 pounds

1 tablespoon soy sauce

3 teaspoons lemon juice

2 teaspoons sugar

4 cups water

STUFFING:

1 clove garlic, minced

1 cup onion, chopped

1 cup tomatoes, chopped

2 tablespoons vegetable oil

¼ cup frozen peas

1 pound ground pork

1 cup potatoes, boiled,
  peeled and diced

2 tablespoons raisins

2 tablespoons sweet pickle
  relish

¼ cup carrot, grated

⅛ teaspoon black pepper

1 teaspoon salt

2 eggs, slightly beaten

Preheat oven to 375° F.

Gently pound the body of the fish with a rolling pin or wooden mallet for approximately 1 hour, or until it is *very* soft throughout. Be careful not to damage or puncture the skin. Break the spine near the tail and just below the head, making sure not to separate the head from the body. Carefully pull the bones and flesh through the opening near the head—they will come out easily if the fish has been pounded thoroughly. Scoop out the rest of the flesh from inside the skin. Remove as much as possible without breaking the skin.

Combine the soy sauce, 2 teaspoons of the lemon juice and sugar and mix well. Pour this mixture over the emptied body of the fish and set aside. Turn the skin occasionally until it is evenly coated with the marinade.

Place the water and remaining 1 teaspoon of lemon juice in a saucepan and bring it to a boil. Add the flesh and bones removed from the fish, bring the water back to a boil, remove from the heat and let stand, covered, for 5 minutes or until the meat becomes firm. Drain the meat and remove all bones. Set the meat aside.

To prepare the stuffing, sauté the garlic, onions and tomatoes in the hot oil. Add the peas and pork and sauté for 5–7 minutes. Add the fish meat, cooked potatoes, raisins, sweet pickle relish, grated carrot, pepper and salt and sauté for another 3 minutes. Allow to cool.

When the stuffing mixture has cooled, add the eggs and mix well. Gently stuff the mixture into the fish skin.

Bake for 45 minutes on a baking pan or cookie sheet lined with oiled aluminum foil. Turn the fish once to brown it evenly. Brush with oil to prevent the skin from drying out.

Allow the fish to cool slightly before slicing it diagonally into 4 or 5 pieces. Makes 4–5 servings.

VARIATION:

Instead of baking, the stuffed fish can be coated with flour and deep fried for 10 minutes on each side. Drain it on paper towels.

Stuffed Milkfish #2
Rellenong Bangus #2

Preheat oven to 350° F.

Mix the tomatoes, onions, bell peppers, garlic, ginger, lemon juice and pepper in a bowl, and let stand for 20 minutes.

Clean and gut the milkfish. Rub it inside and out with the salt. Put the fish on a piece of aluminum foil large enough to wrap it completely.

Fill the cavity of the fish with the vegetables. Pour any leftover liquid over the fish. Wrap it tightly in the foil.

Bake the fish for 45–60 minutes, or until the flesh is flaky.

Makes 4–6 servings.

2 cups tomatoes, chopped

2 cups onions, chopped

1 cup green bell pepper, chopped

4 cloves garlic, minced

2 tablespoons ginger, minced

juice of 2 lemons

1 teaspoon black pepper

1 whole milkfish (bangus), 1½ to 2 pounds

1 teaspoon salt

Stuffed Whole Chicken
Rellenong Manok

1 whole chicken, 3–4 pounds

2 tablespoons lemon juice

3 tablespoons soy sauce

1 teaspoon sugar

STUFFING:

1½ pounds ground pork

¼ pound ham, finely chopped

2 Spanish sausages (chorizo *de Bilbao),* finely chopped

3 tablespoons sweet pickle relish

2 tablespoons catsup

1 teaspoon salt

1 cup onion, finely chopped

2 tablespoons raisins

2 eggs

½ teaspoon white pepper

4 eggs, hard-boiled

2 tablespoons melted butter or margarine

Preheat oven to 350° F.

To prepare the chicken for stuffing, it must be deboned, leaving the skin, wings and legs intact. To do this, rinse chicken in cold water and dry thoroughly. Trim off the fat near the large opening and work your fingers between the skin and the meat until you get to the thighs. Working from inside the skin, isolate the thighs at the drumstick joints and with a knife, cut the thigh meat from the carcass. Pull the skin and legs forward and up, as if about to remove a sweater. When you get to the wings, disjoint and separate the wings from the carcass, leaving them attached to the skin. The carcass should now be able to be removed and the skin left intact, with the legs and wings still in the skin. Set the skin aside, covered with a moist towel.

Remove the meat from the bones. (The bones can be saved for making chicken stock.) Dice the chicken.

Mix the lemon juice, soy sauce and sugar together in a cup. Pour the liquid over the diced chicken meat and marinate for 1 hour.

To prepare the stuffing, combine the marinated chicken, ground pork, ham, Spanish sausage, relish, catsup, salt, onion, raisins, eggs and white pepper.

Stuff the chicken skin with the pork and chicken mixture, shaping the stuffing and skin back into the shape of a chicken. Press the hard-boiled eggs into the stuffing at the middle of the body, 2 eggs on each side of the chicken.

Sew up the opening with needle and thread, crossing the drumsticks over the sewed-up opening and tying back the wings against the stuffed body.

Place the stuffed chicken, breast side up, on a rack over a roasting pan containing a little water. Bake, loosely covered with foil, for 1 hour. Baste with the melted butter occasionally. Remove the foil and bake 15–20 minutes longer.

Remove from the oven and let stand for 30 minutes before slicing.

Serve with catsup or chicken gravy. Makes 6–8 servings.

Stuffed Crabs
RELLENONG ALIMANGO

Wash the crabs, put them in a large pot, and add the water and ½ tablespoon of the salt. Cover and bring to a boil. Lower the heat and simmer for 10–15 minutes, or until the shells turn red. Drain and let cool.

When cool enough to handle, remove the crab meat from the shells, taking care to remove all the pieces of shell and membrane. Clean and save the body shell for stuffing later. Discard the legs, gills, intestines and fat.

In a skillet, sauté the garlic, onions, bell peppers and tomatoes in 2 tablespoons of hot oil. Add the crab meat along with the frozen or canned crab meat, ½ tablespoon of the salt, fish sauce, sugar, pepper and chopped green onions. Sauté for 2–3 minutes. Remove from the heat and allow to cool.

Fill the crab shells with the crab meat mixture, mounding it slightly in the center. Sprinkle bread crumbs over the top, and press lightly.

Heat the remaining 2 cups of oil in a deep pan or wok. Fry the stuffed crab shells, a few at a time, shell side down. Spoon the hot oil over the exposed stuffing occasionally. Cook for 3–5 minutes, until golden brown. Drain on paper towels. Makes 5 servings.

10 medium live blue or rock crabs

1½ cups water

1 tablespoon salt

2 cloves garlic, minced

1 cup onion, chopped

½ cup green bell pepper, chopped

1 cup tomato, chopped

2 cups + 2 tablespoons vegetable oil

4 ounces frozen or canned crab meat (do not use imitation crab meat)

1 tablespoon fish sauce

1 teaspoon sugar

⅛ teaspoon black pepper

2 green onions, chopped

1 cup dried bread crumbs

Squid Stuffed with Pork
RELLENONG PUSIT #1

2 pounds large squid

2 tablespoons vegetable oil

2 cloves garlic, minced

1 cup onions, minced

½ pound ground pork

1 4-ounce can water chestnuts
   (apulid), drained and
   coarsely chopped

1 teaspoon salt

1 tablespoon fish sauce

½ teaspoon black pepper

2 green onions, chopped

1 egg, slightly beaten

To prepare the squid, pull off the tentacles, remove the quill, and wash out the body. Cut off the tentacles below the eye, being careful not to cut the ink sack. Peel off the skin and discard the innards, quill, eye and skin.

Wash the tentacles and body thoroughly. Drain. Chop the tentacles.

Heat the oil in a skillet and sauté the garlic and onions. Add the pork, chopped tentacles and water chestnuts. Cook, stirring for 5 minutes. Add the salt, fish sauce and pepper. Remove from heat and let cool.

Add the green onions and egg to the cooled pork mixture. Loosely stuff the body of the squid with the mixture, to within ½ inch of the opening. Or, if the squid are too small to do this, stuff and then close with a toothpick. Brush the squid lightly with oil.

Grill over hot coals for 3 minutes, turning until cooked evenly. Or place on a rack over a broiling pan and broil for 5 minutes on each side, brushing the sides with more oil. Makes 4–6 servings.

Squid Stuffed with Vegetables
Rellenong Pusit #2

In a bowl, combine all the ingredients except the squid. Mix well and let stand for 30 minutes.

Stuff the squid with the vegetable mixture and seal the opening with a toothpick.

Grill over hot coals for 2 minutes on each side or steam for 5 minutes. Makes 4–6 servings.

6 cloves garlic, minced

1 cup onions, diced

1 cup tomatoes, diced

1 cup green bell pepper, diced

1 tablespoon black pepper

2 teaspoons distilled white vinegar

3 tablespoons green onions, chopped

1 teaspoon salt

1 jalapeño pepper, very finely chopped (optional)

2 pounds large squid, cleaned, skinned and tentacles removed (see instructions for Stuffed Squid, page 94)

Stuffed Cucumbers
Rellenong Pipino

3 cucumbers, zucchini, or
   Chinese fuzzy melon *(upo)*,
   peeled and cut into 1½-inch
   lengths

½ pound frozen crab meat,
   thawed or canned crab
   meat

1 4-ounce can water chestnuts
   (apulid), drained and
   coarsely chopped

2 green onions, chopped

1 tablespoon sesame oil

2 teaspoons fish sauce

1 egg, slightly beaten

1 teaspoon white pepper

Peel the cucumbers and cut in half lengthwise. Remove the seeds and pulp and set aside.

For the stuffing, combine the crab meat, water chestnuts, green onions, sesame oil, fish sauce, egg and pepper and mix well.

Firmly stuff the cucumbers with the crab meat filling.

Put the cucumbers on a dish in a steamer and steam for 5 minutes. Makes 4–6 servings.

VARIATION: Substitute ½ pound ground pork for the crab meat.

Peppers Stuffed with Beef
Rellenong Sili #1

Preheat oven to 350° F.

Cut the bell peppers in half crosswise, remove the stem, seeds and ribs, and set aside until ready to stuff.

In a large skillet, sauté the garlic, onions and tomatoes for 1 minute in the hot oil. With a fork, break the corned beef into smaller pieces, add to the vegetables, and sauté for 5 minutes. Add the cooked rice, chili powder, pepper and fish sauce. Stir well and cook for 3 minutes more.

Stuff the pepper halves with the corned beef and rice mixture. Place in a small baking dish and pour the water into the dish around the peppers. Bake, covered, for 20–25 minutes. Uncover and bake for 3–5 minutes more to brown the tops of the stuffed peppers. Makes 4 servings.

VARIATION:

Use 4–6 Japanese eggplants instead of the bell peppers. Cut them in half lengthwise and scoop out some of the flesh and seeds to make a cavity for the stuffing.

2 large green or red bell peppers
2 cloves garlic, minced
3 cups onions, diced
1 cup tomatoes, diced
2 tablespoons vegetable oil
1 16-ounce can corned beef
2 cups cooked rice
½ teaspoon chili powder
½ teaspoon black pepper
2 teaspoons fish sauce
¼ cup water

Peppers Stuffed with Pork
Rellenong Sili #2

3 large green or red bell
    peppers

4 cloves garlic, crushed

1 cup onion, chopped

2 cups tomatoes, chopped

3 tablespoons vegetable oil

½ pound ground pork

1 teaspoon salt

1 teaspoon black pepper

2 eggs, well beaten

2 cups vegetable oil

Roast the bell peppers in the broiler for 10 minutes, turning them occasionally so that the skin on all sides becomes dark brown or black. Or, hold the peppers over a flame with a pair of tongs and burn the skin until it is black. Remove from the heat and allow to cool. Peel off the skin, cut the peppers crosswise in half, remove stem, ribs and seeds. Set aside until ready to stuff.

In a skillet, sauté the garlic, onions and tomatoes in hot oil until they are soft and translucent, about 5 minutes. Add the pork, salt and pepper and sauté for 10 minutes.

Stuff the peppers with the pork mixture. Dip the stuffed peppers into the beaten eggs and coat them well.

In a large skillet, heat the 2 cups of oil. Deep fry the peppers for 3–5 minutes. Remove from the oil and drain well. Makes 4–6 servings.

VARIATION: The eggplant variation of the previous recipe may be used here also.

Traditional Filipino DISHES

Sinigang

Sinigang are soups with sour broth that stimulate the appetite. Although in many countries soups start a meal, in the Filipino meal, they are part of the main course. *Sinigang* is the most popular Filipino soup and is best when allowed to mellow for a few days in the refrigerator.

Pork in Sour Broth
SINIGANG NA BABOY

1½ pounds pork spareribs, cut into 2-inch lengths

6 cups water

4 medium tomatoes, sliced

1 medium onion, sliced

1½ teaspoons salt

5 tamarind pieces or ½ cup lemon juice

3 cups taro root *(gabi)*, cut into 1-inch cubes (if using small taro, about the size of golf balls, you'll need about 12)

½ pound Chinese long beans, or green beans, cut into 2-inch lengths

1 medium daikon, peeled and cut into 1-inch pieces

½ pound spinach, mustard greens or water spinach

Place the spareribs in a large pot. Add the water, and bring to a boil. Add the tomatoes, onions, salt and tamarind or lemon juice. Reduce the heat and simmer, covered, for 1 hour, or until the pork is tender. Add salt and pepper to taste. (Optional: To make the broth extra sour, remove the tamarind and mash it with some broth. Strain the juice back into pot.)

Add the taro root, Chinese long beans and daikon. Boil, covered, for 10 minutes.

Add the spinach and cook for another 5 minutes.

Serve hot with individual saucers of fish sauce to allow guests to season their broth or to dip their meat. Add lemon juice to the fish sauce for an even more sour taste.

To reduce the fat, refrigerate the soup until the fat comes to top and solidifies. Skim off the fat, heat the soup and serve. Makes 4-6 servings.

VARIATION:

BEEF IN SOUR BROTH — Sinigang na Carne

Substitute 1 pound stewing beef, cut in 2-inch cubes, for the pork. Follow the same instructions. Make a day ahead to allow time to remove the fat by letting the dish sit overnight in the refrigerator and skimming off the solidified fat with a spoon.

Other vegetables can be added or used as substitutes: young pepper leaves *(sili* leaves), sliced green bell pepper, sliced Japanese eggplant, bok choy leaves, cabbage, okra, or young sweet potato leaves.

Chicken in Sour Broth
Sinigang na Manok

Sauté the garlic and ginger in hot oil in a large pot. Add the chicken pieces and brown them on all sides for 10 minutes. Add the onions and tomatoes and cook for 3–5 minutes.

Add the water, salt, pepper, fish sauce and tamarind or lemon juice. Cover and bring to a boil. Reduce the heat and simmer for 30 minutes or until the chicken is tender.

Remove the tamarind pieces and mash with a little broth to extract the juice. Strain and add the juice to the simmering chicken.

Add the daikon and cook for 5 minutes more, until it is just tender.

Add the mustard greens or spinach and green onions, cover and remove from the heat. Let stand for 5 minutes to wilt the greens. Correct the seasonings with fish sauce, salt and pepper, if desired.

Serve with a small bowl of fish sauce for dipping the chicken and vegetables. Makes 4–6 servings.

1 clove garlic, minced

1 tablespoon ginger, minced

2 tablespoons vegetable oil

2½ to 3 pounds chicken, cut up

1 medium onion, sliced thin

2 medium tomatoes, sliced

5 cups water

1½ teaspoons salt

¼ teaspoon black pepper

1 tablespoon fish sauce

6 pieces tamarind or ½ cup lemon juice

1 pound daikon, peeled and cut into 1-inch cubes

½ pound mustard greens or spinach

3 green onions, cut into 1-inch lengths

Milkfish in Sour Broth
SINIGANG NA BANGUS

1 whole milkfish *(bangus)*, about 1½ pounds, dressed

1 teaspoon salt

2 cups water

6 tamarind pods or ½ cup lemon juice

3 medium tomatoes, sliced

1 medium onion, sliced

2 cups green beans or Chinese long beans, cut into 2-inch lengths

1 tablespoon fish sauce

1 14-ounce can banana hearts *(butuan)*, drained (optional)

1 cup spinach, water spinach, or young sweet potato leaves *(camote)*

Slice the fish into 4–6 pieces. Sprinkle with salt, and set aside.

Put the water and tamarind pods in a pot and boil for 15–20 minutes, until the pods are tender. Remove the tamarind, mash it and strain it back into the boiling water. If using lemon juice, add it later.

Add the tomatoes, onions and beans to the boiling water and cook for 15 minutes or until the vegetables are just tender.

Add the fish, fish sauce and the banana hearts, if desired, and bring back to a boil. If using lemon juice instead of tamarind pods, add it. Lower the heat and simmer for 3–5 minutes. Add the greens and boil for another 5 minutes.

Serve with a small dish of fish sauce for dipping the fish and vegetables. Makes 4–6 servings.

VARIATION:

SHRIMP IN SOUR BROTH — Sinigang na Camarones

Substitute 1 pound of shrimp for the milkfish and simmer the shrimp for only 2–3 minutes.

Add clams and/or mussels in addition to the shrimp for a great shellfish soup. Makes 3–4 servings.

Traditional Filipino DISHES

Banana Leaf Wrapped Snacks — Suman

Suman refers to a snack in which flavored rice, cassava or bananas are wrapped in banana leaves, tied in pairs and steamed or boiled. After they are cooked, they are unwrapped and eaten plain or with coconut and sugar. *Suman* is eaten either hot or at room temperature. The banana leaves not only provide a great cooking container but impart a slight earthy, sweet scent to the filling.

Procedure for wrapping *Suman*:

To wrap *suman,* take a 4-inch by 6-inch piece of banana leaf and soften it by passing it lightly over the flame of a kitchen burner or blanching it in hot water for 10–15 seconds. When the leaf is soft, put a strip of filling along the center of the banana leaf, lengthwise, leaving about 1 inch of leaf on either side of the filling. Roll the filling in the leaf like an egg roll or burrito. Fold the open ends of the leaf in toward the side with the center vein. Repeat the procedure to make a second *suman*. Place 2 *sumans* together so the centers and folded ends face each other. Tie the *sumans* together with two or three pieces of kitchen cord to form a tight bundle. Cook as directed.

Sweet Rice in Banana Leaf #1
SUMAN INANTALA

3 cups sweet rice *(malagkit)*

5 cups coconut milk

3 teaspoons salt

12 banana leaves, cut into 4-inch by 6-inch pieces

Sugar

Wash and drain the rice. In a large pot, combine the rice, coconut milk and salt. Bring to a boil over medium-high heat. Reduce the heat and simmer, uncovered, for 15–20 minutes, stirring occasionally.

When the rice has absorbed most of the liquid, cover with a lid and cook for 3 minutes more, stirring occasionally to keep the rice from sticking to the bottom of the pot. Remove from the heat and cool slightly.

Soften the banana leaves and place about 3 heaping tablespoons of the rice on the leaves and wrap them. (See procedure for wrapping *suman,* page 103.)

Place the wrapped bundles in a steamer and steam for 30 minutes.

Unwrap the *suman* and sprinkle with sugar. Makes 12 *suman inantala.*

Rice Flour and Coconut in Banana Leaf
Suman Maruecos

Latik *is available commercially at many stores that sell Asian products. Or, see the recipe for* Latik, *page 228.*

Mix the rice flour, water, coconut milk and sugar in a large pot. Over medium heat, cook, stirring constantly until thick, for 45–50 minutes.

Soften the banana leaves. Put 2–3 heaping tablespoons of this mixture on each leaf. Top each portion with ½ teaspoon of *latik.* Wrap tightly. (See procedure for wrapping *suman,* page 103.)

Place the wrapped bundles in a steamer. Steam for 30 minutes.

Unwrap the leaves. No extra topping is needed. Makes 16–20 *suman maruecos.*

3 cups sweet rice flour

1 cup water

2 cups coconut milk

1 cup sugar

8–10 teaspoons *latik* (page 228)

16–20 banana leaves, cut into 4-inch by 6-inch pieces

Sweet Rice in *Buri* or Corn Husks
Suman sa Ibus

3 cups sweet rice *(malagkit)*

4–5 cups water

2 cups coconut milk

3 tablespoons salt

24 bamboo containers *(buri)* or dried corn husks

12 flat toothpicks, cut in half

Buri *or bamboo containers are made specifically for* suman sa ibus, *and are available in the Philippines. They can be replaced by dried corn husks, available in groceries that carry Latin American ingredients.*

Soak the rice in the water for 2–3 hours, or until the grains are swollen.

Drain the rice and combine it in a mixing bowl with the coconut milk and salt. Mix well.

Fill each *buri* tube ⅔ full. Close the opening with half a toothpick. Tie each *suman* (2 *buri* tubes) with string. If using dried corn husks, put a strip of filling along the center of the husk, leaving 1 inch on each side. Fold the husk like a banana leaf, and tie with a string (see page 103).

Put the *suman* in a deep pot, cover with water and the lid, and bring the water to a boil. Reduce the heat to medium and boil lightly for 2 hours.

Serve with sugar and ripe mangoes or hot chocolate. Makes 24 *suman sa ibus.*

Sweet Rice in Banana Leaf #2
SUMAN SA LIGIA

Soak the rice in water until the grains are swollen, about 2–3 hours.

Wash and drain the rice. Add the lye water and mix in thoroughly.

Soften the banana leaves. Wrap 3 tablespoons of the rice in 2 layers of banana leaves. (See procedure for wrapping *suman*, page 103.)

Put the *suman* in a deep pot, cover with water and a lid, and bring the water to a boil. Reduce the heat to medium. Boil lightly for 2 hours.

Unwrap the leaves and sprinkle with a little grated coconut and sugar. Makes 12 *suman sa ligia*.

3 cups sweet rice *(malagkit)*

4–5 cups water

2 tablespoons lye water *(ligia,* see Author's Notes page 265)

24 banana leaves, cut into 4-inch by 6-inch pieces

Grated coconut

Sugar

Cassava in Banana Leaf
SUMAN CASSAVA

In a bowl, mix all the ingredients except the banana leaves together.

Soften the leaves and put 2 on top of each other. Wrap the mixture in the 2 banana leaves. (See the procedure for wrapping *suman,* page 103.) Repeat until all the leaves are used.

Tie two *suman* together and put the bundled *suman* in a pot and cover them with boiling water. Boil for 45–60 minutes, or until a toothpick inserted in the center comes out clean.

Unwrap the leaves and sprinkle the filling with a little sugar and grated coconut. Makes 6 *suman* cassava.

1 cup cassava, grated

½ cup grated fresh coconut

¾ cup sugar

12 banana leaves, cut into 4-inch by 6-inch pieces

Banana Suman
SUMAN SABA

20–24 saba bananas, ripe but not too soft, peeled

3 cups grated fresh coconut

3 cups (packed) dark brown sugar

1 cup cassava flour or corn flour

48 banana leaves, cut into 4-inch by 6-inch pieces

In a large bowl, using a potato masher or a fork, mash the bananas two at a time, mixing in, a few tablespoons at a time, the grated coconut and brown sugar.

When all the bananas are mashed and the coconut and brown sugar is incorporated, add the cassava or corn flour. Mix well with a spatula or wooden spoon.

Soften the banana leaves. Place 2–3 heaping tablespoons of the bananas onto 2 layers of banana leaves. Wrap tightly. (See procedure for wrapping *suman,* page 103.)

In a large pot, arrange the bundles of *suman,* and cover them with boiling water. Cook for 35–45 minutes or until done.

Unwrap the *suman.* Sprinkle with a little fresh grated coconut. Makes about 24 *suman.*

Beef

Raising cattle for beef was introduced to the Philippines with the arrival of the Spanish. Because of the lack of extensive grazing land needed to grow beef cattle, most beef is raised in pens rather than on pasture land. While this is a more efficient use of land, it increases the cost of raising cattle, making beef an expensive source of protein in the Philippines.

In southern Mindanao, where the religion of Islam, with its strictures against eating pork, is predominant, beef and fish are the primary sources of protein. In this region, closest to Malaysia, beef is usually boiled or stewed and spiced heavily with chile peppers as it is in Malaysian cooking. The farther north in the Philippines one travels, the less spicy the food is.

Beef and Sausage Stew
BEEF POCHERO

2 pounds stewing beef, cut into 2-inch cubes

4 cups water

1½ teaspoons salt

4 green onions, cut into 4-inch lengths

3 ribs celery, cut into 4-inch lengths

1 Spanish sausage (chorizo de Bilbao), whole

2 medium potatoes, peeled and quartered

¼ pound green beans, cut in 2-inch lengths

1 small cabbage, quartered

2 tablespoons vegetable oil

2 cloves garlic, minced

1 medium onion, sliced

½ cup tomato sauce

1 8-ounce can garbanzo beans (chickpeas), drained

Place the stewing beef in a large pot and add enough water to cover. Add the salt, green onions and celery. Bring to a boil, reduce heat and simmer, covered, 1 to 1½ hours, or until the beef is tender. Add the whole sausage and simmer for another 30 minutes. Remove the beef and sausage from the pot and set aside.

Bring the stock to a boil again, add the potatoes and cook for 5 minutes. Add the green beans and cabbage and cook for another 10 minutes or until the vegetables are done. Remove the vegetables, set aside, and reserve the stock.

For the sauce, heat the oil in a large saucepan and sauté the garlic and onion. Add the beef, sausage and tomato sauce. Simmer for 5 minutes. Add 3 cups of the reserved stock and bring to a boil. Add the garbanzo beans and cook on medium heat for about 10 minutes.

To serve, place the beef in a deep serving dish and arrange the vegetables around it. Pour the sauce over the beef and vegetables. Cut the sausage into thin slices and sprinkle over the top as a garnish. Makes 6–8 servings.

Seasoned Dried Beef
BEEF TAPA

Some cooks "cheat" by substituting the vinegar and sugar with Seven-Up.

Combine the soy sauce, sugar, salt, vinegar and garlic thoroughly, pour over the beef, and refrigerate, covered, for 7 days.

To dry the beef, arrange the slices on a foil-lined cookie sheet and put them in a 140° F oven for 5 hours, or follow the directions for a food dehydrator.

Store the dried beef in a cool, dark area until you are ready to cook. Fry in a lightly oiled skillet, or broil to desired doneness, 3–4 minutes on each side for medium-rare. Makes 5–6 servings.

⅓ cup soy sauce

5 tablespoons brown sugar, packed

1 teaspoon salt

⅓ cup cider vinegar

4 cloves garlic, minced

2 pounds boneless beef round, thinly sliced

Beef Teriyaki

½ cup soy sauce

1 tablespoon sugar

¼ cup sherry

1 clove garlic, minced

½ teaspoon ginger, finely
    chopped

1 teaspoon Tabasco sauce

1 pound beef sirloin, cut
    into strips ¼-inch thick

Combine the soy sauce, sugar, sherry, garlic, ginger and Tabasco sauce. Add the beef and marinate for 1–2 hours.

Thread the meat on wood or metal skewers and broil 4 inches from live coals or in a preheated broiler for 3–5 minutes on each side.

Makes 3–4 servings.

Stir-fried Steak
Bistek

2 tablespoons lemon juice

4 tablespoons soy sauce

½ teaspoon salt

1 tablespoon sugar

½ cup water

1½ pounds London Broil
    steak, sliced into strips
    about ¼-inch thick

2 cups onions, sliced thin

3 tablespoons vegetable oil

1 tablespoon cornstarch
    dissolved in 2 tablespoons
    water

Combine the lemon juice, soy sauce, salt, sugar and water in a cup. Pour the mixture over the beef slices and marinate for at least 30 minutes.

In a skillet, sauté the onions in the oil until they are transparent.

Add the beef and marinade liquid to the onions and stir-fry over high heat for 7–10 minutes. Add the cornstarch mixture to the liquid, and cook, stirring, for 2–3 minutes more.

Serve over rice. Makes 3–4 servings.

Braised Beef in Liver Sauce
CALDERETA

This dish is traditionally made with goat meat rather than beef.

Combine the vinegar, peppercorns and garlic in a bowl that is not aluminum, and add the beef cubes. Marinate for 1 or 2 hours.

Pour off the marinade, heat the oil in a skillet, and brown the beef on all sides. Remove the beef from the skillet and set aside.

In the same skillet, sauté the onions in the oil until they are translucent. Add the beef, tomato sauce, potatoes, bay leaves, salt, sugar and hot water. Bring to a boil, lower the heat and simmer, covered, for 1½ hours, or until the beef is tender.

Add the tomatoes, green and red bell peppers and Tabasco sauce. Continue simmering for 10 more minutes. Add the liverwurst, peas and olives. Stir well and cook, uncovered, for another 5 minutes.

Garnish with sliced hard-boiled eggs. Makes 6–8 servings.

*In the Philippines, the canned peas are firmer than those in the U.S., where frozen peas are better for this dish.

½ cup cider vinegar

6 whole peppercorns, crushed

3 cloves garlic, crushed

1½ pounds stewing beef, cut into 1-inch cubes

3 tablespoons vegetable oil

1 cup onion, sliced

½ cup tomato sauce

3 medium potatoes, peeled and quartered

3 bay leaves

2 teaspoons salt

1 teaspoon sugar

1 cup hot water

1 cup tomatoes, coarsely chopped

½ green bell pepper, cut into strips

½ red bell pepper, cut into strips

1 teaspoon Tabasco sauce

3 ounces liverwurst

8 ounces canned or frozen peas*

¼ cup pimiento-stuffed green olives, whole or pieces

2 eggs, hard-boiled and sliced

Tangy Braised Beef
Estofado

1½ pounds stewing beef, cut into 1-inch cubes

1½ teaspoons salt

½ teaspoon black pepper

½ cup flour

¼ cup vegetable oil

2 cloves garlic, minced

1 medium onion, coarsely chopped, or 8–10 pearl onions, peeled

1 medium tomato, chopped

¼ cup cider vinegar

3 bay leaves

1 cup green beans, cut into 1-inch lengths

1 cup carrots, peeled and cut into 1-inch lengths

Sprinkle the beef with the salt and pepper and let stand for 10–15 minutes. Dredge the beef with the flour and in a large pot, brown it in the oil. Remove the meat and set it aside.

Pour off all but 2 tablespoons of oil in the pan, and sauté the garlic, onions and tomatoes until the mixture is soft.

Add the vinegar, bay leaves and enough water to cover the beef. Stir well. Bring to a boil, lower the heat and simmer, covered, for 1½ to 2 hours or until the beef is tender. Add more salt and pepper if desired.

Bring back to a boil, add the green beans and carrots and simmer, covered, until the vegetables are tender, about 10 minutes. Makes 4–5 servings.

Braised Beef Tongue
Lengua Estofada

To prepare the tongue for cooking, rub it with salt and allow it to stand for 15 minutes. Rinse off the salt thoroughly, put the tongue in a large pot and cover it with water. Bring to a boil and parboil for 5 minutes. Remove the tongue from the water and allow it to cool slightly. Peel and scrape off the hard, white outer coating of the tongue. Wash and dry the tongue thoroughly.

Heat the oil in a large pot. Brown the tongue on all sides, remove it from the pot and set it aside. In the same pot, sauté the onions, garlic and tomatoes. Add the peppercorns, bay leaves, vinegar, soy sauce, water and sugar, cover, and simmer for 1½ to 2 hours or until the tongue is tender. Remove the tongue and slice it crosswise into thin pieces. Arrange the slices on a serving platter.

Bring the liquid to a boil over medium heat and cook until the volume is reduced to 1 cup. Strain and pour it over the slices of tongue.

Serve hot or cold. Makes 5–6 servings.

1 whole beef tongue (about 2 pounds)

1½ tablespoons salt

¼ cup vegetable oil

1 medium onion, quartered

3 cloves garlic, minced

8 ounces canned tomatoes

½ teaspoon peppercorns, crushed

2 bay leaves

½ cup native Philippine vinegar (*sukang paombong*) or white wine vinegar

¼ cup soy sauce

1 cup water

3 teaspoons sugar

Braised Flank Steak
Mechado

½ cup *kalamansi* or lemon juice

4 tablespoons soy sauce

2 pounds flank steak, trimmed of fat and silver skin

2 tablespoons vegetable oil

1 large onion, sliced

3 cloves garlic, crushed

3 tablespoons sherry

1½ cups water

1 bay leaf

½ teaspoon salt

1 teaspoon peppercorns, whole

8 ounces tomato sauce

3 potatoes, peeled and quartered

Combine the lemon juice and soy sauce and pour over the flank steak. Cover and refrigerate overnight.

When ready to cook, remove the flank steak from the marinade and reserve the marinade. In a skillet, heat the oil and brown the steak on all sides. Add the marinade liquid, onions, garlic, sherry, water, bay leaf, salt and peppercorns. Simmer, covered, until the beef is tender, about 1 to 1½ hours.

Remove the beef from the pan and slice into thin strips. Strain the liquid and return it to the pan. Add the tomato sauce, the sliced beef and the potatoes and bring to a boil. Reduce the heat and simmer until the potatoes are tender, about 10–15 minutes. Makes 4–6 servings.

Oxtail Stew
Menudo de Rabo

Place the oxtail in a pot, cover with water and season with 1 tablespoon of the salt. Boil, covered, for 2½ to 3 hours or until the oxtail is soft. Skim off the foam occasionally with a slotted spoon. Remove the oxtail from the liquid, reserve 3 cups of the broth, and set both aside.

In a large pot, heat the oil and sauté the onions until soft. Add the tomatoes, oxtail, potatoes and carrots. Cover the pot and cook over high heat until the mixture is almost dry, about 5–7 minutes, stirring occasionally.

Add the garbanzo beans, sausage and soy sauce and continue cooking, covered, for 3 minutes. Add the 3 cups of reserved broth and bring it to a boil. Reduce the heat and simmer for 10 minutes or until the potatoes are soft.

Add the pepper slices and simmer for 3 more minutes. Season with the teaspoon of salt and the pepper. Makes 6–8 servings.

2 pounds oxtail, cut into 2-inch pieces

1 tablespoon + 1 teaspoon salt

3 tablespoons vegetable oil

2 medium onions, sliced

4 medium tomatoes, sliced

2 cups potatoes, peeled and cut into ½-inch cubes

2 cups carrots, peeled and cut into ½-inch cubes

1 cup canned garbanzo beans (chickpeas), drained

1 Spanish sausage (chorizo de Bilbao), diced

1 tablespoon soy sauce

1 medium red bell pepper, sliced into thin strips

1 teaspoon black pepper

Filipino Oxtail Stew
KARE-KARE

2½ pounds oxtail or pork
   hocks, cut into 2-inch
   lengths

½ pound stewing beef
   (optional)

½ cup vegetable oil

2 tablespoons annatto seeds

2 cloves garlic, minced

1 medium onion, sliced

1½ teaspoons salt

3 tablespoons peanut butter

½ pound Chinese long beans
   or green beans, cut into
   2-inch lengths

3 Japanese eggplants, cut in
   half lengthwise and sliced
   into 2-inch lengths

½ pound bokchoy, cut into
   2-inch lengths

1 banana blossom, cut
   crosswise (optional)

½ pound daikon, sliced thin
   (optional)

Place the oxtail pieces or pork hocks and the beef (for a meatier dish) in a large pot, cover with water and bring to a boil. Lower the heat and simmer, covered, for 1½ hours or until tender. Occasionally skim off the foam that rises to surface.

Remove the meat and allow it to cool. Reserve 2 cups of the broth (the extra broth can be saved and used in other recipes).

Heat the vegetable oil in a pan and add the annatto seeds. Sauté until the oil turns red. Discard the seeds and allow the oil to cool. Use this oil to sauté the rest of the ingredients.

Heat 3 tablespoons of the annatto oil in a skillet and sauté the garlic and onions for a few minutes. Add the cooked meat, the 2 cups of reserved broth, and the salt and simmer for 15 minutes. Stir in the peanut butter. Bring back to a simmer and cook for 5 minutes more.

Add the beans, eggplant and bokchoy, and the banana blossom and daikon, if desired, and cook for 10 minutes or until the vegetables are tender, stirring constantly. Add salt and pepper to taste.

Serve with sautéed shrimp paste (page 228). Makes 6–8 servings.

Stuffed Rolled Steak
Morcon

This makes a great dish for parties because it is best if made 3 or 4 days ahead, wrapped in foil and kept in the refrigerator. Do not freeze it before cooking.

Preheat oven to 350° F.

Put the flank steak on a cutting board, and with a long knife, cut it in half parallel to the surface to within ½ inch of one side. Open it and lay flat. Pound the cut flank steak with a mallet to flatten it out further.

Combine the lemon juice, garlic and soy sauce, pour the mixture over the meat, and marinate for 1 hour. Pour off and reserve the marinade.

To stuff the beef, place it on a cutting board or large cookie sheet and arrange the carrots, sausage, bacon, sweet pickles and hard-boiled eggs in alternate rows on top of the meat. Roll the steak carefully from one end to the other like a jellyroll and tie it with string.

In a large, heavy, ovenproof casserole, heat the oil over moderate heat. Dredge the rolled meat in flour and brown it on all sides in the hot oil.

Add the water, reserved marinade, onions, tomatoes, bay leaves, peppercorns and salt. Cover and bake for 1½ to 2 hours, turning the meat once or twice while cooking.

When the meat is tender, transfer to a warm serving dish and remove the strings. Allow it to rest for 15 minutes.

Scrape the sides of the casserole dish and pour the liquid through a strainer into a saucepan. Bring it just to a boil, add the cornstarch and water mixture and cook, stirring, until it thickens into a gravy.

To serve, slice the rolled steak crosswise and pour gravy over the slices. Makes 6–8 servings.

2 pounds flank steak

Juice of ½ lemon

1 clove garlic, minced

3 tablespoons soy sauce

1 medium carrot, peeled and quartered lengthwise

1 Spanish sausage (chorizo de Bilbao), quartered lengthwise

4 slices bacon

2 whole sweet pickles, quartered

2 eggs, hard-boiled and quartered

2 tablespoons vegetable oil

¼ cup flour

4 cups water

2 cups onions, sliced

1 16-ounce can stewed tomatoes

3 bay leaves

½ teaspoon whole peppercorns

1½ teaspoons salt

1 teaspoon cornstarch dissolved in 2 teaspoons water

Shish Kabob

¼ cup onions, finely chopped

Juice of 1 lemon

¼ cup olive oil

2 cloves garlic, crushed

1 teaspoon salt

¼ teaspoon black pepper

1 tablespoon soy sauce

1 tablespoon sugar

1 teaspoon Tabasco sauce or hot chili oil

2 pounds beef sirloin, cut into 2-inch cubes

8 mushroom caps

1 medium tomato, quartered or 4 cherry tomatoes

1 green or red bell pepper, cut into squares

2 red or white onions, quartered

1 medium eggplant, cut into 1½-inch cubes

Combine the onions, lemon juice, oil, garlic, salt, pepper, soy sauce, sugar and hot sauce in a bowl that is not aluminum. Add the beef and refrigerate overnight.

Thread the meat on four 10-inch skewers, alternating it with peppers, mushrooms, onions and eggplants. Put the tomatoes at the end of the skewers so that they can be taken off as soon as they are cooked.

Brush the meat and vegetables with the marinade and grill 4 inches over hot coals, or in a preheated broiler, for 3–4 minutes on each side. Makes 4 servings.

Ground Beef Omelet
TORTANG CARNE

In a skillet, heat 1 tablespoon of the oil and sauté the garlic, onions and tomatoes. Add the ground beef and stir until it is browned, about 5–7 minutes. Drain off any excess fat.

Add the salt, pepper, sugar, parsley or cilantro, potatoes and ¼ cup of water. Cover and cook for 15 minutes or until the potatoes are tender and most of the water has evaporated. Remove from the heat and allow to cool slightly. Stir the beaten eggs into the meat and vegetables.

In a nonstick skillet, heat 2 tablespoons of the oil and coat the bottom of the skillet evenly. Pour the egg and meat mixture into the skillet and let cook undisturbed for 2–3 minutes over medium heat. Loosen the sides with a spatula, place a plate over the omelet and skillet, and turn the skillet upside down so that the torta lands on the plate cooked side up.

Add the remaining 1 tablespoon of oil to the skillet and slide the omelet back into the skillet with the uncooked side down. Cook for 2 minutes more over medium heat. Transfer the omelet to a serving plate. Makes 4–6 servings.

4 tablespoons vegetable oil

2 cloves garlic, minced

1 medium onion, diced

2 medium tomatoes, chopped

1 pound lean ground beef

1½ teaspoons salt

½ teaspoon black pepper

¼ teaspoon sugar

1 teaspoon parsley or cilantro, minced

2 medium potatoes, peeled and diced

¼ cup water

4 eggs, well beaten

Stewed Tripe
CALLOS

1½ pounds tripe

2 tablespoons vegetable oil

2 cloves garlic, minced

1 small onion, thinly sliced

8 ounces tomato sauce

1½ cups water

1 teaspoon salt

1 teaspoon black pepper

2 teaspoons paprika

1 Spanish sausage (chorizo de Bilbao), thinly sliced

2 cups carrots, peeled and cut into 1-inch sticks

1 medium red or green bell pepper, sliced into thin strips or one 4-ounce can pimientos, drained

1 8-ounce can garbanzo beans (chickpeas), drained

Place the tripe in a large pot and cover with water. Bring to a boil and parboil for 5 minutes. Pour off the water and rinse the pot well. Place tripe in the pot again and cover with fresh water. Bring to a boil, lower heat and simmer, covered, for 2½ to 3 hours or until the tripe is tender and the edges are translucent. Drain the tripe and cut it into 1-inch cubes.

Heat the oil in a large skillet and sauté the garlic and onions for a few minutes. Add the tripe, tomato sauce, water, salt, pepper, paprika and sliced sausage. Bring to a boil, lower heat, and simmer, covered, for 20 minutes.

Add the carrots, bell peppers or pimientos and garbanzo beans. Cook, covered, for another 10 minutes or until the carrots are tender. Makes 6 servings.

Pork

In the Philippines, as in other parts of the world that eat pork, every part of the pig is used except for the squeal. Pork is the most popular meat in most of the Philippines because it can be used in so many ways. Pigs are easy and inexpensive to raise and reproduce quickly. Many families in the provinces raise pigs in a pen next to the house, feeding them leftovers and scraps from the table. For many, it is an important way to raise extra cash when needed. Pigs are bred, raised and when necessary, sold to butchers for cash—a living version of a "piggy-bank" for many people in the Philippines.

Braised Pork in Tomato Sauce
Afritada

1 pound pork butt*, cut into
    1-inch cubes

1 teaspoon salt

¼ teaspoon black pepper

2 tablespoons vegetable oil

1 medium onion, sliced thin

2 cloves garlic, minced

½ cup tomato sauce

½ cup water

1 tablespoon fish sauce

2 medium potatoes, peeled
    and quartered

1 small red bell pepper, cut
    into thin strips

1 small green bell pepper,
    cut into thin strips

2 tablespoons cornstarch,
    dissolved in 3 tablespoons
    water

Sprinkle the pork cubes with the salt and pepper. Let stand for 15 minutes.

Heat the oil in a skillet and fry the pork until it is a light brown. Pour off the excess oil.

Add the onions, garlic, tomato sauce, water and fish sauce and simmer, covered, for 40 minutes or until the pork is tender.

Add the potatoes and cook another 10 minutes, or until they are done. Add the bell peppers and cook for 3 minutes more or until the peppers just start to soften. Add salt and pepper to correct seasonings, if desired.

Stir in the cornstarch and water mixture to thicken the sauce.

Serve hot. Makes 4 servings.

*Chicken or a combination of pork and chicken may be used in this recipe.

Barbecued Spareribs

¼ cup soy sauce

2 tablespoons lemon juice

3 cloves garlic, minced

¼ cup brown sugar

1 teaspoon salt

2 pounds pork spareribs

Combine the soy sauce, lemon juice, garlic, sugar and salt. Add the spareribs and let marinate at least 4 hours, or overnight, turning frequently.

Cooking in an oven: Preheat the oven to 350° F. Pour hot water into a roaster pan to a depth of 1 inch. Place the ribs on roaster rack over the water. Bake for 1 hour, turning the ribs once after 30 minutes.

Cooking over charcoal: Cook 4–6 inches above hot coals for 10–15 minutes, turning frequently. Makes 4–5 servings.

Pork and Squid in Tangy Sauce
ASADONG BABOY AT PUSIT

To prepare the squid, twist the tentacles from body of squid. Clean the squid by removing the quill and squeezing out the innards. Remove the skin from the body under running water, using one's fingers. Then take a knife and cut the tentacles just beneath the eye. This makes it possible to discard the beak and the ink sack without being squirted with ink. Wash body and tentacles well and set them aside to drain in a colander.

In a saucepan, bring the water to a boil. Add the pork cubes, lower the heat, and simmer for 15 minutes. Drain the pork and pat it dry with paper towels.

In a heated, dry skillet, sauté the pork in its own fat for 5 minutes. Remove and set aside. Drain all but 1 tablespoon of fat from the skillet.

Sauté the garlic in the same skillet until it is light brown. Add the onions and cook until they are translucent. Add the tomatoes and cook until they become soft. Add the cooked pork and stir-fry for 3 minutes more.

Add the remaining ingredients, except the squid, and bring to a boil without stirring. Lower the heat and simmer for 30 minutes, or until the pork is tender.

Add the cleaned squid and cook for 1–2 minutes, stirring constantly.

Serve hot. Makes 4 servings.

1 pound squid

½ cup water

1 pound pork, cut into 1-inch cubes

3 cloves garlic, minced

1 medium onion, sliced

2 small tomatoes, diced

2 teaspoons salt

½ teaspoon black pepper

2 bay leaves

½ cup distilled white vinegar

1 teaspoon sugar

Pork Blood Stew
Dinuguan Baboy

1 pound pork, diced

2 tablespoons vegetable oil

2 cloves garlic, minced

1 small onion, diced

¼ pound pork liver, diced

2 tablespoons fish sauce

1 teaspoon salt

½ cup red cider vinegar

12 ounces fresh or frozen
   pork blood*

2 teaspoons sugar

3 jalapeño peppers, whole

Put the pork in a saucepan and cover it with water. Simmer for 30 minutes on medium heat. Remove the pork from the broth and reserve 1½ cups of the pork broth.

In a large pan, heat the oil and sauté the garlic and onions for 2–3 minutes. Add the pork, liver, fish sauce and salt. Sauté for 3 minutes more.

Add the vinegar and bring to a boil without stirring. Lower the heat and simmer, uncovered, until the volume of the liquid is reduced by half.

Add the reserved pork broth and simmer for 7–8 minutes. Stir in the pork blood and sugar. (If using frozen blood, make sure it is totally thawed before using.) Continue cooking until the sauce has thickened, stirring continuously to keep the blood from curdling. (The blood makes this dish look black.)

Add the hot peppers and cook for 5 minutes more. For more spiciness, mash the peppers against the side of the pan with a wooden spoon after they have softened.

Serve hot with steamed rice cakes (*puto,* page 68) or over rice. Makes 4 servings.

* *PUBLISHER'S NOTE:* It is important for cooks unfamiliar with this ingredient to be confident of their source for the pork blood.

Stuffed Pork Sausage
Embutido

Thoroughly mix together the ground pork, bread crumbs, sausage, eggs, relish, salt, pepper, onions and raisins.

Spread the mixture over a 12-inch by 18-inch piece of cheesecloth, to make a rectangle 8 inches by 12 inches.

Arrange the hard-boiled eggs in a row at the center lengthwise.

Bringing up the edges of the cheesecloth, roll the meat around the eggs and shape it together. Tie tightly at both ends of the bundle with string.

Place the rolled sausage in a steamer over water and steam for 1 hour. Allow it to rest for 10 minutes. Unwrap and slice crosswise.

To make the sauce, mix together the chicken broth, liverwurst, tomato sauce and catsup in a saucepan and simmer for 5–7 minutes. Thicken with the cornstarch and water mixture.

To serve, arrange the sausage slices on a serving platter. Cover with the sauce. Makes 6–8 servings.

2 pounds ground pork

1 cup bread crumbs, soaked in ½ cup milk

1 Spanish sausage (chorizo de Bilbao), finely chopped

2 eggs, slightly beaten

¼ cup sweet pickle relish

2 teaspoons salt

½ teaspoon black pepper

1 small onion, diced

3 tablespoons raisins

2 eggs, hard-boiled and quartered

SAUCE:

1 cup chicken broth

4 ounces liverwurst or liverspread

8 ounces tomato sauce

3 tablespoons catsup

1 tablespoon cornstarch dissolved in 2 tablespoons water

Grilled Pork Strips
INIHAW NA BABOY

1½ pounds pork shoulder or pork butt, sliced into strips ¼ inch thick

1½ teaspoons salt

1 teaspoon black pepper

Put the pork slices on a platter and sprinkle them with the salt and pepper. Let stand for 20–30 minutes.

Broil on a grill over hot coals until light brown on both sides, approximately 10 minutes on each side.

Serve with Vinegar and Garlic Dipping Sauce (*Suka't Bawang Sawsawan,* page 234).

Pork with Black Bean Sauce
HUMBA

2½ pounds pork hocks, cut into 2-inch pieces or 2 pounds pork butt, cut into 1½-inch cubes

2 cloves garlic, minced

½ cup distilled white vinegar

3 tablespoons brown sugar (packed)

¼ cup soy sauce

2 bay leaves

2 tablespoons fermented black beans *(tausi)*

½ teaspoon black peppercorns, crushed

1 cup water

½ cup unsalted peanuts, coarsely chopped

Combine all the ingredients in a large pot, bring to a boil, lower the heat and simmer until the pork is tender, about 1½ hours for pork hocks, 1 hour for the pork butt.

Remove the bay leaves and serve hot. Makes 6 servings.

Pork with Banana Blossom Heart
LAGAT NA PUSO

Banana blossom hearts are available, canned, in most Asian grocery stores. A 12-ounce can of artichoke hearts, drained and chopped, can be substituted, however.

If using a fresh banana blossom heart, remove the hard covering of the blossom, about 3 petals, and slice the soft inside sections crosswise. Sprinkle the pieces with the salt and squeeze. Rinse and drain well. Set aside.

In a skillet, sauté the pork to a golden brown in 1 tablespoon of the vegetable oil for 5–6 minutes. Remove the pork and set aside.

In the same skillet, add 3 more tablespoons of the oil and heat. Add the garlic and onions and sauté until the onions are translucent.

Add the vinegar and bring to a boil without stirring. Add the shrimp and simmer for 1 minute. Add the cooked pork and simmer for 5 more minutes.

Add the banana blossom hearts and cook until tender, about 5–7 minutes. Season with the salt and pepper. Makes 3–4 servings.

1 12-ounce can banana blossom hearts, drained and chopped or 1 fresh banana blossom heart

1 tablespoon salt, if using fresh banana blossom heart

½ pound pork, diced

4 tablespoons vegetable oil

4 cloves garlic, crushed

1 medium onion, sliced

½ cup native Philippine vinegar (*sukang paombong*)

¼ pound shrimp, peeled and chopped

½ teaspoon salt

½ teaspoon black pepper

Roast Pork
Lechon sa Horno

5 pounds fresh ham roast or
    pork shoulder, skin still on

1 tablespoon salt

Traditional Lechon sa Horno *or* Lechon *involves roasting a whole suckling pig. Since most people do not have ovens large enough to cook a whole pig, we have scaled the size of the cut to a more manageable level. However, if one were inclined to cook a whole pig, the cooking technique is about the same. Note: Roasting pork generates lots of smoke. Ventilate the kitchen and house well.*

Preheat oven to 350° F.

Clean the pork thoroughly and dry with paper towels. Rub it all over with the salt and place in a roasting pan, skin side up, in the oven.

Roast for about 3½ hours, or 40 minutes per pound.

Brush the skin with the drippings every 10 minutes during the last hour of cooking to make the skin crisp.

After the allotted time for cooking, increase the heat to 450° F. and roast for 20–30 minutes more. This will cause the skin to bubble up and become extra golden brown and crisp.

Remove the roast from the oven and allow to rest for 10–15 minutes. Slice and serve with *Lechon* Sauce (page 229).

Pan Roasted Pork
LECHON SA KAWALE

Slice the pork belly into 2 pieces. Put the pieces in a pot, cover with water, and add the salt. Bring the water to a boil, lower the heat, and simmer for 1½ hours.

Remove the pork from the pot and put it on a rack in a roasting pan containing some water. Put the pan in a preheated, 250° F oven and slow roast for 2 hours to remove excess fat. The pork will turn slightly brown.

Put enough oil in a dutch oven or large casserole to a depth of 3 inches. When the oil is hot, fry the pork pieces one at a time for 30 minutes, until the skin becomes bubbly and golden brown.

Remove the meat from the oil and drain well. Cut into 1-inch cubes and serve with *Lechon* Sauce (page 229).

VARIATION:

Cut the pork into 1-inch cubes, place in a pot, cover with water and add the salt. Bring the water to a boil, lower the heat, and simmer for 1½ hours.

Remove the meat from the pot. Heat 2 cups of oil in a wok or *kawale* (a shallow Filipino-style wok) and fry the cubes until they are crisp and golden brown, about 1 to 1½ hours. Must be stirred constantly during the cooking to keep the pieces of pork from sticking together.

Drain the meat on paper towels. Serve with *Lechon* Sauce (page 229) or Vinegar and Garlic Dipping Sauce *(Suka't Bawang Sawsawan,* page 234).

3 pounds pork belly or side of pork *(liempo),* with the skin still on

2 tablespoons salt

3–4 cups vegetable oil

Spiced Pork Sausage
Longanisa

2 pounds pork butt, coarsely ground or chopped

1 pound pork fat, diced

5 cloves garlic, minced

½ teaspoon oregano

3 tablespoons brown sugar (packed)

¼ cup soy sauce

⅓ cup cider vinegar

1½ teaspoons salt

2 tablespoons annatto (atsuete) powder, or paprika

1 teaspoon black pepper

1 teaspoon red pepper flakes (optional)

Sausage casing, natural or artificial

Combine all the ingredients, except for the casing, and marinate at room temperature for 2 hours.

Fill the casing with the pork mixture. Tie the casing with string at 3- to 4-inch intervals. Refrigerate, covered, for 2 days to allow the sausages to age.

When ready to cook, place the desired amount of sausages in a skillet. Using a fork, prick the sausages all over. Cover them halfway with water, and simmer over medium heat until all the water evaporates, about 15–20 minutes. Turn 2 or 3 times during the cooking

Brown the sausages on all sides in their own fat for 3–5 minutes on each side. Makes 6–8 servings.

Pork and Liver Stew
MENUDO

In a large pot, heat the oil and sauté the garlic and onions for 2 minutes. Add the diced pork and sauté until it is light brown.

Add the salt, fish sauce, black pepper, Spanish sausage or ham, tomato sauce, pimientos, paprika and water. Simmer, covered, for 30–40 minutes.

Add the potatoes and garbanzo beans and cook for 10 more minutes, or until the potatoes are tender.

Add the liver and simmer for 5 minutes more. Add salt and pepper to taste. Makes 4–6 servings.

2 tablespoons vegetable oil

2 cloves garlic, minced

1 medium onion, diced

1 pound pork, diced

1½ teaspoons salt

1 tablespoon fish sauce

¼ teaspoon black pepper

1 Spanish sausage (chorizo *de Bilbao),* diced or 1 cup ham, diced

8 ounces tomato sauce

2 ounces canned pimientos

1 tablespoon paprika

1 cup water

2 medium potatoes, peeled and diced

1 cup canned garbanzo beans (chickpeas), drained

½ pound beef or pork liver, diced

Pickled Pork
PAKSIW NA BABOY

1 cup cider vinegar

2 bay leaves

¼ cup soy sauce

¼ cup sugar

1 teaspoon salt

1 teaspoon black pepper

6 cloves garlic, crushed and chopped

1 cup water

2 pounds pork shoulder or butt, cubed

In a ceramic or stainless steel saucepan, combine the vinegar, bay leaves, soy sauce, sugar, salt, pepper, garlic and water. Add the pork and mix well. Cover and simmer for 45–60 minutes, stirring occasionally.

Serve hot or cold. Serves 4–6.

Roast Pork in Liver Sauce
PAKSIW NA LECHON

2 pounds leftover roast pork (lechon), cut into cubes

1½–2 cups leftover *lechon* sauce*

1 bay leaf

3 tablespoons soy sauce

1 teaspoon whole black peppercorns

½ cup distilled white vinegar

¼ cup brown sugar

6 cloves garlic, minced

½ teaspoon thyme

½ teaspoon cinnamon

½ teaspoon salt

This is a simple and tasty way to use leftover roast pork.

In a ceramic or stainless steel saucepan, combine all the ingredients and mix well. Cover and simmer for 30–40 minutes. Serves 4–6.

*If you don't have leftover *lechon* sauce, use the commercially available sauce found in Asian food stores.

Pickled Pork Hocks
PAKSIW NA PATA

Put the pork in a non-aluminum pot and add enough water to cover. Add the remaining ingredients except the plantain, and mix well.

Bring the liquid to a boil, lower the heat, and simmer for 1½ hours, or until the pork is tender.

In a skillet, heat the oil on high and fry the plantain slices for 2 minutes on each side, or until they turn golden brown. Remove and drain on paper towels. Add the fried plantain to the pork during the last 10 minutes of cooking. Serves 6–8.

VARIATION:

Pork shoulder, cut into 1-inch cubes, may be used in place of or in combination with the pork hocks.

3 pounds pork hocks, cut into 2-inch pieces

½ cup cider vinegar

1 teaspoon salt

¼ cup soy sauce

¼ cup brown sugar

½ teaspoon whole black peppercorns

1 bay leaf

2 cloves garlic, crushed

¼ teaspoon oregano

¼ teaspoon whole cloves

½ cup dried banana blossoms, soaked in warm water for 30 minutes (optional)

1 cup vegetable oil

1 plantain, sliced

Grilled Marinated Pork
PORK SATE'

1½ pounds pork butt, cut into strips 2 inches long, 1 inch wide and ¼ inch thick

1 tablespoon salt

2 tablespoons lemon juice

3 cloves garlic, minced

¼ cup peanut butter, creamy or chunky style

3 tablespoons fish sauce

2 teaspoons soy sauce

¼ teaspoon red pepper flakes or crushed red pepper

3 tablespoons brown sugar

3 tablespoons water

Place the strips of pork in a bowl and mix with the salt. Set aside.

Combine the rest of the ingredients in a saucepan, stir, and cook over low heat for 3–5 minutes.

Pour the marinade over the pork, cover with plastic wrap, and refrigerate for 2–3 hours, or overnight.

When ready to barbecue, thread 4 strips of pork per skewer.

Grill over hot coals for 3–4 minutes on each side. Brush with the marinade occasionally. Makes 6–8 servings.

Sweet Marinated Pork
TOSINO

¼ cup sugar

¼ cup cider vinegar

1 tablespoon salt

4 tablespoons red food coloring

2 pounds pork belly or pork butt, cut into ¼-inch-thick strips

2 tablespoons vegetable oil

Combine the sugar, vinegar, salt and red food coloring in a small bowl or cup.

Put the pork slices in a thick plastic storage bag, and pour the mixture of seasonings over the pork slices. Seal the bag tightly with a twist tie and toss the meat and marinade together very well. Marinate in the refrigerator for 3–4 days, tossing it once each day.

When ready to cook, pan-fry the pork in the oil for 4–5 minutes on each side. Or, thread the meat on metal or bamboo skewers and cook over hot coals 4–5 minutes on each side. Makes 6–8 servings.

Pork Adobo

With chunks of pork braised in a sauce of vinegar, garlic and annatto, this dish is best when made from a marbled cut of pork such as the boston butt or picnic shoulder. But most cooks prefer this adobo made with spare ribs because of the gelatin in the spare ribs and the sheer delight of being able to suck the meat off the bone.

Chicken Adobo

The most popular of all Adobo, this and other Adobo are at their best when made one day, allowed to sit for the next few days, reheated and then served. This allows the tangy sauce to "mellow" and the flavors within the meat to intensify.

Shrimp in Coconut Milk

Coconut milk is reduced, then shrimp are added along with slices of bell pepper, ginger and green onions creating a sweet and savory dish that goes well over plain rice.

Stuffed Shrimp

Butterfly cut shrimp and ground pork sausage in a lumpia wrapper then deep fried, this treat is great for parties. Make lots ahead of time and freeze. This and other fried lumpia can be stored for months and then deep fried just before serving. Do not defrost before frying.
If defrosted it will create a mess.

Lumpia

This is the Filipino version of Chinese egg rolls. It tastes great as a snack or part of a main course. Serve with catsup, sweet and sour sauce or garlic and vinegar dipping sauce.

Shrimp Fritters

Great by themselves but enhanced with a drizzle of sauce made from vinegar and garlic,
ukoy are delectable.

Breads

Monay, Pan de Leche, Puto, Ensaymada, Pan de Sal, Bibingkang, Ube Halaya, Cuchinta, Ube Ensaymada.

Pancit palabok

A truly international dish, the rice noodles are Chinese, its garnish is native Filipino dried fish and the sauce is made with annatto which has its roots in Mexican cooking.

Sautéed Rice Noodles

Pancit Bihon is much lighter in taste and texture compared to other pancits because of the thin and delicate bihon noodles used.

Chicken Relleno

Although lots of work, the result is well worth the time spent.

Stuffed Milkfish

The milkfish is stuffed with a relish of tomatoes, peppers, garlic and ginger. When serving a portion of the fish a few tablespoons of the relish should be arranged on the plate. It adds color and lends a sweet and sour taste to this robust fish.

Milkfish in Sour Broth

All Sinigangs start with a sour broth created from tamarind, guavas or lemons and a stock derived
from seafood, fish, beef or pork. The addition of meats and vegetables enhances the dish.
The final result is limited only by the availability of ingredients and the creativity of the cook.

Suman

Suman: To eat, just unwrap like a banana and dip in grated coconut. This makes a great dessert or a highly satisfying snack. *Malagkit:* Sweet rice flavored with lye water and sugar. The banana leaf wrapper imparts not only color but an earthy taste as well. *Pirurutong:* Suman made with a native Filipino purple wild rice and coconut milk. *Cassava:* A hearty and chewy suman made from cassava.

Menudo

It's not unusual in countries with Spanish influences that people enjoy the weekend dancing, singing, eating and drinking. To help overcome the Monday morning hangovers, bowls of Menudo are dished up. Menudo helps clear the mind and invigorate the body.

Kare-kare

Oxtails in peanut sauce would not be Kare-Kare unless it is served with cooked *Bagoong Alamang* (Sautéed Shrimp Paste). It would be like eating a hot dog without mustard or an ice cream sundae without chocolate or caramel sauce. All are good to eat but without the sauce there seems to be something lacking.

Afritada

Although Afritada was originally made with pork or chicken, Filipinos prefer goat meat for this dish.
The most tender and coveted part of the goat is the meat on the head where it is most succulent.

Dinuguan baboy

Pork blood stew is usually served over a bed of rice. But this traditional dish is best enjoyed with puto or steamed sweet rice flour cakes to soak up the sauce.

Stuffed Pork Sausage

A delightful "meatloaf" that is steam cooked rather than baked giving it a more paté like texture.
It is convenient because it can be stored for months in the freezer. When needed it can be
defrosted and quickly baked or pan fried just before it is served.

Roast Pork

Roasted pork with the skin left on and allowed to cook to a crisp is served with a sweet and savory liver sauce.

Marinated Milkfish

Bangus or milkfish like many other fish is extremely versatile. It can be broiled, fried, smoked or made into soups. *Daing Na Bangus* is a very simple dish. Dip the fish in a sauce or vinegar and serve with steamed rice.

Smoked Milkfish

Bangus or milkfish is a great white-flesh fish with good oil and fat content. To smoke the bangus, first clean, lightly salt and rub with a little lemon. Then slow smoke with wood chips derived from fruit trees like apple, pear or cherry. To give the fish a nice glaze brush it occasionally with oil.

Vegetable Stew with Pork

A stew of sautéed vegetables that varies according to what's fresh and available at the market. At its base is bittermelon and *bagoong alamang* which give *pinakbet* its distinctive flavor.

Paella

It looks complicated but Paella can be prepared very easily. All it takes is organization and a touch of the artistic when it comes to the final assembly.

Halo-halo

Here are but a few examples of what can be added to a Halo-Halo: sweetened beans, *nata de pina*, *nata de coco*, *kaong* (palm nut), jackfruit, *macapuno* and *ube* (purple yam) paste. Get yourself a glass of shaved ice, and dallops of each and any of the sweets, top with evaporated milk or vanilla ice cream and mix together. Eat quickly with a spoon. Halo-Halo is at its best when the shaved ice has just started to melt and is still crunchy but not to the point where the water dilutes the flavors.

Seasoned Dried Pork
PORK TAPA

Combine all ingredients except the pork and oil and mix thoroughly. Add the meat, stir well, and marinate, covered, in the refrigerator for 3–4 days.

Arrange the pork slices on a foil-lined cookie sheet and dry them in a 140°F oven for 6 hours. Allow to cool and refrigerate until ready to cook.

To cook: pan-fry in 3 tablespoons of vegetable oil until browned on both sides, about 3–5 minutes on each side. Or broil for 10–12 minutes, turning once. Makes 5–6 servings.

⅓ cup soy sauce

5 tablespoons brown sugar (packed)

1 tablespoon salt

⅓ cup cider vinegar

2 cloves garlic, minced

2 pounds boneless pork butt, sliced thin

3 tablespoons vegetable oil

Thai Marinated Pork
SATE' BABI

Combine the *kalamansi* or lemon juice, brown sugar, soy sauce, rum and garlic together well in a bowl. Add the pork and stir. Marinate, covered, for 3 hours or overnight in the refrigerator.

When ready to cook, remove the pork from the marinade and thread on metal or bamboo skewers, 4–5 cubes on each. Reserve the marinade liquid.

In a bowl, stir together the marinade liquid and the *mafran* sauce.

Grill the pork over hot coals, brushing it with the sauce occasionally, for 5–6 minutes on each side.

Serve with *Sate'* Sauce (page 232). Makes 5–6 servings.

6 tablespoons *kalamansi* or lemon juice

⅔ cup brown sugar (packed)

3 tablespoons soy sauce

4 tablespoons dark rum

3 cloves garlic, minced

2½ pounds pork tenderloin or pork butt, cut into 1-inch cubes

½ cup *mafran* sauce (banana ketchup)

Chicken

Chickens, *manok,* were originally wild fowl that was domesticated by man centuries ago. Even today, in the jungles and forests of the tropics, there are birds that look like the wild ancestors of chickens, but are much harder to catch. Chickens are easy to domesticate and raise because they stay together in flocks and will eat almost anything. So they can be raised in small spaces and fed with scraps from the table.

In the Philippines, one chicken provides three meals. The breast becomes *Fritong Manok* (Fried Chicken, page 145); the dark meat from the thighs and drumsticks is added to *Pancit* (Sautéed Noodles, page 83); the chicken back, wings, neck, liver and gizzards are cooked for a broth as the basis for *Tinola* (Chicken and Green Papaya Stew, page 148) or *Arroz caldo* (Thick Rice Soup, page 206).

Tangy Chicken Stew
ASADONG MANOK

Cut the thigh pieces in half and place the chicken in a medium-sized pan, add the salt, pepper, garlic, bay leaf and vinegar, and cook over medium heat, uncovered, until dry, about 15–20 minutes.

Add the paprika and continue cooking, browning the chicken on all sides.

Add the water and bring to a boil. Add the tomatoes and onions, and simmer for 10 minutes or until the liquid has been reduced by half. Makes 4–5 servings.

2 pounds chicken legs and thighs, or drumsticks and wings

½ teaspoon salt

½ teaspoon black pepper

6 cloves garlic, crushed

1 bay leaf

¼ cup distilled white vinegar

1 tablespoon paprika

1 cup water

1 medium tomato, chopped

1 medium onion, chopped

Ginger and Chicken Stew
NILAGANG MANOK

This dish is also known in the Philippines as Nilaga.

Place the chicken pieces in a large pot, add the water, ginger, peppercorns, salt, onions and celery, and bring to a boil. Lower the heat, cover, and simmer for 30 minutes.

Add the potatoes, and cook for 10–15 minutes.

Add the cabbage and green onions and cook for 10–15 minutes more, or until the cabbage is tender. Add salt and pepper to taste. Makes 5–6 servings.

3 pounds chicken, cut into pieces

5 cups water

3 slices ginger, crushed

½ teaspoon whole peppercorns

2 teaspoons salt

1 medium onion, quartered

1 rib celery, cut into 2-inch lengths

2 medium potatoes, peeled and quartered

1 small cabbage, quartered

3 green onions, cut into 2-inch lengths

Chicken in Ginger Sauce

3 cups water

2 teaspoons salt

3 pounds whole chicken

1 carrot, peeled and sliced

1 medium onion, sliced

1 rib celery, sliced

SAUCE:

4 tablespoons vegetable oil

1 teaspoon salt

1 tablespoon ginger, minced

2 cloves garlic, minced

1 tablespoon cilantro, finely chopped

1 tablespoon green onion, finely chopped

In a large pot, bring the water and 1½ teaspoons of the salt to a boil. Add the chicken, carrots, onions and celery, reduce the heat and simmer, covered, for 20–25 minutes. Remove the chicken and let it cool. Cut the chicken into serving pieces, arrange on a platter, and sprinkle with ½ teaspoon of salt. Cover and refrigerate for 2–3 hours. Refrigerate the liquid and vegetables until the fat rises to the surface and can be skimmed off.

Grind the vegetables in a blender or food processor, return to the broth, and reheat over medium heat.

In a small saucepan or skillet, heat the oil until almost to the smoking point. Add the salt and remove from the heat. Add the ginger and garlic and stir for a few seconds, then add the cilantro and green onions. Return to the heat and fry on medium for 1 minute.

To serve, spread the stir-fried seasonings over the chilled chicken. Serve the warm chicken broth in small bowls on the side. Makes 4 servings.

Chicken in Peanut Sauce

Soak the annatto seeds in the water for 2 hours.

Meanwhile, heat the oil in a large skillet or pot and brown the chicken pieces. Remove the chicken and set aside.

In the same skillet, sauté the garlic and onions for 2 minutes. Add the browned chicken, the hot water, salt, fish sauce and pepper and bring to a boil. Reduce the heat and simmer, covered, for 30 minutes.

Squeeze the soaked annatto seeds in the water, strain, and pour the red liquid in the chicken pot. Discard the seeds. Add the peanut butter and mix well.

Add the green beans and bok choy stalks to the chicken and bring to a boil again. Reduce the heat and simmer for 10 minutes, stirring occasionally. Add the bok choy leaves and stir. Simmer for 3 minutes more.

Remove from heat. Allow to stand for a few minutes before serving. Makes 4–5 servings.

1 tablespoon annatto (*atsuete*) seeds, soaked in ½ cup water for 2 hours

3 tablespoons vegetable oil

3 pounds chicken, cut into bite-size pieces

1 clove garlic, minced

1 small onion, diced

2 cups hot water

1 teaspoon salt

1 tablespoon fish sauce

½ teaspoon black pepper

3 tablespoons chunky-style peanut butter

1 pound bok choy (*pechay*), cut into 2-inch lengths with the stalks separated from the greens

½ pound green beans, cut into 1-inch lengths

Chicken and Sausage Stew
CHICKEN POCHERO

2 pounds chicken, cut up into bite-size pieces

½ pound ham, cut into ¼-inch cubes

1 pound lean pork, diced

6 cloves garlic, crushed

3 tablespoons vegetable oil

1 medium onion, sliced

1 12-ounce can tomato sauce

3 potatoes, peeled and quartered

6 saba bananas or 3 plantains, peeled and sliced

2 Spanish sausages (chorizo de Bilbao), cut into 1-inch lengths

1 cup canned garbanzo beans (chickpeas), drained

1 small cabbage, quartered

½ pound green beans, cut into 2-inch lengths

½ pound bok choy (pechay), cut into strips lengthwise

1 teaspoon salt

½ teaspoon black pepper

1 tablespoon cornstarch dissolved in 2 tablespoons water

Heat 3 cups of water in a pot and bring to a boil. Add the chicken, ham and pork and boil for 15–20 minutes, or until the chicken is tender. Remove the meats and set them aside and reserve the broth.

In a large pot, sauté the garlic in hot oil. Add the onions, tomato sauce and reserved broth and bring to a boil. Reduce the heat and simmer for 5 minutes.

Add the potatoes, bananas, sausage and garbanzo beans and simmer until the potatoes and bananas are tender, about 10 minutes.

Add the cabbage, green beans and bok choy and simmer for another 15 minutes. Add the cooked ham, pork and chicken and simmer for 5 minutes more. Season with the salt and pepper.

To thicken the sauce, stir in the cornstarch and water mixture and continue stirring. Makes 8 servings.

Chicken Blood Stew
DINUGUAN MANOK

The chicken blood that makes this dish so delicious is available, frozen, at most Asian markets. Make sure it is totally thawed before using it.

Heat the oil in a medium saucepan and sauté the garlic for 1 minute. Add the onions and tomatoes and cook until onions have softened.

Stir in the chicken meat, liver and giblets. Cover and cook over medium heat for 5 minutes.

Add the vinegar, salt, pepper and bay leaf and simmer for 5 minutes more.

Add the chicken blood and water mixture and the hot pepper. Continue cooking for 10 minutes, stirring frequently. Makes 3–4 servings.

* See *PUBLISHER'S NOTE*, page 126.

3 tablespoons vegetable oil

3 cloves garlic, minced

1 medium onion, sliced

2 medium tomatoes, sliced

1 pound chicken breast or thigh meat, finely chopped

¼ pound chicken liver, finely chopped

¼ pound chicken giblets, diced

½ cup distilled white vinegar

½ teaspoon salt

¼ teaspoon black pepper

1 bay leaf

1 cup chicken blood dissolved in 1½ cups water *

1 jalapeño pepper, whole

Chicken Blood Stew, Bicol-Style
Dinuguan Manok Bicoleno

3 cloves garlic, crushed

1 tablespoon vegetable oil

1 medium onion, chopped

1 pound chicken breast or
   thigh meat, finely
   chopped

¼ pound chicken liver, finely
   chopped

¼ pound chicken giblets,
   diced

¼ cup distilled white vinegar

1 teaspoon salt

¼ teaspoon peppercorns,
   crushed

1 bay leaf

1 teaspoon oregano

1 cup chicken blood
   dissolved in 1 cup water *

1 jalapeño pepper, minced

¾ cup coconut milk

In a medium saucepan, sauté the garlic in hot oil until golden brown. Add the onions and chicken meat, liver and giblets, stir, and sauté for 3 minutes.

Add the vinegar, salt, crushed peppercorns, bay leaf and oregano and bring to a boil without stirring. Lower the heat and simmer for 5–7 minutes.

Add the chicken blood and water mixture and minced hot pepper, bring to a boil, reduce the heat and simmer, stirring constantly, for 10 minutes.

Add the coconut milk and continue simmering, stirring continuously, for 5 minutes more. Correct seasonings with salt and pepper, if desired. Makes 3–4 servings.

* See *PUBLISHER'S NOTE,* page 126.

Fried Chicken
FRITONG MANOK

In the Philippines, 1-pound fryer chickens are available. Most chickens in the United States are at least 1½ to 2 pounds. Cornish game hens make an excellent substitute for this recipe, in which size is important.

Wash and dry the hens thoroughly.

Combine the salt, pepper and flour and dust the hens inside and out with the mixture. Refrigerate, covered, for 4 hours or overnight.

Heat the oil in a large pot to 375° F. Fry the whole hens for 40–45 minutes, turning occasionally, until they are golden brown all over.

Remove the hens carefully, allowing the oil in the cavity to drain out, and drain them on paper towels. Makes 4 servings.

2 1-pound Cornish game hens or whole chickens

1½ teaspoons salt

1 teaspoon black pepper

1 cup flour

3 cups vegetable oil

Honey Barbecued Chicken

2–3 pounds chicken, quartered

1 teaspoon salt

1 tablespoon lemon juice

2 tablespoons soy sauce

3 tablespoons brown sugar, packed

1½ teaspoons salt

1 teaspoon Tabasco sauce

BASTING SAUCE:

¼ cup honey

1 tablespoon soy sauce

3 tablespoons water

Wash and dry the chicken quarters thoroughly and sprinkle them with the salt. Place them in a shallow dish and set aside.

Combine the lemon juice, soy sauce, sugar, salt and Tabasco sauce and pour it over the chicken. Refrigerate, covered, for at least 4 hours or overnight.

When ready to cook, mix the basting sauce ingredients in a bowl.

To cook in the oven: Preheat the oven to 350° F. Remove the chicken from the marinade and put it on a rack in a roasting pan. Pour 1 cup of water in the bottom of the pan. Cover the chicken loosely with aluminum foil and bake for 30 minutes. Remove the foil and bake for 10 minutes more, basting with the sauce every 5 minutes, until brown on one side. Turn the chicken over and bake another 10 minutes, basting that side.

To cook over charcoal: Cook 4–6 inches above hot coals for 25–30 minutes, turning frequently and basting every 5 minutes. Makes 4 servings.

Oriental Barbecued Chicken

Wash and dry the chicken pieces thoroughly and sprinkle with 1 teaspoon of the salt. Place in a bowl and set aside.

For the marinade, combine all the rest of the ingredients, using only ¼ cup of the oil, in a saucepan and cook over low heat for a few minutes. Pour the marinade over the chicken and refrigerate, covered, for 4–6 hours or overnight, turning the pieces occasionally for an even coating.

Remove the chicken and brush the pieces with the remaining 1 cup of olive oil.

To cook in an oven: Broil the chicken 6 inches from the heat for 15 minutes. Brush with more olive oil, turn the pieces and cook for another 10 minutes, or until done.

To cook over charcoal: Grill the chicken pieces 4–6 inches over hot coals for 15 minutes. Baste with olive oil and cook the other side for 10 more minutes, or until done. Makes 4–5 servings.

2 2½-pound chickens, cut into 8 pieces each

2 teaspoons salt

½ cup soy sauce

1 tablespoon ginger, minced or grated

2 cloves garlic, minced

3 tablespoons sugar

¼ teaspoon red pepper flakes

½ teaspoon black pepper

⅓ cup sake (Japanese rice wine) or sherry

2 tablespoons lemon juice

1¼ cups olive oil

Peppered Chicken Stew
PESANG MANOK

3 pounds chicken, cut up
  into bite-size pieces

5 cups water

2 tablespoons peppercorns,
  crushed

2 teaspoons salt

1 medium onion, quartered

1 rib celery, cut into 2-inch
  lengths

2 medium potatoes, peeled
  and quartered

1 small cabbage, quartered

½ pound bok choy, cut in
  half lengthwise

3 green onions, cut into 2-
  inch lengths

Place the chicken in a large pot, add the water, peppercorns, salt, onions and celery, and bring to a boil. Lower the heat, cover, and simmer for 30 minutes.

Add the potatoes and continue to cook for 10–15 minutes or until the potatoes are just done.

Add the cabbage, bok choy and green onions. Cook for 5 minutes more or until cabbage and bok choy are tender. Add salt and pepper to taste. Makes 5–6 servings.

Chicken and Green Papaya Stew
TINOLANG MANOK

2 tablespoons vegetable oil

2 tablespoons ginger, julienned

2 cloves garlic, crushed

1 medium onion, sliced

3 pounds chicken, cut up
  into bite-size pieces

2 tablespoons fish sauce

1 teaspoon salt

5 cups water

2 cups green papaya, peeled
  and sliced

½ pound pepper leaves or
  spinach

In the Philippines, this dish is also known as Tinola. *The papaya used for this is very green and very hard. If it is not available, you can substitute sliced chayote or zucchini. The pepper leaves, available at Asian markets, add a nice texture and a slightly spicy flavor.*

In a large pot, heat the oil over medium heat and sauté the ginger, garlic and onions for 1 minute. Add the chicken and lightly brown all the pieces.

Add the fish sauce, salt and water and bring to a boil. Lower the heat and simmer, covered, for 30 minutes or until the chicken is tender.

Add the papaya and cook for 5 minutes or until tender. Add the pepper leaves, cover and simmer for 3 more minutes. If using spinach, cover, remove from heat without simmering and let stand for 5 minutes before serving. Makes 5–6 servings.

Fish and Shellfish

Gathering fish from the waters off the Philippines is done not only with the standard fishing pole and net but also with variations on these simple techniques, such as the *baclad*. This is a long, L-shaped fishing net that is floated over a coral reef. The long end of the net is attached to a wooden or bamboo floating pier that is anchored. The short end either lies on the ocean bottom or, if the water is too deep, is kept afloat with buoys.

As the *baclad* stays in the water, algae and plankton get caught in the net, which attract small fish that, in turn, attract larger fish. The largest fish I've ever seen caught in a *baclad* was a pair of marlins, each almost seven feet long.

Fish are harvested from the *baclad* before sunrise and sunset. About two dozen men go out to the *baclad,* grab each line and floating buoy, and start pulling up the short end of the net. For a while nothing happens—only a few fish appear. Then, all of a sudden, the water boils with fish. As the men reel in the net, they toss the fish into a boat behind them. When all the fish are gathered, the net is allowed to settle down above the coral reef, ready for the next catch. The fish are brought back to shore. On the beach, the fishermen are met by their wives, children, and local fish buyers, all curious about the day's catch.

Deep-sea divers also fish in the deep waters off the coast of the Philippines. In the United States, deep-sea divers wear a rubber diving suit, a regulator in mouth, goggles covering their eyes, and a large tank of air strapped to their back.

In the Philippines, however, the deep-sea divers are boys, usually less than 12 years old, dressed in bathing suits and t-shirts, with flat pieces of wood strapped to their feet as fins, their eyes covered by homemade goggles cut from the bottoms of soda bottles and held together with string. The divers are highly tanned and their black hair is bleached blonde by constant exposure to the sun.

The technique they use to catch fish is similar to that of hunters who beat the bush driving their prey before them. But instead of this being done on dry land, it is done on the bottom of the ocean, usually just above a coral reef. Here, a net is allowed to dangle down like curtains, kept afloat at the top with buoys and at the other end weighted down by lead weights and rocks.

The divers swim to the bottom of the water with the air in their lungs their only source of oxygen. They rhythmically lift and drop the weights of the nets that hang above the reefs, moving forward in a long line. As they beat the line and the net moves forward, fish are driven toward another net. The nets come close to each other and are gathered together, with the fish caught between them. The boys do this without underwater breathing devices, holding their breath up to 3–4 minutes and diving as deep as 50 feet.

Large teams of boys exchange positions with one another, allowing them to get a breath of air before having to go back down. The process can last for hours. This technique is quite controversial because many divers suffer pierced eardrums, become crippled, or even die from the bends.

A less controversial and more ecologically friendly technique for getting fish are fish ranches. Low-lying areas of land are surrounded by dikes and levees and flooded, creating fish ponds. Or a fresh-water lake or a slow-moving saltwater bay is partially enclosed with intertwined wood poles or netting. Within these fish pens or ponds, baby fish, called fry, are introduced, fed, grown and protected from predators. As soon as they are mature, they are harvested by net. As the fish populations of the open oceans of the world are slowly depleted, more techniques of growing fish will be employed to create a renewable source of fish and seafood for the tables of the world.

From the eastern shores of the Philippine Sea to the western shores of the South China or Sulu Seas, the Philippine Islands abound with fish and shellfish of all kinds. Such diversity is matched by the variety of ways to prepare the fish and shellfish.

Milkfish in Black Bean Sauce
BANGUS EN TOCHO

Cut the fish into 4–6 slices, sprinkle with the salt and let stand for 15–20 minutes. In a skillet, fry the fish slices in hot oil for 8–10 minutes until they are golden brown on both sides. Drain the fish on paper towels.

In the same oil, fry the onion slices until they are crisp. Drain them on paper towels.

Fry the tofu in the hot oil until it is golden brown, being careful not to touch it until it starts to turn brown to prevent it from breaking and sticking to the spatula. When it is deep golden brown, drain the tofu on paper towels.

Pour off all but 2 tablespoons of the oil from the skillet and sauté the ginger, garlic and tomatoes until the tomatoes are soft.

In a bowl, mix the fermented soybean curd, vinegar, sugar and water. Add this to the sautéed tomatoes. Then add the fried tofu and onions. Stir in the fermented beans. Simmer for 5 minutes, stirring occasionally.

Add the fried fish and simmer for 3 more minutes, turning the fish once. Makes 4–6 servings.

2 pounds milkfish *(bangus)* or any whole fish, dressed

½ teaspoon salt

1 cup vegetable oil

1 medium onion, thinly sliced

8 ounces firm bean curd, cut into ½-inch cubes

2 tablespoons ginger, julienned

2 cloves garlic, minced

4 medium tomatoes, thinly sliced

2 tablespoons fermented soybean curd

2 tablespoons distilled white vinegar

1 tablespoon sugar

¼ cup water

2 tablespoons fermented black beans *(tausi)*

Fish with Vegetables
BULANGLANG

2 pounds whole milkfish
(*bangus*) or bass

1 teaspoon salt

½ cup vegetable oil

1 clove garlic, minced

1 small onion, thinly sliced

2 large tomatoes, chopped

3 tablespoons shrimp paste

2 cups water

2 cups *kabocha* squash or
any other firm-flesh
squash like pumpkin, cut
into 1-inch cubes

1 cup green beans, cut into
1-inch lengths

1 cup bittermelon
(*ampalaya)*, seeded and
cut into 1-inch lengths

2 cups spinach (packed)

Clean the fish and slice it into 4–6 pieces. Sprinkle it with the salt and fry it in hot oil for 8–10 minutes on each side, or until brown on both sides. Remove it from the oil and drain it on paper towels. Set aside.

Pour off all but 2 tablespoons of oil from the skillet. Sauté the garlic, onions and tomatoes in this oil. Add the shrimp paste and water and bring it to a boil.

Add the fried fish, squash, green beans and bittermelon, in that order. Cover, lower the heat and cook for 6–8 minutes or until the vegetables are done.

Add the spinach. Remove the pan from the heat, cover and let stand for about 5 minutes to wilt the spinach. Makes 4 servings.

Marinated Milkfish
DAING NA BANGUS

Cut the fish lengthwise along the back. Lay flat with the skin side down in a shallow dish.

Combine the vinegar, salt, pepper and garlic in a cup and pour over the fish. Let stand, covered, in the refrigerator for at least 8 hours or overnight, turning the fish once or twice.

When ready to cook, remove the fish, dry it thoroughly with paper towels, and dredge it with flour. Heat the oil in a skillet and fry the fish until golden brown, 7–10 minutes on each side. Drain on paper towels.

Serve with Vinegar and Garlic Dipping Sauce (page 234). Makes 4–5 servings.

2 pounds whole milkfish (*bangus*) or whole bass, cleaned

3 tablespoons white distilled vinegar

1 teaspoon salt

¼ teaspoon black pepper

3 cloves garlic, minced

3 tablespoons flour

½ cup vegetable oil

Grilled Whole Fish
INIHAW NA BANGUS

With a sharp knife, cut along the back of the fish and remove the backbone. Rub the fish inside and out with the lemon slices and sprinkle with the salt and pepper.

In a bowl, mix the rest of the ingredients. Stuff the fish with the vegetables through the opening in the back. Place the lemon slices on top of the fish. Wrap the stuffed fish in aluminum foil and seal very well.

Grill over hot coals for 20–30 minutes.

Open the foil and serve the fish with Vinegar and Garlic Dipping Sauce (page 234). Makes 4–6 servings.

2 pounds whole milkfish or any fleshy, white fish, cleaned

4 lemon slices

1½ teaspoons salt

⅛ teaspoon black pepper

½ cup tomatoes, chopped

3 cloves garlic, minced

¼ cup onions, chopped

2 green onions, finely chopped

2 tablespoons ginger, minced

Sweet and Sour Fried Fish
ESCABECHE

2 pounds whole cod or bass, cleaned

1½ teaspoons salt

2 lemon slices

½ cup + 2 tablespoons vegetable oil

2 cloves garlic, minced

1 small onion, sliced thin

2 tablespoons ginger, julienned

½ green bell pepper, cut into thin strips

½ red bell pepper, cut into thin strips

1 small carrot, julienned

¼ cup distilled white vinegar

½ cup water

¼ cup sugar

1 tablespoon soy sauce

2 tablespoons catsup

1 tablespoon cornstarch, dissolved in 2 tablespoons water

Preheat oven to 250° F.

Score the fish 2 or 3 times on both sides, rub all over with the lemon slices, and sprinkle with 1 teaspoon of the salt. Let stand for 15–20 minutes. Drain and pat dry.

In a skillet, heat ½ cup of the oil and fry the fish until it is crispy and golden brown all over, 15–20 minutes on each side. Drain on paper towels. Transfer to a serving dish and keep warm in the oven.

For the sauce, heat the 2 tablespoons of oil in a saucepan and sauté the garlic, onions and ginger until the onions are soft and translucent. Add the bell peppers and carrots and sauté for 3 minutes. Then stir in the vinegar, water, sugar, ½ teaspoon of salt, soy sauce and catsup. Simmer for 3–4 minutes more. Stir the cornstarch and water mixture and add it to the sauce, stirring while it thickens.

Pour the sauce over the fried fish. Makes 4–5 servings.

Fish in Ginger and Soy Sauce
Isda sa Toyo

Preheat oven to 250° F.

If using whole fish, clean well and slice into 4–6 pieces. Rub the pieces or the fillets with the salt and pepper and let stand for 1 hour. Lightly dredge the fish with flour.

In a skillet, heat the ½ cup of oil and fry the fish until golden brown on both sides, 15–20 minutes on each side. Drain on paper towels and keep warm in the oven.

Heat the 2 tablespoons of oil in a saucepan and sauté the ginger, garlic and onions for 2 minutes or until the onions are soft.

Add the soy sauce, sugar and lemon juice and simmer for 2–3 minutes.

Pour the sauce over the fried fish and serve. Makes 4–6 servings.

2 pounds whole milkfish or bass or 1½ pounds fillets

1 teaspoon salt

1 teaspoon black pepper

4 tablespoons flour

½ cup + 2 tablespoons vegetable oil

1 tablespoon ginger, julienned

2 cloves garlic, crushed

4 green onions, cut into 1-inch lengths or 1 small onion, sliced thin

3 tablespoons soy sauce

2 teaspoons sugar

Juice of 1 lemon

Grouper Filets in Fermented Black Bean Sauce

Lapu-lapu at Tausi

2 slices ginger

2 tablespoons water

1 pound grouper fillets

½ teaspoon salt

½ teaspoon black pepper

3 tablespoons cornstarch

1½ cups vegetable oil

8 ounces tofu, cut into 1-inch cubes

1 green onion, cut into 1-inch lengths

1 tablespoon ginger, grated

4 tablespoons fermented black beans (tausi)

1½ cups water

2 tablespoons cornstarch dissolved in 3 tablespoons water

3 medium onions, cut into 8 wedges

3 medium tomatoes, cut into 8 wedges

½ teaspoon sesame oil

Crush the ginger slices and add the 2 tablespoons of water. Soak the fillets in this mixture for 10 minutes. Remove the fish, rinse, pat dry, and sprinkle with the salt and pepper. Roll in the 3 tablespoons of cornstarch.

In a skillet, heat the vegetable oil and fry the fish until golden brown on both sides, or 3–4 minutes a side. Drain on paper towels and set aside.

In the same oil, fry the tofu to a golden brown. Drain on paper towels and set aside.

Pour off all but 2 tablespoons of oil from the skillet and sauté the green onions and grated ginger for 1 minute. Add the fermented black beans and 1½ cups of water, stir, and bring to a low boil. Reduce the heat and add the cornstarch and water mixture, stirring vigorously.

Add the wedges of onion and tomato to the sauce and simmer for 3–4 minutes. Add the fried fish and the tofu. Cover and bring to a boil. Remove from the heat and sprinkle with the sesame oil. Makes 3–4 servings.

Pickled Fish and Vegetables
PAKSIW NA ISDA

Clean the fish, cut it into 4 pieces, rub the pieces with the salt and set aside.

Put the bittermelons, eggplants and garlic in a saucepan that is not aluminum. Add the fish, ginger and peppers on top of the vegetables.

In a bowl, mix the vinegar and water and pour over the fish and vegetables. Cover with a lid.

Bring to a boil without stirring. Reduce the heat and simmer for 5–7 minutes, turning the fish and vegetables once to cook evenly.

Allow to cool, and refrigerate for 1–2 days to mellow.

Serve cold or hot. Serves 3–4.

VARIATION:

The bittermelons and eggplant may be omitted and the fish simply boiled with the vinegar, water and spices.

The degree of sourness can be adjusted by increasing or decreasing the amount of water used.

1½ pounds whole milkfish, bass, cod or any white fish, cleaned

1½ teaspoons salt

2 bittermelons (ampalaya), quartered and seeds removed

2 Japanese eggplants, quartered

6 cloves garlic, crushed

1 teaspoon ginger, crushed

2 jalapeño peppers, whole

½ cup distilled white vinegar

¼ cup water

Gingered Fish and Vegetable Soup
Pesa

1½ to 2 pounds whole bass or cod, cleaned

2 teaspoons salt

4 cups water

½ teaspoon peppercorns, crushed

1 small onion, quartered

1 teaspoon ginger, crushed and chopped

1 small cabbage, quartered

1 small bunch bok choy, separated into individual stalks

4 green onions, cut into 2-inch lengths

¼ cup fish sauce

2 tablespoons lemon juice

Cut the fish into 6 pieces and sprinkle with 1 teaspoon of the salt. Set aside until ready to use.

In a large saucepan, combine the water, 1 teaspoon of the salt, peppercorns, onions and ginger and bring to a boil.

Add the fish, cabbage, bok choy and green onions and cook over medium heat, covered, for 10 minutes or until the fish is tender.

To make the dipping sauce, mix the fish sauce and lemon juice and serve in a bowl with the fish. Makes 3–4 servings.

Miso Sauce for *Pesa* (page 231).

Fish in White Sauce
PESCADO CON SALSA BLANCA

Preheat oven to 350° F.

Clean the fish and squeeze the *kalamansi* or lemon inside and outside the fish. Place the fish in a foil-lined baking dish and sprinkle with salt and pepper.

Add the onion, tomatoes, wine, cilantro and water on top of the fish. Bake in the oven for 40–50 minutes or until the fish flakes easily. Remove the fish from the pan and place on a serving dish. Set the oven at 250°F to keep the fish warm.

Strain and reserve the liquid from the baking dish. Discard the vegetables.

In a saucepan, melt the butter or margarine over low heat. Add the flour slowly, stirring well.

Gradually add the reserved liquid, stirring constantly. Cook over low heat for 4–5 minutes.

Add the milk to the sauce, season to taste with salt and pepper, and continue cooking until the sauce has thickened enough to coat the back of a spoon.

Pour the sauce over the fish just before serving. Makes 3–4 servings.

1½ to 2 pounds bass, cod or trout

2 *kalamansi* or ½ lemon

½ teaspoon salt

¼ teaspoon pepper

1 medium onion, sliced thin

1 medium tomato, sliced thin

3 tablespoons white wine

3 tablespoons cilantro, chopped fine

1½ cups water

2 tablespoons butter or margarine

2 tablespoons flour

⅓ cup evaporated milk

Salt and pepper to taste

Fish in Tomato Sauce
SARCIADONG ISDA

2 pounds cod or striped bass, cleaned

1 teaspoon salt

1 tablespoon lemon juice

½ cup + 1 tablespoon vegetable oil

2 cloves garlic, minced

1 small onion, diced

1 12-ounce can stewed tomatoes

1 4-ounce can tomato paste

½ cup water

1 tablespoon fish sauce

⅛ teaspoon black pepper

2 tablespoons green onions, finely chopped

Cut the fish into 4 pieces and sprinkle with salt and lemon juice. Let stand for 20 minutes.

Heat the ½ cup vegetable oil in a skillet and fry the fish until light brown on both sides, 4–5 minutes a side. Drain on paper towels and set aside.

In a saucepan, heat the 1 tablespoon of oil and sauté the garlic, onion and stewed tomatoes. Add the tomato paste, water, fish sauce and pepper. Mix well and simmer for 4–5 minutes.

Add the fried fish to the simmering sauce. Cover and cook for 3–4 minutes, turning the fish once.

Serve hot, garnished with the chopped green onions. Makes 4 servings.

Smelt in Ginger Sauce
SINUAM NA ISDA

Sprinkle the tablespoon of salt all over the smelt and set aside.

In a saucepan, heat the oil and sauté the ginger, garlic and onions until the onions are soft. Add the fish sauce and 1 teaspoon of salt and sauté for 1 minute. Add the water and bring to a boil.

Add the smelt to the sauce and lightly boil them for 4–5 minutes.

Place the spinach on top of the fish. Cover the pot and remove from the heat. Let stand for 5 minutes to finish cooking the spinach.

To serve, spread the spinach on a serving dish, place the fish on the spinach, and cover with the sauce. Makes 4–5 servings.

1 tablespoon salt

1½ pounds smelt, cleaned

1 tablespoon vegetable oil

1 tablespoon ginger, minced

2 cloves garlic, minced

1 small onion, sliced

1 tablespoon fish sauce

1 teaspoon salt

4 cups water

½ pound spinach, rinsed well

Steamed Fish, Chinese Style

Wash the fish and pat dry with paper towels. Score lightly on both sides at 2-inch intervals. Sprinkle with the salt, including the inside surface, and set aside for 15–20 minutes.

Mix the grated ginger with 1 tablespoon of the chopped green onions. Stuff the slits on one side of the fish with the mixture. Place the lemon slices inside the cavity of the fish.

Place the fish, stuffed side up, on a plate in a bamboo or metal steamer, and steam for 15–20 minutes or until done.

In a small saucepan, heat the vegetable oil and lightly sauté the crushed garlic. Add the soy sauce, chili oil and the remaining green onions (take care, the soy sauce may splatter when it hits the hot oil).

Pour the sauce over the steamed fish. Serve immediately. Makes 4 servings.

1½ pounds bass, cod or trout, cleaned

1½ teaspoons salt

1 teaspoon ginger, grated

2 tablespoons green onions, finely chopped

2–3 lemon slices

1 tablespoon vegetable oil

1 clove garlic, crushed

1 tablespoon soy sauce

1 tablespoon hot chili oil

Crabs in Fermented Black Bean Sauce

2 fresh rock or blue crabs or
  1 fresh dungeness crab

½ teaspoon black pepper

½ teaspoon salt

1 teaspoon ginger, minced

2 tablespoons cornstarch

2 cups vegetable oil

2 cloves garlic, minced

2 tablespoons fermented
  black beans *(tausi)*

1 jalapeño pepper, minced

½ teaspoon sugar

1 tablespoon sherry

1 cup water

½ teaspoon sesame oil

Remove the legs and claws and separate the bodies of the crabs from the shells. Wash the bodies under running water and discard the gills. Cut the bodies in half and crack the claws.

Drain the crab pieces and dry thoroughly with paper towels. Mix with pepper, salt, ginger and cornstarch. Heat the oil and deep-fry the crabs for 2 minutes. Remove from the oil and drain on paper towels.

In a skillet or wok, heat 2 tablespoons of the oil used for frying and sauté the garlic, fermented black beans, hot pepper and sugar for a few minutes. Add the crabs, sherry and water, cover, and simmer for 20 minutes or until most of the liquid has evaporated.

Sprinkle with the sesame oil. Makes 4 servings.

Crab Omelet
TORTANG ALIMASAG

Heat the vegetable oil in a large skillet or wok and sauté the cabbage for 2–3 minutes. Remove from skillet and set aside.

In the same oil, sauté the onions until they just turn translucent.

Add the mushrooms, water chestnuts, crab meat, shrimp, oyster sauce, soy sauce, salt, pepper, Chinese okra and cooked cabbage. Mix well and bring to a boil once. Sprinkle with the sesame oil.

Drain off any excess liquid, pressing the mixture to get all of the liquid out.

Add the eggs and mix well with the vegetables. Cook over medium heat for 6–8 minutes, until the eggs are done, stirring frequently. Makes 8 servings.

3 tablespoons vegetable oil

2 cups cabbage, shredded

1 large onion, sliced thin

3 dried shiitake mushrooms, soaked in water for 30 minutes and minced

8 ounces canned water chestnuts, drained and coarsely chopped

3 cups crab meat

½ pound shrimp, peeled, deveined and coarsely chopped

1 tablespoon oyster sauce

1 tablespoon soy sauce

½ teaspoon salt

½ teaspoon black pepper

1 medium Chinese okra, peeled and cut into 1½-inch wedges

½ teaspoon sesame oil

12 eggs, slightly beaten

Fried Shrimp with Ham and Bacon
CAMARON DORADO CON JAMON

24–28 large shrimp, not less than 3 inches long

3 slices ginger

3 tablespoons water

24–28 thin slices bacon, approximately 1 inch x 1½ inch

24–28 thin slices ham, approximately 1 inch x 1½ inch

3 cups vegetable oil

BATTER:

4 egg whites

¼ cup water

1 teaspoon salt

¼ cup flour

¾ cup cornstarch

Peel the shrimp and slit them deeply at the back so that they can be laid out open and flat. Devein, wash and pat them dry.

In a large bowl, crush the ginger in the 3 tablespoons of water. Put the shrimp in this juice and set aside for 5–7 minutes. Remove the shrimp from the ginger juice, wash them again and pat dry.

Stuff each shrimp with a slice of ham, and wrap them both with a bacon slice. Use one or two toothpicks to secure the wrapping. Run a skewer through this sandwich of ham, shrimp and bacon, and set aside on a plate until ready to deep-fry.

To make the batter, beat the egg whites slightly and add the water, salt, flour and cornstarch. Do not over-stir. The batter should be thick and lumpy.

Dip all the skewered shrimp in the batter so they are fully coated.

Heat the oil in a large skillet over medium-high heat. Deep-fry the shrimp until golden brown, about 4–5 minutes.

Serve hot with Sweet and Sour Sauce (page 233). Makes 6–7 servings.

Fried Shrimp
CAMARON REBOSADO

Preheat oven to 250° F.

Peel and devein the shrimp, leaving the tails on. Sprinkle them with the salt and lemon juice and marinate for 20 minutes.

Combine the egg and ice water in a bowl. In another bowl, mix the flour, baking powder, salt and pepper. Sift the dry ingredients into the egg and water and mix well to form a smooth paste.

In a deep skillet, heat the oil until hot.

Hold the shrimp by the tail, dip in batter and deep-fry, a few at a time, for 2–3 minutes, or until golden brown. Drain on paper towels. Keep the cooked shrimp warm in a 250° F oven until they are all cooked.

Serve with Sweet and Sour Sauce (page 233). Makes 3–4 servings.

12 large shrimp
½ teaspoon salt
1 tablespoon lemon juice
2 cups vegetable oil

BATTER:
1 egg, slightly beaten
1 cup ice water
1½ cups flour
1½ teaspoons baking powder
¼ teaspoon salt
⅛ teaspoon white pepper

Sautéed Shrimp
HALABOS NA HIPON

Put the water and 1 teaspoon of salt in a saucepan and bring to a boil. Add the shrimp, cover, reduce the heat and simmer for 1 minute and drain.

Heat the oil in a skillet over medium heat and sauté the minced garlic for 1 minute. Add the shrimp and sauté for 1–2 minutes. Sprinkle with the pepper.

For the dipping sauce, mix the vinegar, 1 teaspoon of salt and the crushed garlic and serve in a bowl with the shrimp. Makes 2–3 servings.

1 pound large shrimp,
  unpeeled
¼ cup water
2 teaspoons salt
1 tablespoon vegetable oil
1 clove garlic, minced
1 teaspoon black pepper
¼ cup distilled white vinegar
1 teaspoon salt
1 clove garlic, crushed

Grilled Shrimp
Inihaw na Hipon

¼ cup vegetable oil

1 tablespoon cilantro or parsley, finely chopped

2 tablespoons lemon juice

2 cloves garlic, minced

½ teaspoon red pepper flakes

¼ teaspoon sugar

1 teaspoon salt

⅛ teaspoon black pepper

12 large shrimp, peeled and deveined, with tails left on

In a bowl, combine all the ingredients except the shrimp. Pour the marinade over the shrimp and refrigerate covered, for 2 or more hours.

At cooking time, thread the shrimp onto wood or metal skewers. Brush with the marinade and grill over hot coals for 1–2 minutes or under the broiler for 3–4 minutes, turning and basting once. Makes 3–4 servings.

Shrimp in a Tangy Sauce
Lagat na Hipon

¼ cup native Philippine vinegar (*sukang paombong*)

2 cups onion, sliced

½ teaspoon salt

½ teaspoon black peppercorns, crushed

1 pound large shrimp, peeled and deveined

3 tablespoons vegetable oil

4 cloves garlic, crushed

8 *kamias*, sliced crosswise ¼ inch thick

Kamias *are a sour fruit that look like small cucumbers with smooth skin. Available frozen at most Asian markets, they give this dish its distinctive zip.*

In a bowl, combine the vinegar, onion, salt and peppercorns. Add the shrimp and marinate for 20–30 minutes.

Heat the oil in a saucepan and sauté the garlic for 1 minute. Add the shrimp and marinade. Do not stir until the liquid starts boiling, as it will cause the dish to taste too vinegary.

Add the *kamias* and bring back to a boil, and serve. Makes 3–4 servings.

Stir-fried Shrimp and Mushrooms

In a bowl, combine the cornstarch, soy sauce and grated ginger. Add the shrimp, mix well and set aside.

Heat 2 tablespoons of the oil in a skillet and stir-fry the mushrooms, peas, bamboo shoots and baby corn one vegetable at a time for 3 minutes each. Set each aside.

Heat the remaining 2 tablespoons of oil in a skillet and stir-fry the shrimp for 2 minutes. Add the cooked vegetables and chicken broth and mix well. Bring the liquid to a boil, reduce the heat and simmer for 3 minutes. Add the cornstarch and water mixture and simmer, stirring, until the sauce thickens. Remove from the heat.

Serve hot over rice. Makes 4–5 servings.

3 tablespoons cornstarch

2 teaspoons soy sauce

2 teaspoons ginger, grated

1½ pounds large shrimp, peeled and deveined

4 tablespoons vegetable oil

¼ pound fresh mushrooms, sliced

½ cup frozen peas

½ cup canned, sliced bamboo shoots, drained

12 ounces canned baby corn, drained and halved lengthwise

¼ cup chicken broth

1 teaspoon cornstarch dissolved in 2 teaspoons of water

Shrimp and Vegetable Soup
Suam na Sugpo

1 pound large shrimp,
    unpeeled, with heads on

½ teaspoon salt

2 cloves garlic, crushed

1 tablespoon vegetable oil

2 slices ginger, crushed

1 small onion, sliced

4 cups rice water

1 cup *malunggay* leaves or
    spinach

2 tablespoons fish sauce

The use of rice water instead of stock or plain water gives this soup added texture and a distinctive flavor. (See Author's Notes, Rice Water, page 267).

Wash the shrimp, cut the pointers and feelers from the heads, sprinkle with the salt, and set aside.

To make the rice water, reserve the water used for the *second* washing of 3 cups of white rice. (Save the rice for use in other recipes.)

In a medium-sized pot sauté garlic in hot oil until light brtown. Add the ginger and onions and sauté for 2 more minutes.

Add the shrimp and rice water to the pot and bring to a boil.

Add the *malunggay* or spinach leaves and fish sauce, stir well, cover, and remove from heat. Allow to sit for 5 minutes to cook the leaves. Makes 3–4 servings.

Shrimp Omelet
Tortang Hipon

Sauté the garlic and onions in 1 tablespoon of the oil until brown. Add the shrimp, salt and pepper. Cook until the shrimp turn pink, 1–2 minutes. Drain any excess liquid and set aside.

Heat the remaining 3 tablespoons of oil in a pan on high. Pour in the beaten eggs and swirl them about to cover the bottom of the pan evenly. Cook for 2–3 minutes. Pour the shrimp mixture onto one end. Fold the other side of the eggs over the shrimp. Allow the eggs to cook fully for 1 minute. Transfer the omelet to a plate.

Serve plain or top with Patola Sauce (page 231). Makes 4 servings.

- 2 cloves garlic, minced
- 1 medium onion, diced
- 4 tablespoons vegetable oil
- ½ pound shrimp, peeled, deveined and coarsely chopped
- 1 teaspoon salt
- ¼ teaspoon black pepper
- 3 eggs, well beaten

Sautéed Oysters
Oysters Guisado

In a skillet, sauté the garlic in the oil until it is light brown. Add the onions and cook until they just start to wilt. Add the tomatoes and cook for another 3–4 minutes.

Add the oysters and simmer for 2–3 minutes or until the edges of the oysters just start to curl. Season with the salt and pepper and serve. Makes 4 servings.

- 2 cloves garlic, minced
- 2 tablespoons vegetable oil
- 1 medium onion, diced
- 1 medium tomato, diced
- 2 cups oysters, shucked
- ¼ teaspoon salt
- ½ teaspoon black pepper

Clam Omelet
TORTANG TULIA

6 large fresh clams or 3
    tablespoons canned
    chopped clams, drained,
    with 2 tablespoons of the
    clam juice reserved

4 tablespoons vegetable oil

1 medium tomato, diced

1 small onion, diced

1½ teaspoons salt

½ teaspoon black pepper

3 eggs, well beaten

If using fresh clams, bring ¼ cup of water to a boil in a small pan. Drop in the clams, cover and cook until the clams have popped open, about 3–4 minutes. Remove the clams from the shells and chop coarsely. Reserve 2 tablespoons of the water in which the clams were cooked.

Heat 2 tablespoons of the vegetable oil in a skillet. Sauté the onions and tomatoes until the onions are translucent. Add the clams and reserved clam juice. Season with ½ teaspoon salt and pepper. Cook for 1 minute and set aside.

Add 1 teaspoon of the salt to the beaten eggs.

Heat the remaining 2 tablespoons of vegetable oil in another skillet on high. Pour in the eggs and swirl to cover the bottom of the pan evenly. Cook for 2–3 minutes. On one end of the eggs, place the clam and vegetable mixture. Fold the other side of the eggs over this mixture and allow the eggs to cook for 1 minute.

Turn the omelet over and cook for 1–2 minutes.

Serve hot with catsup. Makes 2–3 servings.

Vegetable Dishes

Savory vegetable dishes that can be eaten as the entree or as a side dish.

Bittermelon with Coconut Milk
AMPALAYA AT GATA

1 pound bittermelon
  (ampalaya)

1 tablespoon vegetable oil

2 cloves garlic, crushed

12 ounces coconut milk

⅓ cup shrimp paste

Wash the bittermelon, cut off the ends, slice in half lengthwise, and scoop out the pulp and seeds. Slice into ¾-inch chunks.

In a skillet, heat the oil and sauté the garlic with the shrimp paste until it is light brown.

Add the coconut milk, bring to a boil, reduce the heat and simmer for 15–20 minutes, until the volume has been reduced by about half.

Add the bittermelon, stir, cover, and simmer for 6–8 minutes or until the bittermelon is just tender. Makes 2–3 servings.

Braised Chayote
GUISADONG CHAYOTE

2 cloves garlic, minced

1 small onion, diced

2 tablespoons vegetable oil

½ cup water

1 pound chayote, peeled,
  cored and sliced thin

1 tablespoon shrimp paste

1 tablespoon fish sauce

½ teaspoon black pepper

¼ pound pork butt, cut into
  thin strips

¼ pound shrimp, peeled,
  deveined and chopped

Sauté the garlic and onions in hot oil in a skillet until the garlic is light brown. Add the water and bring it to a boil. Add the chayote, cover, and cook for 8–10 minutes, or until the chayote is slightly tender.

Mix in the shrimp paste, fish sauce, pepper and pork. Bring the liquid back to a boil and simmer for 3–4 minutes.

Add the shrimp, mix well and cook for 2 minutes more. Makes 4–6 servings.

Bittermelon #1
GUISADONG AMPALAYA #1

Cut off the ends of the bittermelon, cut in half lengthwise, and remove the seeds. Cut into thin slices and set aside.

In a heated skillet, sauté the pork for 2–3 minutes.

Add the garlic and sauté until it is light brown. Add the onions and cook until they are transparent. Add the tomatoes and cook until they are soft. Add the fish sauce, sugar, salt and pepper. Mix well.

Add the shrimp and cook for 1–2 minutes. Add the broth or water and bring it to a boil.

Add the bittermelon and stir gently. Cover and simmer for 5–7 minutes or until the bittermelon is tender.

Add the beaten eggs and give the mixture a quick stir. Cook the eggs for 2–3 minutes or until they are firm. Then stir the eggs well into the mixture. Makes 4 servings.

1 pound bittermelon *(ampalaya)*

¼ pound pork, cut into thin strips

1 clove garlic, minced

1 small onion, sliced

1 medium tomato, chopped

1 tablespoon fish sauce

¼ teaspoon sugar

½ teaspoon salt

¼ teaspoon black pepper

¼ pound shrimp, peeled, deveined and chopped

½ cup chicken broth or water

2 eggs, slightly beaten

Bittermelon #2
GUISADONG AMPALAYA #2

2 pounds bittermelon
(ampalaya)

3 cloves garlic, crushed

1 small onion, sliced

3 tablespoons vegetable oil

½ pound pork butt, cut into
thin slices

6 large tomatoes, coarsely
chopped

½ pound shrimp, peeled,
deveined and chopped

1 cup water or chicken
broth

½ cup distilled white vinegar

1 teaspoon salt

½ teaspoon black pepper

Cut off the ends of the bittermelon and cut in half lengthwise. Scoop out the seeds. Cut into thin slices. Set aside.

In a skillet, sauté the garlic and onions in the hot oil for 2 minutes. Add the pork and tomatoes and cook until the tomatoes have softened, about 3–5 minutes.

Add the shrimp and sauté for 1 minute. Add the water or broth, and bring it to a boil. Add the vinegar and cook for 3 minutes more.

Add the sliced bittermelon and continue cooking until it is just tender, about 5–7 minutes. Season with the salt and pepper. Makes 6–8 servings.

Eggplant Salad

3 medium Japanese
eggplants

2 cloves garlic, minced

1 teaspoon salt

3 tablespoons distilled white
vinegar

½ teaspoon black pepper

Over live coals or in a broiler on high, roast the eggplants 3–4 minutes on each side, until the skin is blistered and burned. Set aside to cool.

Peel the burnt skin, chop the eggplants into small pieces, and mash them with a fork.

In a bowl, combine the eggplant, garlic, salt, vinegar and pepper, mix well and let stand for at least 30 minutes. Serve with broiled or fried fish or meat. Makes 3–4 servings.

Cilantro and Snow Peas
Guisadong Kinchay at Sitsaro

Heat the oil in a skillet and carefully add the tofu cubes. Be sure not to touch the tofu with a utensil until it has browned or it will stick to the utensil. Cook the tofu until it is brown on all sides. Remove it from the oil and drain on paper towels. Set aside.

Drain all but 2 tablespoons of the oil from the skillet and sauté the garlic until it is light brown.

Add the onions and cook until they are transparent. Add the tomatoes and sauté until they are soft.

Add the shrimp and sauté for 2 minutes. Add the broth and bring it to a boil. Lower the heat, add the snow peas and cilantro, and simmer for 3–4 minutes, or until the peas are just tender. Season with the salt and pepper.

Add the fried tofu and gently mix it in. Simmer for 2 more minutes. Makes 4 servings.

½ cup vegetable oil

8 ounces tofu, cut into ¼-inch cubes

3 cloves garlic, minced

1 small onion, sliced

1 small tomato, chopped

½ pound shrimp, peeled, deveined and chopped

1 cup chicken broth

1 cup snow peas (sitsaro), tips and strings removed

1 cup cilantro, coarsely chopped

½ teaspoon salt

½ teaspoon black pepper

Braised Bamboo Shoots
GUISADONG LABONG

2 cloves garlic, crushed

1 medium onion, diced

1 medium tomato, chopped

3 tablespoons vegetable oil

½ pound pork, sliced thin

¼ pound shrimp, peeled, deveined and coarsely chopped

1 tablespoon soy sauce

⅛ teaspoon black pepper

1 cup chicken broth

14 ounces canned bamboo shoots, drained and cut into strips

Sauté the garlic, onions and tomato in hot oil in a skillet for 3-4 minutes.

Add the pork and sauté until it is light brown. Add the shrimp and cook for 1 minute. Add the soy sauce, pepper and chicken broth. Bring to a boil, stirring frequently.

Add the bamboo shoots and continue cooking, stirring constantly, for 5 minutes or until they are thoroughly heated. Makes 4 servings.

Corn with Shrimp
GUISADONG MAIS

2 cloves garlic, minced

1 small onion, diced

2 tablespoons vegetable oil

½ pound shrimp, peeled, deveined and chopped

½ cup chicken broth

1 tablespoon fish sauce

1 teaspoon salt

¼ teaspoon black pepper

3 cups canned or frozen corn

1 cup (packed) spinach, washed and drained

Sauté the garlic and onion in hot oil in a medium-sized pan until the onion is translucent, about 2–3 minutes.

Add the shrimp and sauté for 1 minute. Add the chicken broth, fish sauce, salt and pepper. Bring to a boil and reduce heat to medium.

Add the corn and simmer for 3–4 minutes for canned corn and 8–10 minutes for frozen corn.

Stir in the spinach and simmer for 3 minutes more. Makes 4 servings.

Mung Beans with Pork
GUISADONG MUNGO

Spread the mung beans on a plate and discard any fragments mixed in with the beans. Put the beans, water and salt in a pot and bring to a boil over high heat. Lower the heat to moderate and cook partly covered for 45 minutes or until the beans are tender. Drain the beans in a colander and set aside.

In a large pot, heat the oil and lightly brown the pork.

Add the garlic, onions and tomatoes and sauté for 3 minutes.

Add the mung beans, chicken broth, shrimp paste and pepper. Mix well and bring to a boil. Reduce the heat and add more salt and pepper if desired.

If using bittermelon leaves, cut off the 3–4 inches of tender leaves at the tips and discard the rest. Add the leaves or the spinach to the beans and simmer for 3–4 minutes. Makes 4–5 servings.

¾ cup whole mung beans (*mungo*)

3 cups water

1 teaspoon salt

1 tablespoon vegetable oil

½ pound pork butt, diced

2 cloves garlic, minced

1 small onion, diced

1 medium tomato, diced

2 cups chicken broth

3 tablespoons shrimp paste

¼ teaspoon black pepper

1 cup (packed) bittermelon leaves or 1½ cups (packed) spinach, washed and well drained

Braised Cabbage
GUISADONG REPOLLO

2 tablespoons vegetable oil

3 cloves garlic, chopped

1 medium onion, sliced

1 medium tomato, chopped

½ pound pork, cut into thin strips

¼ pound shrimp, peeled, deveined and chopped

1 cup chicken broth

1 pound cabbage, sliced fine

1 teaspoon salt

½ teaspoon black pepper

Heat the oil in a skillet and sauté the garlic until it is light brown. Add the onions and sauté until transparent. Add the tomatoes and sauté until they are soft.

Add the pork and sauté for 2 minutes. Add the shrimp and broth, stir well and bring to a boil.

Add the sliced cabbage, salt and pepper. Cook until the cabbage is just tender, about 5–6 minutes, stirring frequently. Makes 3-4 servings.

Chinese Long Beans
GUISADONG SITAO

3 cloves garlic, minced

1 small onion, diced

2 tablespoons vegetable oil

¼ pound lean pork, diced

½ cup water

1 tablespoon shrimp paste

¼ teaspoon black pepper

½ pound Chinese long beans (sitao) or green beans, cut into 2-inch lengths

Lightly brown the garlic and onions in hot oil in a large skillet. Add the diced pork and sauté for 4–5 minutes.

Add the water, shrimp paste and pepper. Mix well. Bring to a boil and reduce the heat.

Add the Chinese long beans or the green beans. Partially cover and cook until the beans are crispy-tender in texture, about 4–5 minutes, stirring occasionally. Makes 3–4 servings.

Braised Snow Peas
GUISADONG SITSARO

Heat the oil in a skillet and lightly brown the garlic. Add the diced pork and sauté for 2 minutes. Add the onions and sauté until they are translucent.

Add the fish sauce, oyster sauce, shrimp paste and chicken broth. Bring to a boil and reduce the heat to medium.

Add the snow peas and water chestnuts and cover. Simmer for 2–3 minutes or until the peas are just tender.

Uncover, add the shrimp and cook for 2 minutes more, stirring constantly. Makes 4 servings.

2 tablespoons vegetable oil

3 cloves garlic, minced

½ pound pork, diced

1 small onion, sliced

1 tablespoon fish sauce

2 tablespoons oyster sauce

1 tablespoon shrimp paste

½ cup chicken broth

½ pound snow peas *(sitsaro)*, **tips and strings removed**

6 water chestnuts *(apulid)*, **chopped**

¼ pound shrimp, peeled, deveined and chopped

Chinese Fuzzy Melon
GUISADONG UPO

2 cups Chinese fuzzy melon (*upo*) or zucchini, cut into ½-inch cubes

2 tablespoons vegetable oil

2 cloves garlic, crushed

1 small onion, diced

½ cup chicken broth

1 tablespoon shrimp paste

¼ teaspoon black pepper

¼ pound shrimp, peeled, deveined and chopped

Peel the fuzzy melon and slice crosswise into ½-inch-thick slices. Cut the slices into quarters.

Heat the oil in a large skillet and lightly brown garlic. Add the onions and sauté for 2–3 minutes or until they turn translucent.

Add the chicken broth, shrimp paste and pepper. Bring to a boil and add the fuzzy melon or zucchini. Cover and cook until it is just tender, about 5–7 minutes. Stir occasionally to prevent scorching the fuzzy melon.

Stir in the shrimp and cook for another 2 minutes, stirring constantly. Makes 4 servings.

Japanese Squash with Coconut Milk
KALABASA AT GATA

3 tablespoons vegetable oil

3 cloves garlic, crushed

1 small onion, diced

½ cup water or chicken broth

1 teaspoon salt

½ teaspoon pepper

1 pound Japanese squash (*kalabasa*), or 1 pound *kabocha*, peeled, seeded and sliced thin

½ pound shrimp, peeled, deveined and chopped

12 ounces coconut milk

Heat the oil in a large skillet, add the garlic and onions and sauté until the onions are translucent.

Add the water or broth, salt, pepper and squash. Bring to a boil, cover, lower the heat, and simmer for 10 minutes, or until the squash is tender.

Add the shrimp and cook for 2 minutes.

Add the coconut milk and simmer for 4 minutes, stirring well. Correct the seasonings if desired. Makes 3–4 servings.

Japanese Squash with Shrimp
KALABASA AT HIPON

Brown the garlic in hot oil in a large pan or wok. Add the diced pork and brown it on all sides.

Add the onions, tomatoes, shrimp, shrimp paste and pepper. Mix well and sauté for 5 minutes, stirring occasionally.

Add the chicken broth and bring to a boil. Add the squash, cover, lower the heat, and simmer for 10 minutes or until the squash is tender. Correct the seasonings if desired. Makes 4–6 servings.

5 cloves garlic, chopped

3 tablespoons vegetable oil

¼ pound pork, diced

1 small onion, sliced

1 medium tomato, chopped

¼ pound shrimp, peeled, deveined and chopped

1 tablespoon shrimp paste

½ teaspoon black pepper

1 cup chicken broth

1½ pounds Japanese squash (*kalabasa*), or *kabocha*, peeled, seeded and sliced thin

Water Spinach and Tomato Salad
KANG KONG AT CAMATIS

Discard the tough stems of the water spinach. Wash the leaves well, place in a steamer and steam for 4–5 minutes, until wilted but still slightly crisp. Plunge it in ice water to stop the cooking process. Drain and squeeze out all the water.

In a large bowl, toss all the ingredients together. Chill the salad for a few minutes in the refrigerator. Makes 4 servings.

2 pounds water spinach (*kang kong*)

2 large tomatoes, sliced

1 red bell pepper, sliced

1 green bell pepper, sliced

1 cup jicama, peeled and shredded

¼ pound shrimp, peeled, boiled and coarsely chopped

½ cup bottled salad dressing, French, Italian or ranch

Water Spinach in a Tangy Sauce
KANG KONG AT SUKA

3 cups (packed) water spinach
(*kang kong*)

2 tablespoons vegetable oil

3 cloves garlic, chopped

¼ pound pork, diced

1 small onion, diced

1 medium tomato, chopped

½ pound shrimp, peeled,
deveined, and chopped

½ cup water

½ cup chicken broth

½ cup native Philippine vinegar
(*sukang paombong*)

1 teaspoon salt

¼ teaspoon black pepper

Wash the water spinach very well, discard the stems, and slice the leaves into thin strips.

Heat the oil in a skillet and sauté the garlic for 1 minute. Add the pork and sauté until it is lightly browned. Add the onions and sauté until they are translucent. Add the tomatoes and sauté for 3–4 minutes, or until they are soft.

Add the shrimp and sauté for 1 minute. Add the water and chicken broth, bring to a boil, and add the vinegar. Cook for a few minutes without stirring.

Add the water spinach and cook until it is just tender, about 3–4 minutes. Stir in the salt and pepper. Makes 3–4 servings.

Braised Chinese Okra and Shrimp
PATOLA AT CAMARON REBOSADO

Sprinkle the shrimp with the salt and marinate for 20 minutes. Dust them lightly with 2 tablespoons of the flour, and dip each shrimp in the eggs. Dredge the shrimp in the remaining flour. Shake off any excess flour. In a skillet, heat 1 cup of the oil and fry the shrimp to a golden brown. Drain on paper towels and set aside.

In a saucepan, heat the remaining 2 tablespoons of oil and sauté the garlic until it is light brown. Add the onions and sauté until they are translucent.

Add the chicken broth, fish sauce and pepper and bring to a boil. Reduce the heat, add the Chinese okra and simmer for 5–6 minutes.

Remove from the heat and add the fried shrimp. Serve immediately. Makes 4 servings.

12 large shrimp, peeled and deveined

1 teaspoon salt

½ cup flour

2 eggs, well beaten

1 cup + 2 tablespoons vegetable oil

2 cloves garlic, minced

1 small onion, sliced

2 cups chicken broth

1 tablespoon fish sauce

½ teaspoon black pepper

1½ pounds Chinese okra or zucchini, peeled and sliced crosswise into 1-inch-thick pieces

Vegetable Stew with Pork
PINAKBET

2 tablespoons vegetable oil

2 cloves garlic, crushed

1 tablespoon ginger, minced

1 small onion, diced

½ pound pork, diced

1 medium tomato, chopped

3 tablespoons shrimp paste

½ cup water

½ pound Japanese eggplant,
sliced in 1-inch rounds

½ pound okra, whole

½ pound bittermelon
(ampalaya), seeds and
pulp removed and sliced
crosswise into thin slices

In a large saucepan, heat the oil and sauté the garlic, ginger and onions for 2 minutes. Add the pork and sauté until lightly browned on all sides.

Add the tomatoes, shrimp paste and water. Bring to a boil, reduce the heat, and simmer, covered, for 5 minutes.

Add the eggplant, okra and bittermelon and cook, covered, for 15 minutes, stirring occasionally. Add more shrimp paste or salt if desired. Makes 4–6 servings.

Braised Japanese Squash Blossoms
Puso na Kalabasa

Heat the oil in a large skillet, add the garlic and sauté until it is golden brown. Add the tomatoes and sauté until soft, about 4–5 minutes.

Add the pork, fish sauce and pepper and sauté for 10–15 minutes, or until the meat is tender.

Add the water and bring to a boil. Add the squash blossoms or the bok choy and cook for 1–2 minutes. Do not overcook. Makes 3 servings.

2 tablespoons vegetable oil

2 cloves garlic, crushed

1 large tomato, chopped

¼ pound pork, diced

1 tablespoon fish sauce

¼ teaspoon white pepper

¼ cup water

20 Japanese squash blossoms *(puso na kalabasa),* stem and calyx removed, or 10 zucchini blossoms, or 6 baby bok choy, quartered

Chinese Fuzzy Melon and Pork
Upo Dinengdeng

In a large saucepan, heat the oil and lightly brown the garlic. Add the pork and sauté until it is well browned. Drain off any excess oil.

Add the water, tomatoes and shrimp paste. Bring to a boil, reduce the heat and simmer for 2 minutes.

Add the fuzzy melon, salt and pepper and mix well. Cover and cook for 8–10 minutes or until the melon is just tender. Makes 4–5 servings.

2 tablespoons vegetable oil

2 cloves garlic, minced

¾ pound ground pork

⅔ cup water

1 medium tomato, diced

2 tablespoons shrimp paste

3 cups Chinese fuzzy melon *(upo),* cut into 1-inch cubes

1 teaspoon salt

½ teaspoon white pepper

Pickles & Preserves

In the days before refrigeration, pickling foods with vinegar or other acidic products and preserving foods with salt was an absolute necessity, especially in preparation for the inevitable times of food shortage due to weather and the seasons. Today, pickling and preserving foods is strictly done for the wonderful flavors and textures that can be created by such techniques.

Pickled Green Papaya
Achara

In a bowl, combine the grated papaya and coarse salt. Using your hands, knead them together for a few minutes. Wrap the papaya 1 cup at a time in cheesecloth and squeeze to express the juice.

Pour the vinegar over the papaya and let stand overnight. The next day, squeeze as much of the vinegar as possible through the cheesecloth.

Combine the papaya with the rest of the ingredients in a large ceramic bowl and mix thoroughly.

Pack in sterilized jars and pour a hot pickling solution (below) over the vegetables. Let cool to room temperature, remove any air bubbles, and cover the jars tightly and refrigerate. Allow to ripen 1 week before serving. Makes 1 quart.

PICKLING SOLUTIONS:

For Sour Pickle: 1 cup white distilled vinegar, ½ cup sugar, 1 teaspoon salt

For Sweet and Sour Pickle: 1 cup white distilled vinegar, ⅔ cup sugar, 1 teaspoon salt

For Sweet Pickle: 1 cup white distilled vinegar, ¾ cup sugar, 1 teaspoon salt

Combine the vinegar, sugar and salt in a stainless steel, teflon-coated or Pyrex saucepan. Do not use aluminum.

Place over medium heat, stirring until sugar is dissolved. Bring to a boil, lower the heat and simmer for 3–4 minutes. Remove from the heat and let cool slightly. Pour over the vegetables to be pickled.

4 cups green papaya, grated

½ cup salt

1 cup distilled white vinegar

1 small carrot, peeled and cut into 1-inch sticks

1 small red bell pepper, cut into thin strips

1 small green bell pepper, cut into thin strips

4 tablespoons ginger, julienned

½ cup onions, thinly sliced or 10 pearl onions, peeled

5 cloves garlic, diced

2 tablespoons raisins

Pickled Vegetables
ACHARANG GULAY

3 Japanese eggplants, stems and tips removed

1 cucumber, peeled

1 medium carrot, peeled

1 bittermelon, stem and seeds removed

1 medium onion, sliced thin

1 green bell pepper

1 red bell pepper

¼ cup salt

PICKLING SOLUTION:

½ cup coarse salt

1½ cups sugar

1½ cups distilled white vinegar

3 cloves garlic, crushed

2 tablespoons ginger, julienned

Cut all the vegetables, except the onions, into 2½-inch by 1½-inch strips. Arrange them in layers in a glass or ceramic jar, sprinkling ½ tablespoon of the salt on each layer. Let stand at room temperature for at least 12 hours.

Rinse the vegetables thoroughly with water 3 or 4 times and drain well.

Combine all the ingredients for the pickling solution in a stainless steel or ceramic saucepan and bring to a boil. Reduce the heat and simmer for 10 minutes.

Pack the vegetables into sterile glass jars, pour the hot pickling solution over them, and let cool at room temperature. Cover and refrigerate. Allow to ripen for at least two weeks before serving. Makes 1 quart.

Pickled Water Spinach
ACHARANG KANG KONG

Spread the water spinach out on a cutting board. Remove any soft or wilted leaves and cut off the hard stems. Wash thoroughly with water, changing the water between each wash. Cut the leaves and tender stems into 2- to 3-inch lengths. Separate leaves from stems. Dry between cotton towels or in a salad spinner. Set aside.

Mix the rest of the ingredients in a large ceramic or stainless steel saucepan and bring to a boil. Do not stir this pickling solution, because it will taste too vinegary.

Put the water spinach stems into the pickling solution and cover. Simmer for 5 minutes.

Add the leaves, cover, and simmer for 3 minutes more. Allow to cool to room temperature.

Serve at room temperature or cold. Makes 3–4 cups.

1½ pounds water spinach

1 tablespoon ginger, julienned

1 small onion, sliced thin

2 teaspoons salt

1 teaspoon pepper

2 tablespoons sugar

½ cup native Philippine vinegar (*sukang paombong*) **or** distilled white vinegar

½ cup water

Pickled Cucumbers
ACHARANG PIPINO

10 pickling cucumbers, 3–4
  inches long

¼ cup salt

2 medium onions, sliced thin

PICKLING SOLUTION:

1 tablespoon ginger, minced

3 cloves garlic, minced

1 cup white distilled vinegar

⅔ cup sugar

1 teaspoon salt

5 native Philippine hot peppers
  (siling labuyo) or 2 jalapeño
  peppers (optional)

Wash and dry the cucumbers and cut them crosswise into thin slices. Do not peel them.

Place a layer of the cucumber slices in the bottom of a ceramic dish. Sprinkle with ½ tablespoon of the salt. Add a layer of sliced onions and sprinkle with ½ tablespoon of the salt. Continue alternating layers of cucumber and onions, sprinkling each with salt, until all the vegetables are in the dish. Cover with a lid or plastic wrap and let stand overnight at room temperature.

Rinse well with water several times, changing the water between rinses to remove all salt. Drain completely in a colander.

Mix the pickling solution ingredients in a stainless steel or ceramic saucepan. Simmer until the sugar has completely dissolved. Remove from the heat and cool to room temperature.

Place the drained cucumber and onions in sterile jars. Pour the pickling solution over the vegetables. Remove any trapped air and cover. Refrigerate 3–4 days before serving. Makes 1 quart.

Salted Mustard Greens
BURONG MUSTASA

Wash the rice thoroughly. Put it in a medium saucepan, add the water, and bring it to a boil. Lower the heat, cover and simmer until the rice is done, or about 20 minutes. Drain and reserve the rice water. Save the rice for use in other recipes.

Remove any soft or discolored areas from the mustard leaves. Wash each leaf under cold running water and dry *thoroughly* (if any moisture is left on the leaves, mold will form).

Put the greens in a large bowl and add the salt. Mix together thoroughly. Squeeze out the juices.

Pack the leaves in a sterile 1-quart glass jar. Pour the cooled rice water over the leaves, to cover by at least 1 inch.

Put plastic wrap over the mouth of the jar and seal jar with the lid. Place in a cool, dark place for at least 1 week. Afterward, store in the refrigerator. The best flavor and texture occur in 3–4 weeks.

To serve: Thoroughly chop up a few of the mustard green leaves. In a small bowl, mix the greens and a few tablespoons of the liquid. A diced, ripe tomato can also be mixed in. Serve as a vegetable side dish. Makes 1 quart.

½ cup white rice

6 cups water

3 pounds mustard greens
  (mustasa)

½ cup salt

1 tomato, diced (optional)

Sautéed Mustard Greens
GUINISANG BURONG MUSTASA

2 cloves garlic, minced

2 tablespoons vegetable oil

1 small onion, sliced

1 medium tomato, sliced

1½ cups salted mustard
greens *(burong mustasa)*,
drained and chopped
(page 191)

3 eggs, slightly beaten

1 teaspoon salt

¼ teaspoon black pepper

In a skillet, sauté the garlic in the hot oil until it is light brown. Add the onions and tomatoes and sauté until the tomatoes are soft.

Add the mustard greens and sauté for 3 minutes.

Add the beaten eggs, salt and pepper and stir well and frequently until eggs are cooked, or 3–4 minutes.

Serve hot. Makes 4–5 servings.

Salted Eggs
ITLOG MA-ALAT

Use eggs that have thick shells with no cracks. Put them in a wide-mouth glass jar or a porcelain crock.

To make the brine, pour the hot water into a large glass or plastic pitcher and gradually stir in 2 cups of the salt. Continue stirring until the salt is completely dissolved. Add more salt until it will no longer dissolve, and instead, settles to the bottom of the pitcher. At this point, stop and allow the brine to cool.

Pour the cooled brine over the eggs in the jar or crock. The eggs will float, so put a plate smaller than the opening of the jar or crock on top of the eggs, with a weight on the plate to keep the eggs immersed in the brine.

Cover the jar or crock with foil and let stand in a cool, dark place for 3 weeks.

After 3 weeks, remove the eggs from the brine. Brine may be used again to cure more eggs.

Place the eggs in a large pot, cover with water, and gently bring them to a boil over medium-high heat. Reduce the heat and simmer for 15 minutes. Remove from the heat. Pour cold running water into the pot to cool the eggs. (Because the salted eggs look fresh, it is customary to dye or mark them. In the Philippines, salted chicken eggs are marked with an "X" using a felt-tip marker. Salted duck eggs are often dyed like Easter eggs with red or purple food coloring.)

To serve: Peel and slice or chop 1 salted egg into small, thin pieces. Coarsely chop 2 medium tomatoes, and mix the tomatoes with the eggs. Garnish with 1 tablespoon of finely chopped green onions and a few dashes of fish sauce.

Serve cold as an accompaniment to fried fish or meats. Makes 2 dozen salted eggs.

24 chicken or duck eggs
8 cups hot water
2½ cups coarse salt

Pickled Green Mangoes

6 large green mangoes*

2 medium green bell peppers, cut into thin strips

2 medium red bell peppers, cut into thin strips

2 jalapeño peppers, cut into thin strips

8 cloves garlic, crushed

4 tablespoons ginger, julienned

20 pearl onions or 2 medium onions, sliced

½ cup raisins

PICKLING SOLUTION:

2 cups distilled white vinegar

6 cups sugar

4 teaspoons salt

Peel and thinly slice the mangoes into pieces ⅛ inch thick and 3 inches long. Set the slices aside.

To make the pickling solution, mix the vinegar, sugar and salt in a stainless steel or ceramic pan. Cook over medium heat until the sugar has dissolved. Increase the heat and let mixture simmer and thicken slightly.

When the syrup has thickened, add the mango slices. Continue cooking until the mangoes are transparent, about 15 minutes.

Add the peppers, garlic, ginger and onions and simmer for 10 minutes. Add the raisins and remove the pan from the heat.

Pour the mixture, while hot, into sterilized jars and cover. Cool to room temperature. Store in the refrigerator until ready to serve, in about a week.

Serve at room temperature or cool. Makes 1 quart.

*The mangoes should be very hard and show no signs of yellow or orange on the skin.

Pickled Green Tomatoes

Wash the tomatoes and remove the hard core and stem. Cut them into ¼-inch slices.

Arrange the tomatoes and onions in layers in a glass or ceramic bowl. Sprinkle the salt on each layer. Let stand at room temperature for at least 12 hours.

Rinse the tomatoes and onions several times, changing water between each rinse to remove the salt.

In a stainless steel or ceramic pan, combine the ingredients for the pickling solution and bring to a boil. Reduce the heat and simmer for 10 minutes.

Pack the tomatoes and onions in a sterile jar. Pour the hot pickling solution over the vegetables and let cool to room temperature. Cover and place in the refrigerator. Ripen for 2 weeks before serving. May be kept refrigerated for up to 6–8 weeks.

Serve cold. Makes 1 quart.

12 medium green tomatoes
1 medium onion, sliced thin
½ cup coarse salt

PICKLING SOLUTION:
1 cup distilled white vinegar
1 cup sugar
4 whole cloves

Jicama Relish
SINGKAMAS

6 cups water

1½ cups salt

6 cups jicama *(singkamas)*, peeled and grated

12 pearl onions, peeled, or 1 medium onion, chopped coarsely

3 cloves garlic, peeled and halved

3 tablespoons ginger, julienned

1 large green bell pepper, diced

1 large red bell pepper, diced

6 native Philippine hot peppers *(siling labuyo)* or 2 jalapeño peppers, whole

PICKLING SOLUTION:

2 cups distilled white vinegar

⅔ cup sugar

Mix the water and salt in a large bowl. Add the jicama and cover the bowl. Let stand overnight at room temperature.

Rinse the jicama with running water to remove all the salt and drain in a colander. Squeeze out any excess liquid by hand.

Put the drained jicama in a large bowl and add the onions, garlic, ginger and peppers. Mix well and pack in a sterilized 1-quart jar.

In a non-aluminum pan, mix the pickling solution ingredients and bring them to a boil. Reduce the heat and simmer for 5 minutes.

Pour the hot pickling solution over the vegetables in the jar. Allow to cool to room temperature. Cover with a lid and seal tightly. Store in the refrigerator for at least 1 week before using.

Serve cold. Makes 1 quart.

Pickled Spiced Eggs

Place the eggs in a large pot, cover with water and boil for 5–6 minutes, or until the eggs are hard-boiled. Plunge the eggs into a bowl of ice water to stop the cooking process. Peel, and set the hard-boiled eggs aside.

Tie the cinnamon stick, star anise, cloves and peppercorns in a small piece of cheesecloth and set aside.

To make the spiced syrup, mix the vinegar, sugar and salt together in a stainless steel or ceramic saucepan and bring to a boil. Reduce the heat and add the bag of spices. Simmer for 10 minutes.

Add the hard-boiled eggs and simmer for another 5 minutes. Discard the bag of spices.

Put the eggs and syrup into sterilized jars. Cover with a lid and seal tightly. Plunge the jars into a pot of boiling water for 25 minutes to sterilize the contents for longer shelf life. Allow to cool to room temperature before storing in the refrigerator. Ripen for at least 1 week before using. (The longer the eggs age, the better their flavor.)

Serve cold. Makes 12 pickled spiced eggs.

12 eggs

PICKLING SOLUTION:
1 cinnamon stick
4 whole star anise
6 whole cloves
6 whole black peppercorns
1 cup distilled white vinegar
½ cup sugar
1 teaspoon salt

Rice Dishes

Underwood & Underwood/Corbis–Bettman

The vast canyon-like rice terraces of Banaue rise from the deep valleys of northern Luzon. The Ifugao people still tend the 3000-year-old terraces.

For Filipinos, and most people in Asia, a meal without rice is almost inconceivable. In parts of the Philippines, especially parts of southern Luzon and Visayas, substituting root crops such as sweet potatoes, yams and cassava for rice is a sign of desperate poverty.

The rice terraces of Banaue are located four thousand feet up the steep-sided mountains of northern Luzon's central Cordilla mountain range. Built about 1000 BC, today they cover over 100 square miles and are considered an engineering marvel. The rice paddies are irrigated by a system of rock retaining walls that catch the water at the top of the mountains and allow it to trickle down to the lower terraces and eventually into the valleys below.

Today these terraces are maintained by a tribe of Filipinos called the Ifugao, who believe that rice has a soul and provides life. In January, the rice is planted, and by March, all the terraces are green. As the rice matures, it turns golden and the terraces of Banaue are transformed to an awe-inspiring mountain of gold. In June and July the rice is harvested and ritual ceremonies of thanksgiving are performed. In August, September and October, the paddies are repaired. In November and December the paddies are prepared for planting, and in January, the cycle starts again.

The Rice Terraces of the Ifugaos— They were built by the ancestors of the present dwellers here.

The International Rice Institute (IRI) is headquartered in the Philippines. Its mission is to locate and preserve, throughout the world, the hundreds of different varieties of cultivated and wild rice, and, using sophisticated genetic and bioengineering techniques, to create new hybrid strains of rice for growth around the world.

Although there are many ways to cook rice, most Filipinos simply boil it in water in a heavy pan on top of the stove or in an electric rice cooker. Or they add extra water or broth to make it into a thick rice soup or gruel, called *arroz caldo.* When meat is added it makes a hearty cold-weather dish.

Many of the rice or *arroz* dishes are based on the famous Spanish rice dish, *paella.* To this, other ingredients have been added and the original recipe adapted to the Filipino taste.

Catalan Rice
Arroz a la Catalana

½ cup + 3 tablespoons olive oil

2 pounds chicken, cut into bite-size pieces

½ pound lean pork, diced

½ pound fresh squid, cleaned (see instructions, page 94)

¼ cup light rum

6 large shrimp

¼ cup clam juice

12 large clams

4 cloves garlic, crushed

2 small onions, diced

3 cups white rice, washed and drained

1 8-ounce can tomato paste

1 teaspoon salt

¼ teaspoon black pepper

6 cups water

8 ounces canned peas, drained

2 Spanish sausages (chorizo de Bilbao), sliced thin

In a wok or large skillet, heat the 3 tablespoons of olive oil and lightly brown the chicken pieces. Drain and set aside. In the same oil, sauté the diced pork for 3–4 minutes. Drain and set aside. Sauté the squid for 2 minutes, drain and set aside.

In a small saucepan, heat the rum. (NOTE: As the alcohol evaporates, the rum may flame up; just let it burn off.) Add the shrimp and simmer for 3 minutes. Remove the pan from the heat and let stand.

In another saucepan, heat the clam juice to a light boil. Add the clams, cover, and steam for 4–5 minutes. Remove the clams from the liquid and set both aside. Discard any clams that have not opened.

In the wok in which the chicken, squid and pork were sautéed, pour the ½ cup of olive oil and heat on high. Add the garlic and fry until it is golden brown.

Add the onions and rice. Stir the mixture in the oil for 2 minutes. Add the tomato paste, salt and pepper and stir.

Add the reserved clam liquid and the water, cover, and bring to a boil. Lower the heat and simmer a few minutes.

Stir in the chicken, squid, pork and Spanish sausage. Cover and continue simmering until the rice is tender, about 20–25 minutes.

Add the peas and mix well. Reduce the heat to low.

Arrange the clams and shrimp on the rice mixture, cover and heat for 5 minutes more. Makes 6–8 servings.

Cuban Rice
ARROZ A LA CUBANA

Heat 2 tablespoons of the vegetable oil in a skillet and sauté the garlic, onions and tomatoes for 3–4 minutes. Add the pork and beef, and sauté until they are browned.

Add the raisins, beef broth, salt and pepper. Simmer, stirring occasionally, until most of the liquid has evaporated.

Add the frozen peas and continue cooking until they are cooked and the mixture is quite dry. Remove from the heat.

In another skillet, heat 3 tablespoons of the oil and fry the banana slices until they are golden brown on all sides. Remove the bananas and set aside.

Wipe the skillet in which the bananas were fried with a paper towel. Heat the remaining 3 tablespoons of oil and fry the eggs, sunny side up.

To serve, mound the rice in the middle of a large platter or take individual cups of rice and overturn onto individual plates. Arrange the fried bananas around the rice. Spoon the meat and raisin mixture over the rice, and put the fried eggs on top. Makes 6 servings.

½ cup vegetable oil

2 cloves garlic, minced

1 medium onion, diced

1 medium tomato, chopped

½ pound ground pork

½ pound ground beef

4 tablespoons raisins

½ cup beef broth

1 teaspoon salt

½ teaspoon black pepper

½ cup frozen peas

6 cups cooked rice

4 saba bananas, peeled and cut in half lengthwise, or 2 plantains, peeled and sliced diagonally into ¼-inch-thick slices

6 eggs

Filipino Rice
ARROZ A LA FILIPINA

2 cups sweet rice *(malagkit)*, washed and drained

2 cups white rice, washed and drained

8 cups water

3 tablespoons vegetable oil

3 cloves garlic, crushed

2 pounds chicken, cut into bite-size pieces

1 medium onion, diced

3 medium tomatoes, chopped

1 cup chicken broth

2 medium green bell peppers, sliced into thin strips

1 tablespoon annatto *(atsuete)* seeds soaked in ¼ cup water for 30 minutes

4 tablespoons raisins

1 teaspoon salt

½ teaspoon black pepper

3 hard-boiled eggs, halved

Malagkit *or sweet or glutinous rice is quite heavy and filling. If preferred, it can be replaced with plain white rice.*

Put the washed and drained sweet and white rice in a pot with the water. Bring to a boil, reduce the heat, cover, and simmer for 25–30 minutes.

Heat the oil in a large pot and sauté the garlic until it is light brown. Add the chicken pieces and brown.

Add the onions and tomatoes and cook until the onions are soft.

Add the chicken broth, cover, and simmer for 8-10 minutes or until the chicken is tender.

Add the sliced bell peppers, cover, and cook for 3 minutes more.

Remove the annatto seeds from the water and stir the water into the vegetables for an orange color. (Be sure not to add any of the seeds.)

Add the cooked rice, raisins, salt and pepper and mix well. Continue cooking over low heat for 10 minutes, stirring occasionally to prevent burning.

Garnish with the hard-boiled egg halves. Makes 6–8 servings.

Luzon Rice
ARROZ A LA LUZONIA

Put the washed and drained sweet rice and the water into a pot, bring to a boil, cover, and reduce the heat. Simmer for 25–30 minutes.

Heat 2 tablespoons of the oil in a large skillet and sauté the garlic for 1 minute. Add the onions and sauté until they are translucent.

Add the chicken and pork and sauté for 4–5 minutes. Add the shrimp and cook for 1 minute more.

Stir in the cooked rice, salt, pepper and the water the seeds were soaked in. (Be sure all seeds are discarded.) Stir well to give the rice a nice yellow-brown color. Remove the pan from the heat and allow to cool.

Add the eggs and mix well.

Grease well a mold or bowl with the butter. Line the bottom with the hard-boiled eggs and red bell pepper slices.

Fill the mold with the rice mixture. Pack well and cover with wax paper. Put the mold in a steamer and steam for 30 minutes.

In a skillet, fry the bananas in 3 tablespoons of the oil until they are golden brown on both sides. Drain on paper towels and set aside.

Remove the mold or bowl from the steamer and let rest for a few minutes before unmolding.

Turn the mold onto a platter. Arrange the fried bananas around the rice. Makes 4–6 servings.

3 cups sweet rice *(malagkit)*, washed and drained

6 cups water

5 tablespoons vegetable oil

3 cloves garlic, minced

1 small onion, diced

½ pound chicken breast meat, diced

½ pound lean pork, diced

¼ pound shrimp, peeled and chopped

1 teaspoon salt

½ teaspoon black pepper

1 tablespoon annatto *(atsuete)* seeds soaked in ¼ cup water for 30 minutes or 1 teaspoon paprika

2 eggs, slightly beaten

2 tablespoons butter or margarine

1 hard-boiled egg, peeled and sliced

1 red bell pepper, cut into 6 slices

4 saba bananas, peeled and sliced in half lengthwise or 2 plantains, peeled and sliced diagonally ¼-inch-thick

Valencian Rice
ARROZ A LA VALENCIANA

2 pounds chicken, cut into
    bite-size pieces

1 pound lean pork, cut into
    thin strips

1 teaspoon salt

½ teaspoon black pepper

½ cup + 3 tablespoons olive
    oil

3 cups white rice, washed
    and drained

3 cups water

2 cups coconut milk

2 cloves garlic, crushed

1 medium onion, sliced

1 medium tomato, diced

6 potatoes, peeled and
    quartered

5 ounces Spanish sausage
    (chorizo *de Bilbao),* sliced
    thin

¼ cup water

8 ounces canned peas,
    drained

4 ounces canned chopped
    black olives, drained

½ small red bell pepper,
    diced

½ small red bell pepper, cut
    into thin strips

3 hard-boiled eggs, halved

12 stuffed green olives

Sprinkle the chicken pieces and pork with the salt and pepper. Heat 3 tablespoons of the oil in a wok or large skillet and lightly brown the chicken. Remove the chicken and set aside. Sauté the pork in the same hot oil for 3–4 minutes. Drain and set the pork aside.

In a pot, combine the washed and drained rice, the 3 cups of water and the coconut milk. Stir and bring to a boil. Cover, reduce the heat, and simmer for 25–30 minutes.

In the wok, heat the ½ cup of the oil. Fry the garlic until it is golden brown. Add the onions and tomatoes and sauté for 2 minutes.

Add the potatoes and cook for 3–4 minutes. Add the chicken, pork, Spanish sausage and ¼ cup water. Mix well, cover, and cook until the potatoes are tender, about 10 minutes.

Add the peas, olives and red bell peppers and simmer for 4–5 minutes. Remove ½ cup of the liquid from the wok and set it aside.

Add the cooked rice to the meat mixture. Mix thoroughly with a wooden spoon.

Add the reserved liquid back to the wok. Season to taste with salt and pepper. Cook on low heat until the mixture becomes quite dry, about 10–15 minutes. Stir occasionally.

Serve on a large dish or platter. Arrange the red pepper strips, hard-boiled eggs and stuffed green olives on top. Makes 6–8 servings.

Thick Rice Soup with Tripe
Arroz Caldo at Goto

Place the tripe in a pan and cover it with water. Bring to a boil and cook for 5 minutes. Discard the water. Cover again with water and boil until tender, 1½ hours. Drain, cool and cut the tripe into thin slices. Set aside.

Heat the oil in a large pot and sauté the garlic, onions, ginger and rice for 2 minutes.

Add the chicken broth and water and bring to a boil. Reduce the heat and simmer, covered, until the rice is almost done, 15–20 minutes.

Stir in the sliced tripe, fish sauce and pepper and simmer for 10 minutes more.

In a small pan, heat the oil for the garnish and fry the garlic until it is golden brown. Drain it on a paper towel.

To serve, ladle the soup into individual bowls. Garnish each portion with ½ tablespoon of garlic and ½ teaspoon of green onions. Makes 6 servings.

1 pound tripe *(goto)*, boiled and sliced thin

3 tablespoons vegetable oil

2 cloves garlic, minced

1 small onion, diced

1 tablespoon ginger, minced

1½ cups white rice

4 cups chicken broth

2 cups water

2 tablespoons fish sauce

¼ teaspoon black pepper

GARNISH:

3 tablespoons vegetable oil

3 tablespoons garlic, crushed

3 tablespoons green onion, finely chopped

Thick Rice Soup with Chicken
Arroz Caldo at Manok

2 tablespoons vegetable oil

1 tablespoon ginger, minced

2 cloves garlic, minced

1 small onion, sliced

2 pounds chicken, cut into bite-size pieces

2 tablespoons fish sauce

1 cup white rice, washed and drained

4 cups water

1 teaspoon white pepper

3 tablespoons green onions, finely chopped

In a large pot, heat the vegetable oil and sauté the ginger, garlic and onions for 1 minute.

Add the chicken pieces and fish sauce, cover, and simmer for 3 minutes, stirring occasionally.

Add the rice and water, stirring well. Bring the water to a boil, reduce the heat to low and simmer for 20 minutes, or until chicken and rice are cooked.

Remove from the heat and stir in the green onion. Makes 6 servings.

Paella

In a mortar and pestle, grind together the oregano, garlic, 1 teaspoon of the salt, and peppercorns with 2 tablespoons of the oil. Rub the chicken pieces with this mixture. Let stand for 30 minutes.

Bring the water and the remaining 3 teaspoons of salt to a boil. Add the shrimp and boil for 1 minute. Remove the shrimp and set aside. In the same water, boil the crabs for 4 minutes. Remove them from the water and cut into quarters. Set them aside. Boil the clams for 3 minutes or until they open. (If any fail to open, discard.) Remove them from the water and set aside. Reserve at least 4 cups of this fish broth.

In a wok or large skillet, heat 2 tablespoons of the oil. Brown the marinated chicken and the pork lightly over medium heat.

Add the onions, ham, Spanish sausage and salt pork. Cook for 10 minutes.

Stir in the rice and sauté it for 5 minutes. Add the 4 cups of reserved fish broth, tomato sauce, paprika, saffron and bell pepper strips. Mix well and bring to a boil. Reduce the heat and cover. Cook until all the liquid is absorbed and rice is cooked, about 20 minutes.

Remove the cover and stir well. Add the peas and stir again. Arrange the shrimp, crab quarters and clams on top of the rice. Cover again and heat for 5 minutes more. Makes 4–6 servings.

½ teaspoon oregano

2 cloves garlic, minced

4 teaspoons salt

6 peppercorns

4 tablespoons vegetable oil

2 pounds chicken, cut into bite-size pieces

6 cups water

12 large shrimp, boiled

2 crabs

12 large clams

1 pound pork butt, cut into 1-inch cubes

2 large onions, sliced

¼ pound ham, diced

1 Spanish sausage (chorizo de Bilbao), diced

¼ pound salt pork

2 cups white rice, washed and drained

8 ounces tomato sauce

½ teaspoon paprika

½ teaspoon saffron

1 large green bell pepper, cut into strips

1 large red bell pepper, cut into strips

½ cup canned peas, drained

Soups

Meatball Soup
ALMONDIGAS

Combine all the ingredients for the meatballs and shape into walnut-sized balls. Set aside on a plate covered with a moist towel or plastic wrap.

In a saucepan, sauté the garlic and onions in the oil. Add the chicken broth, fish sauce, salt and pepper and bring to a boil.

Reduce the heat and add the meatballs to the broth gently. Cover and simmer for 10 minutes.

Add the noodles and cook for 1–2 minutes or until they are tender.

Garnish with the green onions. Makes 4 servings.

MEATBALLS:

½ pound ground pork

½ pound shrimp, peeled and chopped

2 cloves garlic, minced

1 egg, slightly beaten

½ cup onion, chopped

½ teaspoon salt

½ teaspoon black pepper

SOUP:

1 clove garlic, minced

½ cup onion, chopped

1 tablespoon vegetable oil

4 cups chicken broth

1 tablespoon fish sauce

½ teaspoon salt

½ teaspoon black pepper

2 ounces thin wheat noodles (*misua*) or angel hair pasta

2 tablespoons green onions, finely chopped

Pork Liver and Kidney Soup
BACHOY

1 tablespoon vegetable oil

2 cloves garlic, minced

¾ cup onion, chopped

½ teaspoon ginger, julienned

½ pound pork tenderloin, diced

½ pound pork liver, diced

½ pound pork kidney, white outer membrane removed, and diced

4 cups beef broth or water

1 tablespoon fish sauce

1 teaspoon salt

½ teaspoon black pepper

¼ cup green onions, finely chopped

In a large pot, heat the oil and sauté the garlic, onions and ginger until the onions are transparent, about 2–3 minutes.

Add the pork meat, liver and kidney and stir-fry for 5 minutes.

Add the broth or water, fish sauce, salt and pepper and bring to a boil. Lower the heat, cover, and simmer for 10 minutes.

Garnish with the green onions. Makes 4–5 servings.

VARIATIONS:

Add ½ cup pork brains, cleaned and diced, in the last 3 minutes of cooking.

Add 2 ounces of thin noodles to the soup in the last minute of cooking.

Chicken and Bean Thread Soup
BAM-I

In a skillet, heat the oil and sauté the pork for 2–3 minutes. Set aside.

Sauté the garlic and onion in the oil until the onions are soft.

Add the broth and fish sauce and bring to a boil.

Add the black tree fungus, jicama, noodles, chicken and pork. Stir well and bring back to a boil. Reduce the heat and simmer for 15–20 minutes or until the bean thread is soft and transparent. Stir in the salt and pepper. Makes 8 servings.

3 tablespoons vegetable oil

1 cup lean pork, cut into thin strips 1 inch long

6 cloves garlic, minced

½ cup onion, chopped

8 cups chicken broth

3 tablespoons fish sauce

½ cup black tree fungus *(taingang daga)*, soaked in water for 30 minutes and cut into small strips

¾ cup jicama, julienned, or water chestnuts *(apulid)*, sliced thin

8 ounces dried bean thread noodles *(sotanghon)*, soaked in water 20–30 minutes and cut to a length of 4 inches

2 cups chicken breast meat, cooked and shredded

¼ teaspoon salt

¼ teaspoon black pepper

Chicken and Coconut Soup
Manok Binakol

6 cloves garlic, crushed

1 cup onion, chopped

1 teaspoon ginger, minced

3 tablespoons vegetable oil

3 tablespoons fish sauce

2 pounds chicken, deboned and cut into bite-sized pieces

6 cups chicken broth

1 green young coconut (*buko*), thawed and shredded or cut into 1-inch pieces and the coconut juice reserved

¼ teaspoon salt

¼ teaspoon black pepper

Green, young coconut (buko) *is available frozen, whole or shredded, at Asian markets.*

In a pot, sauté the garlic, onions and ginger in the oil until the onions are soft. Do not allow the garlic to brown.

Add the fish sauce and cook for 2 minutes.

Add the chicken and brown slightly, for 5 minutes.

Pour in the broth and bring it to a boil. Reduce the heat and simmer for 30 minutes or until the chicken is tender.

Add the coconut and coconut juice and cook for 2–3 minutes more. Stir in the salt and pepper. Makes 6–8 servings.

Chinese Chicken Noodle Soup
MANOK MAMI

Heat the oil in a small skillet and fry the crushed garlic until it is golden brown. Drain on paper towels, mince into fine pieces and set aside.

Put the Chinese-style noodles in warm salted water to separate them. If using dried egg noodles, cook in salted, boiling water until the noodles are just tender.

Drain the noodles in a colander and divide into 6 equal portions and place in soup bowls. Sprinkle the chicken, chopped egg and green onions on top of the noodles.

In a saucepan, bring the chicken broth to a boil. Stir in the fish sauce, salt and pepper.

Pour the hot broth into each bowl and garnish with the fried garlic. Makes 6 servings.

VARIATION:

Pork *Mami* — Substitute 1 cup of thin-sliced cooked pork or ham for the chicken.

¼ cup vegetable oil

6 cloves garlic, crushed

½ pound Chinese-style thick wheat noodles *(mami)* or ¼ pound wide egg noodles

1 cup diced, cooked chicken

1 hard-boiled egg, chopped coarsely

¼ cup green onions, finely chopped

5 cups chicken broth

1 tablespoon fish sauce

¼ teaspoon salt

½ teaspoon black pepper

Sour Chicken Soup
SINAMPALOCAN MANOK

2½-pound chicken, cut into pieces

4 teaspoons salt

6 cloves garlic, crushed

1 tablespoon ginger, minced

3 tablespoons vegetable oil

1 medium onion, sliced

2 large tomatoes, chopped

8 cups water

2 tablespoons fish sauce

2 cups tamarind leaves tied in cheesecloth, or juice of 2 lemons

1 teaspoon black pepper

Sprinkle the chicken pieces with 3 teaspoons of the salt and set it aside to marinate.

In a pot, sauté the garlic and ginger in hot oil. Add the onions and tomatoes and cook until the tomatoes are very soft.

Add the chicken pieces and cook until the liquid is almost gone, about 15–20 minutes.

Add the water and bring to a boil. Add the fish sauce and the tamarind leaves in cheesecloth, or the lemon juice.

Reduce the heat and simmer for 30–40 minutes or until the chicken is tender. Add the remaining teaspoon of salt and the pepper.

Just before serving, remove the bundle of tamarind leaves and discard. Makes 8 servings.

Corn and Beef Soup

In a medium-sized saucepan, heat the oil and sauté the sirloin strips until they are browned, about 2–3 minutes. Remove from the pan and set aside.

Pour the beef broth into the saucepan and bring it to a boil. Stir in the corn and bring back to a boil. Add the salt and pepper, beef and spinach, lower the heat and simmer for 3–4 minutes, stirring occasionally.

Add the cornstarch and water mixture and cook, stirring constantly for 1 minute, until the soup is thickened. Garnish with the green onions. Makes 3–4 servings.

1 tablespoon vegetable oil

½ pound beef sirloin, sliced into thin strips

3 cups beef broth

10 ounces canned whole kernel corn, drained

1½ teaspoons salt

⅛ teaspoon black pepper

2 cups spinach, washed and coarsely cut or 1 package frozen spinach, thawed and squeezed dry

2 tablespoons cornstarch dissolved in 3 tablespoons water

2 tablespoons green onions, finely chopped

Corn and Chicken Soup

In a medium-sized saucepan, sauté the chicken strips in the oil until browned, about 3 minutes. Remove from the pan and set aside.

Pour the broth in the pan and bring it to a boil. Stir in the creamed corn and bring it back to a boil.

Add the cooked chicken, salt and pepper and simmer for 2 minutes, stirring occasionally.

Add the cornstarch and water mixture and stir constantly until the soup is thick.

Garnish each serving with chopped egg. Makes 3–4 servings.

½ pound chicken, sliced into thin strips

1 tablespoon vegetable oil

3 cups chicken broth

10 ounces canned creamed corn

1½ teaspoons salt

⅛ teaspoon black pepper

2 tablespoons cornstarch dissolved in 3 tablespoons water

1 hard-boiled egg, chopped

Corn and Egg White Soup

1 tablespoon vegetable oil

1 clove garlic, minced

3 tablespoons green onions, finely chopped

3 cups chicken broth

10 ounces canned creamed corn

½ cup frozen peas

1½ teaspoons salt

¼ teaspoon white pepper

2 tablespoons cornstarch dissolved in 3 tablespoons water

2 egg whites, well beaten

2 tablespoons parsley or cilantro, finely chopped

In a medium-sized saucepan, heat the oil and sauté the garlic and green onions for 1 minute.

Add the chicken broth and bring it to a boil.

Add the corn, frozen peas, salt and pepper and bring to a second boil. Reduce the heat and simmer for 3–4 minutes.

Stir in the cornstarch and water mixture to thicken the soup.

Beat the egg whites again until they are frothy. Add them to the hot broth a few drops at a time, stirring constantly to create ribbons of egg in the soup.

Garnish with the parsley or cilantro. Makes 3 servings.

Noodle Soup with Eggs
Misua with Eggs

1 clove garlic, chopped

1 tablespoon vegetable oil

1 small onion, sliced

3 cups water

1 teaspoon salt

1 teaspoon black pepper

3 eggs, unbeaten

4 ounces Chinese-style thin wheat noodles (misua)

In a saucepan, sauté the garlic in the oil until brown. Add the onions and sauté until they are soft.

Add the water, salt and pepper and bring to a boil.

Add the eggs one at a time, stirring a minute or so between each egg.

Break the noodles into smaller lengths and add them to the liquid. Simmer for 3–4 minutes or until they are tender. Makes 3 servings.

Noodle Soup with Pork
MISUA WITH PORK

Luffa gourd is available fresh at Asian markets. It can be replaced with the same amount of zucchini.

Heat the oil in a saucepan and sauté the garlic and onions until they are light brown.

Add the pork and sauté for 6–8 minutes, until the meat is firm.

Add the water, salt and pepper and bring to a boil.

Reduce the heat and add the luffa gourd slices. Simmer for 4–5 minutes or until they are soft.

Add the noodles and simmer for 3–4 minutes or until tender. Stir in the fish sauce and remove from the heat. Makes 3 servings.

1 tablespoon vegetable oil

1 clove garlic, crushed

1 small onion, sliced

¼ pound lean pork, diced

3 cups water

1 teaspoon salt

1 teaspoon black pepper

1 luffa gourd *(patola),* or 1 zucchini, peeled and sliced into 1-inch slices

4 ounces Chinese-style thin white noodles *(misua)*

1 tablespoon fish sauce

Filipino Dumpling Soup
PANCIT MOLO

FILLING:

½ pound ground pork

½ cup cooked and shredded
chicken breast meat

1 egg, unbeaten

3 tablespoons green onions,
chopped

½ pound shrimp, peeled,
deveined and chopped

3 tablespoons garlic, minced

½ cup onions, diced

¼ cup water chestnuts (*apulid*)
or jicama, diced

½ teaspoon sesame oil

1 teaspoon salt

1 teaspoon black pepper

1 tablespoon soy sauce

WRAPPERS:

24 wonton wrappers
  - or -
1 cup white flour

¼ teaspoon salt

2 egg yolks

2 cups water

BROTH:

2 tablespoons garlic, crushed

½ cup onions, chopped

3 tablespoons vegetable oil

12 cups chicken broth

4 tablespoons fish sauce

1 teaspoon salt

1½ teaspoons black pepper

3 tablespoons green onions,
finely chopped

If you don't have time to make your own wrappers, commercial wonton wrappers are a fine substitute.

Instructions for Filling: Combine and mix well all the filling ingredients. Divide into 2 halves—one half will go in the broth and the other will fill the wrappers.

Instructions for Wrappers:Combine the flour and salt on a smooth flat surface. Make a well in the center and add the eggs and water. Stir into a fine paste. Knead the dough until it is smooth and form it into a large ball. Dust the work surface with more flour and roll out the ball of dough until it is paper-thin. Cut into triangles or squares 3 inches long on each side.

Place 1 tablespoon of filling in the middle of each wonton wrapper. Fold over one corner of the wrapper until it meets the opposite corner. Seal the edges with water. Set aside on a plate, covered with plastic wrap until ready to add to the soup.

Instructions for Broth: Sauté the garlic and onions in a large pot in the hot oil for 1 minute.

Add the remaining half of the filling mixture and cook for 5 minutes or until lightly browned. Add the chicken broth and fish sauce and bring to a boil.

Gently add the stuffed wrappers to the broth and stir.

Cover the pot and boil for 15 minutes, stirring gently occasionally. Add the salt and pepper. Garnish with the green onions. Makes 10–12 servings.

Chinese Okra and Noodle Soup
PATOLA AT MISUA

In a large pot, heat the oil and sauté the garlic and onions until the onions are translucent. Add the Chinese okra and sauté for 4–5 minutes.

Add the chicken broth and bring to a boil. Reduce the heat and simmer for 3–4 minutes.

Add the noodles, fish sauce and pepper. Simmer, stirring constantly, for 3–4 minutes or until the noodles are cooked. Season to taste with more fish sauce and pepper. Makes 2–3 servings.

2 tablespoons vegetable oil

3 cloves garlic, minced

1 small onion, diced

1 pound Chinese okra (*patola*), peeled and sliced crosswise ¼ inch thick

2 cups chicken broth

8 ounces thin wheat noodles (*misua*), cut into 4-inch lengths

1 tablespoon fish sauce

¼ teaspoon black pepper

Ground Beef and Potato Soup
PICADILLO

In a medium saucepan, heat the oil. Sauté the garlic and onions in hot oil until the onions just turn transparent. Add the tomatoes and sauté for 3–5 minutes.

Add the ground beef and sauté until brown. With a spoon, remove any excess fat. Add the fish sauce, salt, pepper and sugar.

Add the water and bring to a boil. Add the potatoes, cover, and simmer for 20 minutes or until they are tender. Makes 6 servings.

1 tablespoon vegetable oil

2 cloves garlic, minced

1 small onion, sliced thin

1 medium tomato, chopped

½ pound ground beef

2 tablespoons fish sauce

1 teaspoon salt

1 teaspoon black pepper

½ teaspoon sugar

5 cups water

2 medium potatoes, peeled and diced

Garlic Soup
SOPA DE AJO

8 slices bread

6 tablespoons olive oil

1 tablespoon garlic, minced
(can use more or less, to
taste)

2 tablespoons onions,
chopped

4 cups chicken broth

½ teaspoon salt

½ teaspoon black pepper

4 hard-boiled eggs,
sliced in half

Lightly toast the bread in a conventional toaster or in 3 table-spoons of the olive oil in a skillet.

Heat the remaining 3 tablespoons of oil in a medium-sized saucepan and sauté the garlic and onions until soft. Do not allow them to brown.

Add the broth, salt and pepper. Bring to a boil and remove from the heat.

Break the toasted bread into bite-size pieces and place in each soup bowl, along with 2 egg halves. Ladle the soup over the eggs and bread. Makes 4 servings.

Macaroni Soup
SOPA DE FIDEOS

2 cloves garlic, minced

1 medium onion, sliced thin

2 tablespoons vegetable oil

1 cup chicken breast meat,
diced

½ cup chicken giblets, diced

½ cup chicken livers, diced

1 tablespoon fish sauce

1 teaspoon salt

6 cups chicken broth

1 cup elbow or shell macaroni

½ teaspoon white pepper

4 tablespoons green onions,
finely chopped

In a medium saucepan, sauté the garlic and onions in hot oil until the onions are transparent. Add the chicken, giblets, liver, fish sauce and salt. Sauté for 2–3 minutes.

Add the broth and bring to a boil.

Add the macaroni and return to a boil. Cover, lower the heat to medium, and simmer for 15 minutes or until the macaroni is tender. Stir occasionally to keep the macaroni from sticking together.

Add the pepper and garnish with the green onions. Makes 6 servings.

Spanish Sausage and Bread Soup
SOPA DE PAN A LA DIABLA

Heat the oil in a skillet, add the bread cubes, and sauté until they are golden brown all over. Set aside.

In a medium saucepan, sauté the diced sausages for 3–4 minutes. Remove from the pan and drain on paper towels.

Pour off all but 1 tablespoon of the oil in the pan that cooked the sausages. Sauté the onions in that oil until they are translucent.

Add the broth and the drained sausages and bring to a boil.

Add the salt and pepper.

Garnish each serving with the toasted bread cubes. Makes 5 servings.

2 tablespoons olive oil

1 cup bread cut into ¼-inch cubes, or croutons

2 Spanish sausages (chorizo *de Bilbao*), diced

1 medium onion, sliced thin

5 cups beef broth

½ teaspoon salt

¼ teaspoon black pepper

Mung Bean Thread Soup
SOTANGHON

2 tablespoons vegetable oil

6 cloves garlic, minced

1 medium onion, chopped

½ pound chicken or pork, diced

6 cups chicken broth

12 ounces mung bean thread noodles *(sotanghon),* soaked in warm water for 30 minutes

½ teaspoon salt

1 teaspoon black pepper

1 cup black tree fungus (wood's ear), soaked in water for 30 minutes and sliced into thin strips

2 tablespoons fish sauce

4 tablespoons green onions, finely chopped

Heat the oil in a large pot and sauté the garlic and onions until translucent.

Add the chicken or pork and sauté for 3–4 minutes.

Add the chicken broth and bring to a boil.

Add the noodles, pepper, salt, black tree fungus and fish sauce. Simmer for 15–20 minutes. Garnish with the green onion. Makes 6 servings.

Meatballs and Noodle Soup
SOTANGHON AT ALMONDIGAS

Combine the pork, diced onion, egg, flour, salt, and ¼ teaspoon of pepper. Form into balls about 1 inch in diameter. Set aside.

Sauté the garlic in hot oil in a medium pot for 1 minute. Add the sliced onions and sauté for another 2 minutes. Add the broth and bring to a boil.

Gently add the meatballs one at a time to the boiling liquid. Simmer for 5 minutes. Add the noodles and cook for 5 minutes longer. Stir in the soy sauce and 1 teaspoon of pepper. Garnish with green onions. Makes 3–4 servings.

½ pound ground pork

2 tablespoons onion, diced

1 egg, well beaten

1 tablespoon white flour

1 teaspoon salt

1¼ teaspoons black pepper

2 cloves garlic, minced

2 tablespoons vegetable oil

1 small onion, sliced

3 cups chicken broth

4 ounces mung bean thread noodles *(sotanghon)*, soaked in water for 30 minutes and cut into 4-inch lengths

2 teaspoons soy sauce

3 tablespoons green onions, finely chopped

Peanut-Pork Balls and Noodle Soup
SOTANGHON AT MANI

½ pound raw, unshelled peanuts

2 cups water

½ pound ground pork

1 teaspoon salt

1 teaspoon white pepper

3 tablespoons green onions, finely chopped

1 egg, well beaten

2 cloves garlic, minced

1 small onion, diced

1 tablespoon vegetable oil

3 cups chicken broth

4 ounces mung bean thread noodles (sotanghon), soaked in water for 30 minutes and cut into 4-inch lengths

1 tablespoon fish sauce

Wash the peanuts well, and place them in the water in a medium saucepan. Cover and boil for 45–60 minutes. The peanuts are done when they are firm but not woody in texture. Drain and let cool for 15 minutes. Shell and chop the peanuts.

In a bowl, mix the peanuts, pork, salt, ½ teaspoon of the white pepper, green onions and egg together. Form into balls about 1 inch in diameter. Set aside on a plate.

Sauté the garlic and onions in hot oil in a medium pan until both are soft. Add the broth and bring to a boil.

Put the meatballs into the boiling liquid one at a time. Simmer for 5 minutes.

Add the soaked noodles, fish sauce and remaining ½ teaspoon of white pepper. Cook for 5 more minutes. Makes 3–4 servings.

Chicken and Mung Bean Thread Soup
SOTANGHON AT MANOK

In a large pot, sauté the garlic in hot oil until golden brown. Add the onions and sauté for 2 minutes. Add the chicken and sauté for 3–4 minutes.

Squeeze any remaining water from the black tree fungus and add to the chicken mixture. Add the fish sauce, salt and pepper.

Add the broth and bring to a boil. Add the drained noodles and simmer for 10 minutes or until they are tender. Garnish with the green onions. Makes 6 servings.

2 cloves garlic, minced

2 tablespoons vegetable oil

1 medium onion, chopped coarsely

½ pound chicken breast meat, diced

¼ pound black tree fungus, soaked in water for 30 minutes and sliced into thin strips

2 tablespoons fish sauce

1 teaspoon salt

¼ teaspoon white pepper

6 cups chicken broth

½ pound mung bean thread noodles *(sotanghon)*, soaked in water for 30 minutes and cut into 4-inch lengths

2 tablespoons green onions, finely chopped

Tofu and Mushroom Soup

1 tablespoon vegetable oil

¼ pound pork, cut into thin strips

6 cups chicken broth

1 tablespoon fish sauce

1 tablespoon soy sauce

1 teaspoon white pepper

2 large dried shiitake mushrooms, soaked in water for 30 minutes, stems discarded, and cut into thin strips

1 pound tofu, cut into ¼-inch cubes

2 tablespoons distilled white vinegar

2 tablespoons cornstarch dissolved in 3 tablespoons water

1 egg, slightly beaten

4 tablespoons green onions, finely chopped

In a pot, heat the oil and sauté the pork for 3–5 minutes, until slightly browned.

Add the broth, fish sauce, soy sauce, pepper and the shiitake mushrooms. Bring to a boil, lower the heat and simmer for 5 minutes.

Add the tofu and bring to a boil again.

Add the vinegar and cornstarch and water mixture and stir until the soup thickens.

Gently stir in the beaten egg, a few drops at a time, to make ribbons of egg in the soup.

Remove from the heat and garnish with the green onions. Makes 6 servings.

Sauces

The recipes in this section are for sauces that accompany specific dishes mentioned in other parts of this cookbook.

Shrimp Paste Sautéed with Pork
BAGOONG GUISADO

4 cloves garlic, crushed

2 tablespoons vegetable oil

¼ pound lean pork, chopped

½ cup shrimp paste (bagoong alamang)

2 tablespoons distilled white vinegar

1 teaspoon sugar (or more, to taste)

An indispensable condiment for many Filipino dishes, especially Kare-kare (page 118).

Sauté the garlic in hot oil in a skillet. Add the pork and cook until crisp. Drain off any excess oil.

Stir in the shrimp paste, vinegar and sugar and simmer for 3–5 minutes. Makes ¾ cup.

LATIK

3 14-ounce cans coconut milk

Used in many Filipino dishes. See Introduction to Guinataan, page 10.

Pour the coconut milk into a saucepan and bring to a boil. Reduce the heat and let it simmer for 45–60 minutes. The coconut oil will rise to the top, and a cheese-like substance will form at the bottom and turn a delicate brown color. This is the *latik*.

Drain the oil from the top of the *latik* and save it for use in recipes or to grease plates and molds. Save the *latik* to use to flavor or top many dishes.

Store both, covered, in the refrigerator up to 10 days.

Liver Sauce #1
LECHON SAUCE #1

Preheat oven to 350° F.

Season the liver with 1 tablespoon of the salt and let stand for 20 minutes.

Place the liver in a roasting pan and cook in the oven for 35–45 minutes. Let cool and chop into small pieces.

In a blender or food processor, puree a few pieces of the liver with ½ cup of the water. Slowly add the rest of the liver and the garlic and puree, adding more water if needed.

Sauté the onions in hot oil in a saucepan until they are soft. Add the pureed liver and garlic, the rest of the water, the vinegar, sugar, pepper and remainder of the salt. Bring to a light boil, reduce the heat and simmer for 10 minutes.

Add the bread crumbs slowly and continue cooking and stirring the sauce until it has thickened to the desired consistency.

Serve warm with Roast Pork *(Lechon sa Horno,* page 130). Makes 6 cups.

2 pounds pork liver

2 tablespoons salt

1½ cups water

12 cloves garlic, peeled

1 small onion, chopped

2 tablespoons vegetable oil

½ cup distilled white vinegar

½ cup sugar

1 teaspoon black pepper

½ cup fine bread crumbs

Liver Sauce #2
LECHON SAUCE #2

2 tablespoons vegetable oil

8 cloves garlic, minced

2 tablespoons onions, finely chopped

4 ounces liver paste or liverwurst spread

1 teaspoon salt

1 teaspoon black pepper

1½ cups water

¼ cup distilled white vinegar

¼ cup sugar

¼ cup bread crumbs

Heat the oil in a saucepan, add the garlic and sauté until it is brown. Add the chopped onions and cook 1–2 minutes more.

Add the liver paste, salt and pepper, and stir well. Gradually stir in the water.

Add the vinegar and sugar and bring the mixture to a boil. Stir in the bread crumbs slowly and cook until the sauce has thickened to the desired consistency.

Serve with roast pork dishes. Makes 2–3 cups of sauce.

Miso Sauce for *Pesa*

In a saucepan, sauté the garlic, onions and tomatoes in the oil until the tomatoes are soft.

Add the miso and water mixture and the fish sauce and simmer for 3–5 minutes.

Use as a dipping sauce for Gingered Fish and Vegetable Soup, *(Pesa,* page 158). Makes ½ cup.

1 clove garlic, minced

2 tablespoons onions, chopped

1 medium tomato, chopped

1 tablespoon vegetable oil

3 tablespoons miso (fermented soybean paste), mashed in ½ cup water

1 tablespoon fish sauce

Sauce for Shrimp Omelet
PATOLA SAUCE

In a small pan, bring the clam juice to a light boil.

Add the Chinese okra or zucchini and cook over medium heat for 5 minutes.

Add the soy sauce, sugar and cornstarch dissolved in water. Lower the heat and cook until the sauce has thickened, about 1 minute, stirring constantly.

Pour over the Shrimp Omelet *(Tortang Hipon,* page 169). Makes ½ cup.

¼ cup clam juice

1 medium Chinese okra, peeled and sliced thin, or 2 small zucchini, sliced thin

1 teaspoon soy sauce

½ teaspoon sugar

1 tablespoon cornstarch dissolved in 2 tablespoons water

Sauce for Thai Marinated Pork
SATE' SAUCE

3 tablespoons creamy-style peanut butter

½ cup water

4 tablespoons soy sauce

3 tablespoons *kalamansi* or lemon juice

3 tablespoons sugar

6 cloves garlic, minced

1 small onion, diced

1 jalapeño pepper, minced

2 teaspoons butter or margarine

2 tablespoons peanuts, chopped fine

½ teaspoon salt

¼ teaspoon black pepper

In a saucepan, stir together the peanut butter and water. Add the soy sauce, *kalamansi* or lemon juice and sugar. Set aside.

In a mortar and pestle or blender, grind together the garlic, onion, and jalapeño pepper until you get a thin paste. If needed, add 1 tablespoon of water. Add this paste to the peanut butter mixture and bring to a boil over low heat.

Remove from the heat and stir in the butter, chopped peanuts, salt and pepper.

Serve over Thai Marinated Pork *(Saté Babi,* page 137). Makes 1 cup.

Dipping Sauce for Fried Egg Rolls

In a small saucepan, sauté the garlic in hot oil until it is golden brown. Remove it from the oil, drain on paper towels, and set it aside.

To the garlic-flavored oil, add the soy sauce, water and brown sugar and mix well to dissolve the sugar. Bring the mixture to a light boil over medium heat. Reduce the heat and simmer for 1 minute, stirring frequently.

Add the cornstarch and water mixture and cook, stirring constantly, until the sauce is thick.

Remove the sauce from the heat and top with the fried garlic. Makes 1½ cups of sauce.

4 cloves garlic, crushed

2 tablespoons vegetable oil

¼ cup soy sauce

1 cup water

⅓ cup dark brown sugar, firmly packed

1 tablespoon cornstarch dissolved in 2 tablespoons water

Sweet and Sour Sauce

Combine the vinegar, water, sugar, salt, catsup and oyster sauce in a small saucepan and bring it to a boil. Add the peppers if desired.

Stir in the cornstarch and water mixture and stir until the sauce has thickened. Makes 1 cup.

2 tablespoons cider vinegar

1 cup water

6 tablespoons sugar

½ teaspoon salt

1 tablespoon catsup

1 teaspoon oyster sauce

½ teaspoon jalapeño pepper, finely chopped (optional)

1 tablespoon cornstarch dissolved in 2 tablespoons of water

Dipping Sauce for Fresh Springrolls

¼ cup sugar

1 teaspoon salt

2 tablespoons soy sauce

1 cup water

1 tablespoon cornstarch dissolved in 2 tablespoons water

3 cloves garlic, minced

Combine the sugar, salt, soy sauce and water in a saucepan. Bring to a light boil over medium heat. Add the cornstarch and water mixture and stir until the sauce has thickened, about 1 minute.

Remove the pan from heat and stir in the fresh garlic. Makes 1½ cups. Drizzle over fresh lumpia or springrolls.

Vinegar and Garlic Dipping Sauce
SUKA'T BAWANG SAWSAWAN

¼ cup distilled white vinegar

3 cloves garlic, crushed

½ teaspoon salt

Serve this sauce in small bowls with grilled meats, vegetables and egg rolls.

Thoroughly mix the vinegar, garlic and salt in a small bowl. Makes 1 serving.

Desserts & Snacks

The Philippines is a country overflowing with tropical fruits, coconuts and sugar. Their use has been influenced not only by its native population but also by the Chinese, Spanish and Americans. It is no wonder that Filipinos are so fond of sweet things to finish the end of a meal or to satisfy their desires between meals.

Banana Chips

6 unripe saba bananas or 3
   plantains

1 cup sugar

2 cups vegetable oil

Peel and slice the bananas into thin rounds or lengths. Roll each slice in the sugar.

In a large skillet, heat the oil and fry a few slices of banana at a time until they are golden brown and crisp. Because of the differences in the starch and sugar content of each banana, some chips will darken more than others.

Using a slotted spoon, remove the cooked bananas and drain them well on paper towels. Let cool to room temperature. Store in a well-sealed jar or container after they have cooled thoroughly. Makes about 2 cups of banana chips.

Rolled Wafer Cookies
BARQUILLOS

¾ cup milk

5 egg yolks, lightly beaten

¼ cup white flour, sifted

1 cup sugar

1 teaspoon vanilla extract

1 tablespoon grated lemon
   zest

Preheat oven to 375° F.

In a bowl, mix the milk and egg yolks.

Slowly add the sifted flour and mix well to a smooth batter. Add the sugar, vanilla and grated lemon zest and mix well.

Onto a non-stick cookie sheet, using a small ladle or spoon, pour out the batter in 2–3 tablespoon portions to make circular wafers about 3 to 4 inches in diameter and ⅛ inch thick.

Bake for 12–15 minutes, or until the wafers are deep brown.

Remove from the oven and while they are still soft and warm, lift up one edge with a spatula and roll. Set aside on a plate to cool and harden. Makes 12–15 cookies.

Coconut Candy Bars
BUKAYO

Using a large knife, chop the grated coconut fine. In a large bowl, mix the chopped coconut, powdered sugar, cornstarch and water together.

Place the mixture in a double boiler over gently boiling water and cook until it reaches 200° F, using a candy thermometer, or until it no longer sticks to a finger when touched. Stir constantly to avoid burning.

Pour the mixture onto a greased board or surface and roll it into a sheet 12 inches long, 3 inches wide and ½ inch thick. Set aside to cool and harden.

Using a sharp knife, cut it into bars at intervals of ½ inch.

Wrap each bar with a piece of wax paper and store in an airtight container. Makes about 48 bars.

6 cups grated fresh coconut

3 cups powdered sugar

¾ cup cornstarch

1½ cups water

Wax paper, cut into 48 strips 4 inches long and 1 inch wide

Cashew Tarts
CASUY TARTS

Preheat oven to 350° F.

Separate the whites and yolks of the eggs. Beat the yolks well and add the sugar, cashews, vanilla, milk, butter and lemon zest.

Beat the egg whites until they are stiff. Fold them into the yolk mixture.

Fill the tart shells about ⅔ full with the cashew filling. Arrange them on a cookie sheet and bake for 30 minutes.

Allow to cool slightly and top with vanilla ice cream just before serving. Makes 12 tarts.

4 eggs

1½ cups sugar

1½ cups cashews *(casuy)*, chopped coarse

2 teaspoons vanilla extract

2 tablespoons evaporated milk

½ cup melted butter or margarine

2 tablespoons lemon zest

12 pre-made tart shells

Coconut Pastries
BUKO PASTELLITOS

FILLING:

1 cup shredded fresh young coconut (*buko*) or young coconut preserves

⅔ cup sugar (if using fresh young coconut)

½ cup milk

1 egg yolk

1 tablespoon butter or margarine

1 tablespoon flour

PASTRY:

2 cups flour, sifted

½ teaspoon baking powder

1 teaspoon salt

½ cup vegetable shortening

4 tablespoons ice water

2 eggs, well beaten

Preheat oven to 350° F.

To make the filling, mix the fresh young coconut, sugar and milk in a saucepan. Over medium heat, cook this mixture until it is very thick, about 20–25 minutes, stirring constantly. If using the preserves, eliminate the sugar and cook the mixture for 5–7 minutes.

Add the egg yolk, butter and flour and mix thoroughly. Cook for 5 minutes more. Remove from the heat and set aside.

To make the pastry, in a bowl, sift the flour, baking powder and salt together.

Using 2 forks or knives, cut the vegetable shortening into the dry ingredients. Add the ice water one tablespoon at a time and mix between each addition.

On a floured board or surface, roll the dough thin, about ¼ inch thick. Cut into 1½-inch squares, making 36–48 squares of pastry.

To assemble, spread 1 teaspoon of the filling on a square of the dough and cover with another square. Arrange on a cookie sheet with space between each. Brush the top of each with a little of the beaten eggs.

Bake for 12–15 minutes, or until brown.

Cool before serving. Store in an airtight container. Makes 18–24 *buko pastellitos.*

Coconut Brittle

In a non-stick skillet over medium-high heat, toast the grated coconut to a golden brown, stirring constantly for 15–20 minutes. Remove from the heat and set aside to cool slightly.

In a medium saucepan, dissolve the sugar in the water over low heat. Increase the heat to high and bring the water to a boil. Cook for 5–7 minutes. Brush the sides of the pan with a wet pastry brush to keep sugar crystals from forming. Watch carefully—this can burn easily.

When the syrup is cooked, add the butter or margarine 1 tablespoon at a time, stirring well between each addition.

Mix in the toasted coconut and salt and cook for another 7–10 minutes, stirring constantly.

Line a cookie sheet with wax paper. Spoon the mixture, 2–3 heaping tablespoons at a time, onto the wax paper. Allow to cool and harden at room temperature. Store in an airtight container.

Serve alone or with ice cream. Makes about 12 coconut brittle.

1 cup grated coconut

1 cup sugar

1 cup water

4 tablespoons butter or margarine

1 teaspoon salt

Coconut Meringue Cookies

PASTRY:

3 egg whites

6 tablespoons sugar

1 tablespoon water

½ cup flour

½ teaspoon baking powder

FILLING:

1½ cups grated coconut

1 cup sugar

½ cup water

1 teaspoon vanilla extract

2 egg whites, well beaten

Preheat oven to 400° F.

To make the pastry, beat the egg whites until they are stiff. Add the sugar and water. Sift the flour and baking powder together and gently fold into the egg whites.

Spread the dough thin on a lightly greased baking sheet. Bake for 10–15 minutes or until it is golden brown. Watch carefully to avoid burning.

Remove from the oven and while the pastry is still hot, cut it into 2-inch squares with a sharp knife.

To make the filling, mix the grated coconut, sugar, water and vanilla in a saucepan. Over medium heat cook the mixture, stirring constantly, for 12–15 minutes.

Reduce the heat and fold in the egg whites gently. Cook for another 3–4 minutes.

To assemble, place 1 tablespoon of filling on each pastry square. Allow to cool and store in an airtight container. Makes 12–15 cookies.

Filipino Fruit Salad

In a large serving bowl, combine all the fruit. If using the cream, fold it in and mix well. Chill for at least 1 hour before serving. Makes 12–15 servings.

14 ounces canned fruit cocktail, drained

8 ounces canned mandarin oranges, drained

1 red or golden delicious apple, peeled, cored and cubed

12 ounces frozen young coconut *(buko)*, thawed and drained

12 ounces canned or bottled palm nuts *(kaong)*, drained

12 ounces canned or bottled pineapple gel *(nata de piña)* or coconut gel *(nata de coco)*, drained

2 ripe bananas, peeled and sliced

1 cup seedless grapes, washed

2 8-ounce Nestles canned cream or 1 pint whipping cream, whipped with 2 tablespoons sugar until stiff (optional)

Filipino Fruit Sundae
Halo-halo

3 heaping tablespoons:
   palm nuts *(kaong)*
   purple yam preserves *(ube jam)*
   preserved shredded young coconut *(macapuno)*
   jackfruit *(langka),* diced
   sweetened red mung beans
   creamed corn
6 heaping tablespoons shaved ice
4 tablespoons evaporated milk
1 scoop vanilla ice cream (optional)

Halo-halo, *literally translated, means "mix-mix." It is a snack or dessert of fruits, sweet preserves, evaporated milk and shaved ice mixed together. The amount and combination of each is up to the cook. Here is one of an infinite possible combinations.*

In a clean, dry 16-ounce glass, layer the palm nuts, purple yam preserves, preserved shredded young coconut, jackfruit, sweetened red mung beans and creamed corn.

Top with shaved ice and evaporated milk. Top it all with a scoop of vanilla ice cream, if desired.

Mix well with a long spoon and eat like a sundae. Serves 1.

VARIATIONS:

The following can be substituted or added to the sundae:
melons, diced
mango, diced
sweetened white beans
sweetened red kidney beans
sweetened garbanzo beans (chickpeas)
boiled tapioca pearls (sago)
boiled sweet potatoes, diced
boiled taro root, diced
agar-agar *(gulaman)*
coconut gel *(nata de coco)*
pineapple gel *(nata de piña)*

Gelled Coconut Milk
GULAMAN

Agar-agar (gulaman) *is gelatin derived from seaweed that stays solid at warm temperatures. It is available in stores that carry Asian food products and natural food stores. It comes in a variety of colors.*

Chill the coconut milk and water mixture in the refrigerator.

Rinse the agar-agar in cold water to soften it. Drain and shred it.

In a saucepan, bring the water to a boil and add the sugar and shredded agar-agar. Stir until they are dissolved completely.

Strain the liquid through a fine sieve or 2–3 layers of cheesecloth to remove any undissolved pieces of agar-agar. Chill in a shallow dish until it is set, about 2 hours in a cool place. Do not refrigerate.

TO SERVE: Chop the gel coarsely and place 4 heaping tablespoons in a glass. Fill each glass with 1 cup of the chilled coconut milk. Sweeten with sugar, if desired.

VARIATION:

Add 1 cup of diced pineapple, banana, mango or lychee nuts to the strained sugar water before gelling it.

3 cups coconut milk diluted with 3 cups water

1 bar agar-agar (gulaman)

3 cups water

½ cup sugar

FLAN

2 cups sugar

⅓ cup water

8 egg yolks

1½ cups milk

8 ounces condensed milk

1 teaspoon vanilla extract

1 teaspoon lemon juice

Preheat oven to 300° F.

Stir 1 cup of the sugar and the water in a heavy, medium saucepan over low heat until the sugar dissolves. Increase the heat to high and boil without stirring until the caramel mixture turns deep amber, about 10 minutes. Swirl the pan occasionally, and brush the sides of the pan with a wet pastry brush to keep sugar crystals from forming. Pour the caramel into 8 custard cups, dividing evenly to cover the bottoms of the cups only. Set aside to cool.

In a bowl, beat the yolks well and add the remaining 1 cup of sugar gradually, stirring to mix thoroughly.

To the yolk mixture add the milk, condensed milk, vanilla and lemon juice and mix well.

Pour this custard over the caramel in the cups, dividing it evenly. Put the cups in a large baking pan. Pour enough hot water into the pan to come halfway up the sides of the cups.

Bake for 1½ hours, or until the custards are almost set but still slightly soft in the center. Remove the cups from the pan and let the custards cool completely.

To unmold, run a small, sharp knife around the edges of the cups to loosen the custard. Invert the molds onto plates, letting the caramel drizzle over the custards.

Serve cold or at room temperature. Makes 8 flan.

Flan with Coconut Milk
FLAN AT GATA

Preheat oven to 300° F.

Stir ¾ cup of the sugar into the water in a heavy, medium saucepan over low heat until the sugar dissolves. Increase the heat to high and boil, without stirring, until the caramel mixture turns deep amber. Swirl the pan occasionally, and cook for about 10 minutes. Brush the sides of the pan with a wet pastry brush to keep sugar crystals from forming. Pour ¾ of the caramel into 6, ¾-cup custard cups, dividing evenly, to just cover the bottom of the cups.

Stir the coconut milk into the caramel remaining in the pan. Place over low heat and stir continuously until all the caramel is dissolved.

In a bowl, combine the egg yolks and egg whites and beat together lightly to mix thoroughly.

Add the remaining 1 cup of sugar, the lemon juice, the coconut milk and caramel mixture and mix together well.

Strain this custard through a cheesecloth and pour it over the caramel in the custard cups, dividing it evenly. Place the cups in a large baking pan. Pour enough hot water into the pan to come halfway up the sides of the cups.

Bake for 1½ hours, or until the custards are almost set but still slightly soft in the center. Remove the cups from the pan and let the custards cool completely.

Just before serving, sprinkle 1 tablespoon of the brown sugar over each custard. Melt the sugar by applying a heated metal utensil or lightly flaming it with a propane torch (available at any hardware store) to form a nice crust of melted sugar over the custard.

To unmold, run a small sharp knife around the edge of the cups. Invert the custard onto plates, letting the caramel drizzle over the custards.

Serve cold. Makes 6 flan.

1¾ cups sugar

¼ cup water

2 cups coconut milk

6 egg yolks

4 egg whites, lightly beaten

1 teaspoon lemon juice

6 tablespoons brown sugar

Coconut Meringue Cookies #2
Macapuno

3 egg whites

¼ teaspoon baking powder

1½ cups sugar

⅛ teaspoon ground anise

12 ounces shredded young coconut preserves (*macapuno*)

Preheat oven to 250° F.

In a bowl, beat the egg whites to stiff peaks. Add the baking powder.

Add the sugar a few tablespoons at a time until it is all incorporated. Add the ground anise and set the meringue aside.

Divide the coconut preserves into 1-heaping-tablespoon portions and shape into balls using 2 spoons.

Coat the balls with the meringue. Arrange them 1 inch apart on greased cookie sheets.

Bake for 12–15 minutes, until the meringue is dry. Cool the cookies on a rack. Store in an airtight container between sheets of wax paper. Makes 18–24 cookies.

Coconut Pudding
Kalamay

5 cups coconut milk

2 cups dark brown sugar

1 cup white sugar

Mix the ingredients in a large saucepan and cook over medium heat, stirring constantly, until it is very thick, about 2½ to 3 hours.

Let cool and cut into paper-thin slices with a sharp knife. Makes about 12 servings.

Mocha and Coconut Roll
Macapuno Roll

Preheat oven to 350° F. Line a cookie sheet with waxed paper.

Sift the flour, baking powder and salt together.

Separate the eggs. Beat the yolks well, gradually beat in the sugar, and mix well.

Sift the flour mixture into the yolks, add the vanilla, and gently fold into the yolks. Beat the egg whites until the peaks are stiff. Gently fold the whites into the flour mixture.

Pour the batter onto the lined cookie sheet and spread it evenly. Bake for 12–15 minutes, or until the cake is light brown and springs back when gently touched with a finger.

Turn the cake onto a few layers of cheesecloth or a towel dusted with powdered sugar. Peel off the waxed paper carefully and trim off the crusty edges. Roll the cake *and towel* very gently along the narrow end. Let cool for 10 minutes.

Unroll the cake and towel and spread the mocha icing and then the shredded young coconut preserves (*macapuno*) over it evenly. Roll the cake again, gently, leaving the towel flat.

Wrap the roll in waxed paper until ready to serve. Just before serving, remove the paper and sprinkle powdered sugar on top. Slice crosswise. Makes 6–8 servings.

PASTRY:

1 cup flour

2 teaspoons baking powder

¼ teaspoon salt

3 eggs

¾ cup sugar

1 teaspoon vanilla extract

Powdered sugar

FILLING:

12 ounces shredded young coconut preserves (*macapuno*)

2 cups mocha icing (page 252)

Coconut Tarts
Macapuno Tarts

8 egg yolks

6 tablespoons sugar

4 tablespoons flour

2 tablespoons melted butter
or margarine

24 ounces shredded young
coconut preserves
(*macapuno*)

1 teaspoon lemon zest

12 pre-made tart shells

Preheat oven to 375° F.

In a bowl, beat the egg yolks and sugar together.

Mix the flour and melted butter together in another bowl and add it to the egg yolks. Add the shredded young coconut preserves (*macapuno*) and lemon zest and mix the ingredients thoroughly.

Fill each tart shell ⅔ full with the filling.

Arrange the tarts on a cookie sheet and bake for 15 minutes.

Let cool slightly and top with vanilla ice cream before serving. Makes 12 tarts.

VARIATION:

Jackfruit (*langka*) preserves can be substituted for the shredded young coconut preserves to make jackfruit tarts.

Sweet Potatoes in Syrup
MATAMIS NA KAMOTE

Preheat oven to 350° F.

Put the sweet potatoes in a baking dish and sprinkle them with the brown sugar. Bake for 35–45 minutes, or until they are very soft.

In a heavy, medium saucepan, dissolve the white sugar and salt in the water over low heat. When they are dissolved, increase the heat to medium and bring the syrup to a boil. Do not stir. Cook for 10 minutes, or until it is brown. Swirl occasionally. Brush the sides of the pan with a wet pastry brush to keep sugar crystals from forming.

Grind the sweet potatoes in a food processor or mash them with a fork. Leave them a little lumpy for texture.

Add the sweet potatoes to the syrup and mix well. Cook for another 5 minutes.

Serve warm, alone or with ice cream. Makes 4–6 servings.

3 pounds sweet potatoes or yams, peeled and sliced lengthwise into quarters

¼ cup brown sugar

1 cup white sugar

¼ teaspoon salt

1½ cups water

Bananas in Syrup
MATAMIS NA SAGING

In a heavy, medium saucepan, dissolve the sugar and salt in the water over low heat. When they are dissolved, increase heat to medium and bring the syrup to a boil. Do not stir. Cook for 10 minutes or until it is brown. Swirl occasionally. Brush the sides of the pan with a wet pastry brush to keep sugar crystals from forming.

Add the banana slices to the simmering syrup and continue cooking for about 10 minutes.

Serve warm or cold, alone or with ice cream. Makes 4–6 servings.

1 cup sugar

¼ teaspoon salt

1½ cups water

3 ripe saba bananas or plantains, peeled and cut diagonally into ½-inch slices

Milk Bars
PASTILLAS DE LECHE

14 ounces condensed milk
2 cups powdered milk
½ cup corn starch
1 tablespoon lemon zest
Powdered sugar

In a heavy saucepan, combine the condensed milk, powdered milk and lemon zest. Cook, stirring, over low heat until the mixture forms a ball, in 20–25 minutes. Remove from the heat and allow to cool.

Dust a board or flat surface with powdered sugar. Turn the milk mixture onto the surface and flatten with a rolling pin dusted with powdered sugar, until it is about ¼ inch thick. Cut into bars about 2½ inches long by ½ inch wide.

Separate the bars and allow to fully harden for 30–40 minutes. Lightly dust them with more powdered sugar. Wrap the individual bars in waxed paper. Store in an airtight container. Makes about 36 milk bars.

VARIATIONS:

MILK BARS WITH ALMONDS—*Pastillas de Almendras*

Substitute 1 cup of powdered milk with 1 cup of finely chopped blanched almonds. Proceed as above.

MILK BARS WITH PEANUTS—*Pastillas de Mani*

Substitute ½ cup of the powdered milk with ¾ cup of finely chopped, blanched or roasted unsalted peanuts. Proceed as above.

MILK BARS WITH PURPLE YAM—*Pastillas de Ube*

Substitute ½ cup of powdered milk with ½ cup of purple yam (*ube*) powder. Omit the lemon zest. Proceed as above.

Peanut Brittle

In a heavy saucepan, dissolve the sugar in the water over low heat. Increase the heat to high and bring the water to a boil. Cook for 5–7 minutes. Brush the sides of the pan with a wet pastry brush to keep sugar crystals from forming. Watch carefully to prevent burning.

Add the butter or margarine 1 tablespoon at a time, stirring well between each addition.

Mix in the peanuts and salt. Cook for another 7–10 minutes, stirring constantly.

Pour the mixture onto a greased board and spread it thin with a greased rolling pin. Roll as thin as possible. Allow to cool and harden.

Break or cut into desired forms. Store in an airtight container between layers of wax paper.

1 cup sugar

1 cup water

4 tablespoons butter or margarine

1 cup chopped, unsalted, roasted peanuts

1 teaspoon salt

Cashew Torte
Sans Rival

FILLING:

6 egg yolks

½ cup corn syrup

2 tablespoons water

¼ cup sugar

½ pound softened butter or margarine

½ cup roasted, unsalted cashews, finely chopped

MOCHA ICING:

¾ pound butter or margarine

1¼ cups sugar

14 ounces evaporated milk

1 teaspoon (heaping) instant coffee

WAFERS:

10 egg whites

1 cup sugar

2 cups roasted, unsalted cashews, finely chopped

Preheat oven to 325° F.

To make the filling, beat the egg yolks very well.

Heat the corn syrup, water and sugar over low heat in a heavy saucepan, stirring to dissolve the sugar. Let it come to a slow boil and cook for 2 minutes.

Pour the hot syrup slowly in a thin stream into the egg yolks, beating continuously. Refrigerate for 10 minutes.

Cream the softened butter or margarine, using an electric beater. Gradually beat in the cooled egg yolk mixture and beat well. Set aside, along with the chopped cashews, until later.

To make the mocha icing, put the butter in a bowl and using an electric beater, start on slow and gradually increase the speed until the butter is smooth and creamy.

Gradually add the sugar and evaporated milk, beating at medium speed.

Add the instant coffee and beat for 5–7 minutes, or until the icing is the consistency for spreading. Keep cool until ready to use. (Makes 2 cups of mocha icing.)

Generously grease and flour three cookie sheets.

To make the wafers, using a beater, beat the egg whites until soft peaks are formed. Beat in the sugar a few tablespoons at a time until the peaks are stiff and all the sugar is added.

Gently fold the 2 cups of chopped cashews into the whites.

Spread the mixture ¼ inch thick evenly on the cookie sheets. Bake for 30 minutes or until golden brown. (Put the cookie sheets in the oven at 5-minute intervals so there will be time to work on each baked wafer while it is still warm.)

Put sheets of waxed paper a little larger than the cookie sheets on a flat surface. As soon as the wafer sheets are baked, cut each in half. Set aside to cool on the waxed paper.

To assemble, spread the filling thinly on top of each wafer and sprinkle with the chopped cashew nuts. Stack the wafers in 6 layers.

Spread the mocha icing over the top and sides of the torte and sprinkle with more chopped cashews.

Cover with plastic wrap. Use toothpicks to keep the wrap from touching the torte. Chill in the refrigerator for 2-3 hours before serving. Makes 10-12 servings.

Milk Candy
POLVORONES

In a non-stick skillet, toast the flour until it is a light brown, about 15–20 minutes. Remove from the heat and cool thoroughly.

In a large mixing bowl, sift together the toasted flour, powdered milk and sugar. Mix well.

Add the softened butter. Using your hands, mix thoroughly and form into a ball of dough.

Pinch off enough dough to form balls about ¾ inch in diameter. Dust a cookie sheet with powdered milk. Place the dough balls on the cookie sheet and slightly flatten them.

Let the balls stand for 30 minutes to harden. Wrap each in waxed paper.

Serve immediately or store in an airtight container. Makes approximately 2 dozen candies.

4 cups flour
¾ cup powdered milk
1½ cups sugar
1 cup softened butter or margarine

Almond Brittle in a Wafer
Turrones de Almendras

FILLING:

2 cups roasted almonds,
coarsely chopped

1 cup sugar

½ cup honey

WAFER:

2 cups water

½ cup flour

½ cup sugar

Preheat oven to 375° F.

To make the filling, grind the roasted almonds and sugar in a mortar and pestle, a blender or food processor until the almonds are very fine in consistency.

Put the almonds and sugar in a heavy saucepan with the honey over low heat and stir until the sugar dissolves. Increase the heat to medium and stir constantly until it begins to turn brown, about 10–15 minutes.

Pour the mixture onto a well-greased wooden board or surface. With a greased rolling pin, roll it out until it is ¼-inch thick.

Allow to cool slightly and cut into bars 3-inches long by ¼-inch wide. Separate the bars and cool thoroughly before wrapping them in the wafer.

Grease a cookie sheet with oil.

To make the wrapper, mix the water, flour and sugar together to make a smooth batter.

Onto the cookie sheet, spoon out 2–3 tablespoon portions of the batter to make wafers 3 to 4 inches in diameter and ⅛-inch thick.

Bake for 12–15 minutes, or until the wafer is a golden or deep brown.

To assemble, while the wafer is still warm and pliable, put it on a plate.

Put a bar of the filling on one end and roll it in the wafer. Set aside to cool.

Serve immediately or wrap with waxed paper and store in an air-tight container. Makes about 18–24 *turrones*.

Cashew Brittle in a Wafer
Turrones de Casuy

Preheat oven to 375° F.

In a heavy saucepan, mix the honey and sugar together over low heat until the sugar fully dissolves. Increase the heat to medium and cook the syrup about 7–10 minutes, or until it spins a thread when a spoon is lifted out of the syrup.

In a bowl, beat the egg whites until stiff peaks form. Slowly add the syrup and cashews. Mix well. Pour the mixture onto a well-greased wooden board or surface and roll with a greased rolling pin until it is ¼-inch thick.

Allow to cool slightly and cut into bars 3 inches long by ¼-inch wide. Separate the bars and cool thoroughly before wrapping them in the wafer.

Grease several cookie sheets with oil.

To make the wafer, mix the water, flour and sugar together to make a smooth batter. Onto the well-greased cookie sheet, spoon two 2–3-tablespoon portions of the batter to make two wafers 3–4 inches in diameter and ⅛-inch thick.

Put in the oven at 5-minute intervals and bake for 12–15 minutes or until the wafers are a golden or deep brown.

To assemble, while the wafers are still warm and pliable, place them on a plate. Immediately put a bar of filling on one end of each wafer and roll. Set aside to cool. Continue to assemble as soon as each cookie sheet is removed from the oven.

When thoroughly cooled, serve, or wrap with waxed paper and store in an airtight container. Makes about 18–24 *turrones*.

FILLING:

1 cup honey

2 cups sugar

5 egg whites

2 cups cashews (*casuy*), chopped fine

WAFER:

2 cups water

½ cup flour

½ cup sugar

Purple Yam Pudding
UBE HALAYA

2 cups milk

4 ounces powdered purple yam (*ube*)

14 ounces condensed milk

2 egg yolks, lightly beaten

2 tablespoons butter or margarine

Pour the 2 cups of milk into a heavy saucepan. Stir in the powdered purple yam until it is smooth. Add the condensed milk and cook over medium heat until the mixture thickens, about 15–20 minutes, stirring constantly.

Gradually stir ¼ cup of the milk mixture into the beaten egg yolks, then slowly add the yolks to the rest of the mixture. Add the butter or margarine and continue to simmer, stirring constantly, for 50–60 minutes more, or until the pudding is very thick.

Put the pudding into a well-oiled 3-cup mold or bowl. Cover with plastic wrap and cool for 20–25 minutes at room temperature. Then refrigerate until ready to serve.

Just before serving, run a small knife along the edges of the bowl and unmold the pudding onto a platter. Makes 8–10 servings.

Egg Candies
YEMA

14 ounces condensed milk

1 cup milk

10 egg yolks, lightly beaten

1 cup instant mashed potato flakes

1 teaspoon vanilla extract

Powdered sugar

In a heavy saucepan, mix the two milks together well. Cook over low heat until they reach a light boil. Remove from the heat and allow to cool slightly.

Add a few tablespoons of the hot milk to the egg yolks and then add them to the milk. (This is to prevent the eggs from curdling.) Mix well and return the pan to the heat.

Add the instant mashed potato flakes and vanilla and cook for 2 minutes, or until the mixture is thick enough to shape into small balls.

Remove from the heat and cool. Shape into small balls about 1 inch in diameter, using two spoons. Arrange on a plate and flatten the balls slightly with the tips of the fingers. Sprinkle with powdered sugar. Let stand for 5 minutes to harden.

Wrap each *yema* in waxed paper and store in an airtight container. Makes 16–20 candies.

Author's Notes

AGAR-AGAR ◦ Gulaman

Agar-agar is a natural gelatin extracted from seaweed. It sets without the need for refrigeration and has a firmer texture than packaged gelatin. *Gulaman* is sold in red, green, yellow, white and orange colored bars that make colorful and delicious desserts when mixed with canned or fresh fruits.

ANNATTO SEEDS ◦ Atsuete

Annatto seeds are used as a natural food coloring that lends an orange tint to ingredients. The tiny seeds are from the annatto fruit brought to the Philippines centuries ago by Spaniards who found the trees in Mexico.

The orange food color is extracted by steeping the seeds in hot water or hot oil. The food coloring comes in a variety of forms, either as whole seeds, powder or liquid extract. It is sold in packets or bottles at Asian and Latin American markets.

BANANAS

Cavendish

The bananas found in the Philippines are the Baston or Cavendish, Latundan, Lacatan, Senorita and the Saba.

The Baston or Cavandish is the type of banana sold fresh in stores around the world.

Saba

The Latundan is oblong with a whitish flesh. The Lacatan is long and slender with a yellowish flesh. The Senorita is a small banana only 3–4 inches long and is sold in bunches. These three are favorite dessert or snack fruits.

The Saba is flat, rounded and thick-skinned. It is one variety of banana that must be cooked to be enjoyed. Saba are simply boiled until tender, then peeled and sliced. The sliced Saba, added to a sugar syrup and served with

Latundan

Senorita

shaved ice makes a delicious dessert. In cooking, it is incorporated in some originally Spanish dishes that have been adjusted to the Filipino taste such as *puchero, estofado* and *arroz a la Cubana.*

In the Philippines, the bulk of the Saba supply is claimed by vendors of the Banana-Q and the *saging na turon,* a sort of banana *lumpia* or egg roll. The Banana-Q is a peeled Saba banana, skewered onto bamboo sticks, and roasted over live coals.

Lacatan

BASIC FILIPINO COOKING TECHNIQUES & TERMS

Binuro – Process of using salt as a preservative.

Dinaing – Any fish that has been butterfly-cut, marinated with salt, pepper and vinegar and broiled or fried.

Guinataan – Stewed fish, shellfish, vegetables and yams or sweet potatoes in coconut milk.

Guinisa – Fish, meat, fowl or vegetables sautéed in oil with garlic and onions.

Halabos – Shellfish or crustaceans steamed using naturally occurring fluids with a little salt and water just to start the cooking process.

Inadobo – Braised meat, fish, fowl or vegetables simmered in vinegar and spices.

Inasnan – Meat, fish or vegetables that have been preserved with salt and then broiled.

Inihaw – Meat, fish or tubers like sweet potatoes or yams, broiled over live charcoals.

Nilaga – Fish, fowl or meat boiled in water spiced with whole peppercorns.

Pangat – Fish cooked in a little water with or without a souring agent derived from fruits or vegetables.

Pasingao – Steamed fish, meat, fowl or shellfish.

Pesa – Sautéed fish or fowl boiled with ginger, vegetables and fish sauce.

Pinaksiw – Fish cooked in vinegar, a small amount of water and spices.

Pinausukan – Fish, meat and fowl that have been lightly smoked just before being eaten. The smoke is used to provide flavor rather than as a preservative.

Sinigang – Dishes of meats or seafood boiled with sour fruit. Sour fruits commonly used are tamarind, *kamias* or guavas.

Sinuam – Sautéed fish or shellfish boiled in ginger and pepper leaves.

Tinapa – The process of soaking salted and smoked fish in water to remove any excess salt. The fish is then pan-fried with a little oil until golden brown on both sides.

BITTERMELON ◦ Ampalaya

Bittermelon is a gourd-like vegetable with green wrinkly skin that is highly nutritious but has a very bitter taste. For some that bitterness is distasteful, to others it is irresistible. For *ampalaya* lovers it is an acquired taste. Once the taste for *ampalaya* is acquired it is hard to resist when offered as part of a meal.

Many Asian peoples familiar with the use of bittermelons have specific preferences for its stage of maturity or ripeness reflecting the amount of its bitterness. Indians prefer bittermelons that are green, firm and just barely mature enough for harvest with a medium amount of bitterness. Chinese prefer it more mature, sweet, soft, slightly yellowing and the seeds loose within the gourd. It even comes in a candied form available in some specialty Chinese stores. Filipinos prefer it immature. The more immature, the more bitter the taste. Filipinos also enjoy the leaves of the bittermelon plant. The growing tips of the vine are harvested and added to chicken soup or steamed and used to flavor shrimp, fish paste or fish sauce. Nutritionally, it helps stimulate digestive juices and is high in iron.

To temper the bitter bite, soak the bittermelon slices in warm water with salt before cooking or mash with rock salt to squeeze out the bitter juice.

CASSAVA

Cassava, also known as *kamoteng kahoy,* is a root crop or tuber used as a staple food product not only in the Philippines but throughout the world, especially Central America and western tropical Africa. It is similar to taro root but is much more wood-like in consistency. Dug from the ground, it is washed and allowed to dry in the sun. It is available fresh or fresh-frozen at many Asian and Latin American markets.

Cassava is used like a potato. The thick bark is peeled off and the starchy, fibrous, white meat is steamed or boiled. It can be mashed. If eaten whole, it is tasty when dipped in sugar. It can also be added to stews. It is used in such native Filipino delicacies as *suman* or *bibingka*.

For use in *suman* or *bibingka,* the cassava is washed in water and brushed to remove any dirt. It is then sliced into smaller pieces and a cut is made in the skin to peel off the bark. Any discolored or damaged portions are removed. The peeled cassava is grated and washed well with water to remove toxins naturally occurring in cassava. The cassava pulp is squeezed dry and the resulting flour saved.

CASTAÑAS FOR CHRISTMAS

Castañas, or chestnuts, are tender, sweet nuts covered by a fuzz-lined, leathery brown shell. They are best when roasted, rendering the meat soft and almost chewy. They were originally introduced by the Spanish and are now exported to the Philippines from such countries as Italy and China.

Castañas are considered holiday treats in the Philippines. It has become a tradition to have *castañas* on the *Noche Buena* table, along with apples and grapes, to symbolize prosperity.

During World War II and the Japanese occupation of the Philippines, importation was banned, so a substitute for *castañas* was invented just to keep up the tradition. When roasted over charcoal, mature coconut meat becomes tender and chewy, with a sweet, nutty flavor. The result is *castaniyog.*

CHINESE BOK CHOY ◦ Tagalog pechay

Chinese bok choy belongs to the cabbage family. Its longish, wide, dark green leaves and white stalks provide a substantial amount of vitamins and minerals. Except for the base, it is almost entirely edible. *Pechay* leaves can be added to stews or used as edible wrappers for fish. It is equally delicious when chopped and sautéed.

CILANTRO ◦ Wansoy

Cilantro, or fresh coriander, is used as a garnish for soups and noodle dishes or as a flavoring for dipping sauces. Whole or chopped, it adds a distinct bite to any dish. It is also served chopped and mixed with chopped ripe tomatoes and a few tablespoons of fish sauce.

CITRUS FRUIT ◦ Kalamansi

Kalamansi is a round citrus fruit about half the diameter of a golf ball that grows on a lush green bush in the Philippines. Its very thin outer skin can be green, yellow or orange and its flesh is a very bright orange. It is exceptionally juicy and fragrant. The scent is a cross between a lemon and a ripe orange. *Kalamansi* makes a great lemonade. It flavors cold teas and perfumes hot ones.

COLD DRINKS ∘ Sa malamig

These are cool, refreshing drinks sold out of large plastic or glass jars at bus terminals, bus stops and market exits. They come in a variety of flavors and colors. For a few pesos, one can have a glass of tapioca pearls and gelatin, refreshing pineapple juice, *buko* juice (liquid from a fresh, young coconut), melon juice from melons that are in season or *kalamansi* juice with slices of the fruit floating on top, similar to a lemonade.

Vendors shout the phrase *sa malamig* over and over again to attract passersby, usually commuters or tired shoppers, who cannot resist buying a cold drink to quench their thirst.

CURRY

Curry is actually a combination of several spices. The curry powder that is commercially available is usually a mixture of turmeric, coriander, cumin, chili powder, fennel and fenugreek. Other spices that are sometimes included in curry are ginger, mustard, cloves, cardamon, allspice, mace and pepper. Good cooks worldwide like to grind or pound whole spices together to create their own specific blends and tastes of curry.

Dinengdeng

Dinengdeng is a dish composed of vegetables cooked in a fermented-fish-flavored broth. The favorite vegetable for dinengdeng is *saluyot* or okra leaves.

FERMENTED SAUCES

In the Philippines, there are many fermented sauces, mostly made from fish and other seafood that enhance the flavor of many dishes.

The three major categories of fermented fish and seafood sauces are: *buro,* fermented rice and fish; *bagoong,* fermented fish paste; and *patis* or fish sauce that is a by-product of the *bagoong*-making process.

Buro is made by placing well-cleaned and gutted small catfish or mudfish in raw uncooked rice along with generous salt and a little water. It is allowed to ferment for 3–4 months in sealed clay jars. The concoction takes on a sour taste and smell along with a distinctive pink color. *Buro* is very popular with people from the Rizal province.

Bagoong is made by combining, in a one-to-one ratio, fish, shellfish and salt. For every portion of fish, there is one portion of salt. This is layered into large clay jars, covered and allowed to ferment for six months to one year. As time goes on, the fish breaks down and settles to the bottom as a sediment, the *bagoong*. The brown liquid that floats to the top is skimmed off. This is the *patis*.

To accelerate the process, the fish and salt-filled jars are well sealed and buried in the ground. A fire is built above the jars. As the fire dies down the ashes are spread out over the jars. This cooks the fish so the *bagoong* needs to ferment for only 1–2 months. But, the taste and texture are quite different from the *bagoong* made using a longer processing time.

Bagoong can be made from a variety of fish and other seafoods:

Bagoong padas – made from little flat fish caught in the waters off the Philippines. It is used as a sauce or condiment for dishes that are drier in consistency, like broiled or boiled fish.

Bagoong monamon or *bagoong balayan* – made from anchovies. In *bagoong monamon* the anchovies are allowed to stay whole, whereas in *bagoong balayan* the anchovies are dissolved into a brown sauce. Both are used for stews or dishes that have a bit of sauce or broth in them such as *dinengdeng*.

Bagoong sisi – made from small oysters or clams. It is very popular in Visayas, where lots of clams and oysters are harvested.

Bagoong macabebe – made from larger varieties of oysters. Also popular in Visayas but because of the size difference in the oysters used, it has a taste and texture different from *bagoong sisi*.

Bagoong alamang – popular not only in the Philippines but throughout Asia, and known also as shrimp paste. The *patis* derived from *bagoong alamang* is called *beko*.

Bagoong ipon – made from small fried fish.

Bagoong has also been made out of fish eggs to make a caviar-like *bagoong*.

If it were not for the fermented sauces many of the dishes associated with the Philippines just would not be the same.

FILIPINO BREAKFASTS

A typical Filipino breakfast consists of garlic fried rice, using leftover rice from the night before, scrambled or fried egg and a broiled meat or fish dish with a dipping sauce of native vinegar and crushed garlic.

The broiled dish can be any of the following: beef tapa, pork *tocino*, beef or pork *longganiza*, or dried salted fish. Filipino breakfast fare can include canned goods, like sautéed corned beef or sardines, and fried luncheon meat.

Some may opt for a lighter breakfast of rolls and white cheese with coffee, or cheese buns with hot cocoa. But to the Pinoy who needs to work a long day, nothing can be more satisfying than a full meal to start the day. A full meal is incomplete without a healthy serving of rice.

FILIPINO FAST FOOD ◦ Turo-turo

Turo-turo, or Point-point, refers to a Filipino fast-food stand located not only along the side of the road but in bus terminals and the modern malls of metro Manila. Here, an array of hot dishes is displayed before the hungry diner. All she or he has to do is point to the desired dish and it is served accordingly. A bowl of soup is sometimes included and always a cup of rice. Service is fast and personalized. The food is inexpensive but filling.

FLAN

The recipe for this favorite of Filipino desserts was brought to the Philippines by the Spaniards in the 1500s. In the provincial or rural areas of the Philippines, the people claimed that their Spanish ancestors used egg whites or albumin as part of the cement or plaster to reinforce the structure of churches. More than likely, the egg whites were used by the Spaniards of old as part of the process of making wines or sherries. But, whatever way they were used, this left bowls and bowls of egg yolks. Instead of throwing them away, they were made into delicious desserts such as flan and *tocino del cielo.*

FRESH OR DRIED PEPPERS ◦ Sili

Siling labuyo – a very small and hot pepper, currently holds a world record for being the hottest variety of pepper.

Siling mahaba – a long, thin flat pepper.

Siling bilog – any form of bell pepper.

GINGER

Ginger is one of the world's oldest spices. It was considered so precious by the ancient Romans that it was taxed. Today, it is readily available all over the world as fresh gingerroot or powdered ginger.

Depending on the recipe, fresh ginger may be smashed, sliced into rounds, cut into strips or grated. Mature ginger root has a strong flavor that can be used to eliminate fishy and gamey tastes. Young ginger has a very subtle flavor that adds interest to the taste of a dish.

Salabat is a favorite Filipino beverage made with ginger. This delicious ginger tea is traditionally taken along with *bibingka* or *puto bumbong* on cold December mornings after *Simbang Gabi,* a series of morning masses or religious services held each day a week before Christmas. It is also believed that drinking *salabat* regularly will improve and strengthen one's voice and vocal cords.

GOAT MEAT

Goat meat is popular in certain regions of the Philippines. In some areas of metro Manila, live goats are purchased from enterprising families who raise the animals on empty lots. The goat should not be younger that 8 months or older than 2 years.

Some popular Ilocano dishes make use of spicy flavored goat meat.

GREEN MANGOES   ∘   Manggang hilaw

Unripened, hard, green mangoes are eaten by Pinoys as a welcome snack to munch between meals or as a complement to a meal.

Some like their mangoes green, crunchy and very sour. Others prefer them with a hint of yellow and some sweetness. Part of the fun of eating unripe mangoes is the lip-puckering, face-grimacing reaction when one bites into a thin slice of *manggang hilaw.*

The perfect match for *manggang hilaw* is shrimp paste that has been sautéed with lots of garlic and small bits of pork. To the Pinoy it is a combination that is as inseparable as hot dogs and mustard or strawberries and cream. *Bagoong alamang* is used as a dipping sauce for the thin slices of green mangoes. However, some like to have their own *sawsawan* of rock salt, fish sauce, native Philippine vinegar, sugar or a combination of these.

JACKFRUIT   ∘   Langka

Jackfruit is one of the largest fruits grown in the world. It grows to a length of 1½ to 2 feet, with short blunt spines covering its body.

When ripe, it gives off a very distinct aroma. The fruit is often wrapped with plastic while still hanging from the tree to prevent birds and insects from feasting on the irresistibly sweet smelling and succulent flesh. It is delicious when made into preserves for *Halo-halo* or served fresh on a bed of ice.

The unripe whitish pulp is usually cooked like a vegetable. It is stewed in coconut milk with shrimp and pork. The large seeds are boiled until tender, peeled and eaten with sugar.

LEMON GRASS   ○   Tanglad

Lemon grass is a plant with tall, slender leaves and a creamy, bulbous base. The lower part of the stalk is peeled and mashed to impart a lemony fragrance and flavor to soups and roasts. It is not only used by Filipinos but more extensively by the Thai and Vietnamese in their cooking.

LYE WATER   ○   Ligia

Lye water is made from the ashes of a wood-burning stove, a common feature of most homes in the provinces and rural areas of the Philippines. The ashes are placed in a clay pot with a slight crack at the bottom, which is then filled with water. The water that drips through the crack is collected in a jar or bowl placed beneath. This is the lye water. The active ingredient is potassium carbonate. It is used to make steamed sweet rice cakes, rice wrapped in leaves and steamed gelatin cakes. In the old days, it was used to make soap. Of course, today it is available commercially in small bottles.

MILKFISH   ○   Bangus

Milkfish, a very popular fish in the Philippines, is cultivated in fish ponds. It has a taste quite similar to many white fish but is much firmer in texture and very bony.

In the Philippines, it is available fresh, but throughout the rest of the world it is only available frozen whole, in a multitude of sizes. Milkfish is available in a butterfly cut, marinated with vinegar and salt and sold frozen. It is possible to purchase it canned or as a smoked and frozen whole fish.

MORTAR & PESTLE

The mortar and pestle is an indispensable fixture in every Filipino kitchen. Usually made of stone or marble, it is used for pounding cloves of garlic to loosen the skin, cracking whole black peppercorns or mashing shrimp heads to obtain shrimp extract for flavoring.

OREGANO

Oregano was introduced to the Filipinos by the Spaniards who came via Mexico. It is a member of the mint family and originated in the Mediterranean. The word oregano comes from the Greek words *orus,* which means mountain, and *ganus,* meaning joy. For the Greeks, it was truly joy from the mountain, where it grew lusciously wild. It was used not only for cooking but for healing certain ailments.

PAPAYA

One of the more common fruits in the Philippines, the papaya is available all year round. Crunchy when unripe, it is cooked as a vegetable, pickled as *achara,* or eaten raw with rock salt. Ripe papayas have a refreshingly sweet and tender meat, best when eaten chilled with a squeeze of lemon juice. Papayas are also made into dried fruit preserves, juices and jams.

The enzyme papase is found in the papaya fruit, seeds and leaves. This is a natural meat tenderizer that breaks down the protein fibers in tough cuts of beef or pork.

PEPPER ◦ Black & white

Pepper comes from the Sanskrit word *pippali,* meaning berry. Pepper bushes grow in tropical climates, producing hundreds of green berries each year. These are picked just before ripening and dried in the sun. After ten to twelve days, the berries turn into black peppercorns.

White peppercorns come from the same berries, but are allowed to ripen on the bush until they turn red. They too are dried under the sun, then soaked in running water to loosen the outer shells. Traditionally, workmen trampled upon the dried berries with their bare feet. This process is now done mechanically. The husks are completely removed, revealing whole white peppercorns. Ground white pepper is ideal for white or light-colored sauces and dressings. It is less sharp in flavor and less pungent in aroma than black pepper.

PILI NUT

In the Bikol region of the Philippines is an area called Camarines Sur, where the *pili* nut is grown. The *pili* nut is a thick-shelled nut that is difficult to crack. But, once past the shell, the delicious white meat is similar to a Brazil nut. The *pili* nut is used in the Philippines to make a variety of sweets that call for almonds because the almond tree does not grow well in the Philippines. Sweets made from the pili nut are in great demand around Christmas and Easter or Holy Week, when they are given out by families and friends who go visiting during these times.

The *pili* nuts are mostly grown on plantations, but it is not unusual to find them growing wild or planted in backyard orchards or gardens of homes throughout Bikol. Usually they are found in pairs, for without cross-pollination, the fruit is small, ugly and stunted in growth.

The *pili* season begins in March. *Pili* fruits can be harvested by shaking the trees. This can damage the fruit, especially if one is after the fleshy pulp that surrounds the nut. The least harmful way to harvest *pili* fruits is by detaching each one with pruning scissors attached to a pole with a small net. The net is positioned directly beneath the pili fruit. The stem is cut with the pruning scissors and the fruit falls undamaged. The process is similar to harvesting avocados here in the United States. A good *pili* fruit is one that is undamaged, unblemished and has a large "eye."

The fleshy pulp that surrounds the nut is referred to as fresh *pili*. When cooked, the flesh becomes soft to the touch. If the flesh is hard, the fruit is old. Good quality *pili* is fine and smooth, not fibrous. Cooked *pili* must be eaten at once because it discolors quickly and loses its taste. Fresh, uncooked *pili* cannot be kept for more than a few days, even under refrigeration. The people of the Bikol region are the only Filipinos accustomed to eating fresh *pili*.

Fresh *pili* is prepared by blanching in boiling hot water for 20–30 minutes with no flame or heat beneath. When tender, the *pili's* dark purple skin peels off. Fresh *pili* has a tangy, resin-like taste.

RICE WATER

To obtain rice water, pour water into a bowl of uncooked rice. Swish rice and water around with the fingers until the mixture becomes cloudy and tiny particles, such as unhusked rice and tiny pebbles, float on top. Throw out the first rinse. Repeat the procedure for the second rinse and save the water. This rice washing contains water-soluble nutrients from the rice that provide a light, somewhat viscous broth for many dishes.

ROAST SUCKLING PIG ∘ Lechon

Roast suckling pig is very popular in the Philippines. It is served at many gatherings and parties. It is also sold sliced or in chunks at most places that sell hot food. The whole pig is roasted in an oven or *horno*. Because of the size of a whole pig, most are cooked at the oven of a local bakery or in a pit dug in the ground, covered with hot coals, and wrapped in banana leaves. If cooked in the oven, the roast pork is referred to as *lechon sa horno*.

The sauce that accompanies the *lechon* varies from region to region in the Philippines. In Batangas, pork liver is broiled or roasted and pounded into a paste using a mortar and pestle or pureed into a thick sauce with a food processor or blender. The tough, fibrous ligaments of the liver are removed. The pounded or pureed liver is then mixed with vinegar, sugar and herbs. To further thicken and bind the sauce, bread crumbs are added. This is the basic *lechon* sauce recipe found throughout the Tagalog-speaking regions of the Philippines.

SALTED DRIED CODFISH ∘ Bacalao

Bacalao is usually cooked with olive oil, whole tomatoes, pimientos, garbanzos and potatoes. This imported fish has always been expensive, and it is a rare treat for the family to have. It is usually served during Holy Week, when adults abstain from eating meat. When *bacalao* is part of the one meal allowed on Good Friday, the fasting becomes an easier sacrifice.

SALTED EGGS ∘ Itlog-ma-alat

These are salted duck or chicken eggs. The eggs are pickled in a salt or saline solution and hard-boiled. To distinguish them from regular eggs, they are dyed like Easter eggs, red for chicken eggs and purple for duck eggs.

They are peeled and chopped, then mixed with fresh tomatoes or cooked vegetables like collard or mustard greens. Serve as a salad or side dish.

Saluyot & Alugbati

Saluyot and *alugbati* are vegetables. When cooked they have a slippery texture similar to okra. This is why *saluyot* is sometimes referred to as okra leaves. *Saluyot* is a bushy plant that grows in almost any type of soil. It is a rich source of iron, calcium and vitamins, while providing texture to any dish. It can also be dried and ground to make powder, which is used as a healthy substitute for tea by the Japanese because it does not contain caffeine.

Alugbati is a red-stemmed vine that grows well even in harsh conditions. Its dark green leaves are used in many dishes.

SMOKED FISH ∘ Tinapa

Smoked fish, particularly mackerel, sardines and milkfish, is very popular in the Philippines, especially in Lent. Many Catholics reduce their consumption of meat during that period. Smoked fish is popular in the tropics because food can easily spoil without refrigeration and the process of smoking fish not only preserves it but also imparts a special flavor.

Smoked fish is also versatile. It can be broiled or pan-fried in a little oil and eaten with rice. Before mixing with other ingredients the meat should be carefully taken off the tiny bones.

SPANISH PORK SAUSAGE ∘ Chorizo *de Bilbao*

For Filipinos, chorizo *de Bilbao* refers to any dried Spanish-style pork sausage packed in paprika-colored lard. The early Spaniards imported it for their cooking and then later produced it commercially in the Philippines for local consumption. It is used in Spanish dishes, authentic or Filipinized, such as paella, *puchero,* and *cocido.*

Chorizo *de Bilbao* comes canned, frozen and sometimes fresh. The canned sausages come packed in lard or oil, which many use for cooking. The paprika lends meats and vegetables not only the flavor of the sausage but the red color as well. The frozen sausage comes in pairs wrapped in vacuum-packed plastic. It is available fresh from stores that sell Latin American meat products and sausages. All are now made in the United States.

SPONGE GOURD ∘ Patola

A tropical vegetable whose flesh is similar to a cucumber but has a totally different outward appearance. It has a light green skin that is tough and dry to the touch with deep grooves. It can be peeled and added to soups or eaten like a vegetable after being steamed or lightly boiled. It is called sponge gourd because it can be dried and used in the bath just like a sponge.

TARO LEAVES

In the Philippines and sometimes in the United States, when buying taro leaves from the market choose those that are already wilted but not so dry that the leaves crumble. Vendors in the Philippines hang them from a pole in their stalls until they are ready to be sold. In the United States, they are usually available as fresh leaves from stores that sell Oriental food products. If you happen to get fresh leaves, dry them first under the sun for a day to eliminate the surface irritants that may cause discomfort upon ingestion. Medium-sized leaves are best because the stalks of the bigger ones tend to be fibrous, while the small ones are not large enough for wrapping. The taro leaves can be used in such dishes as *laing* and *pinangat,* in which the leaves are dried, chopped and reconstituted with coconut milk to make a thick stew of vegetables and meat or fish.

TUNA ∘ Tulingan

Tulingan belongs to a species of the tuna family. It is a fatty fish, but when cooked, its meat is somewhat dry. Medium-sized *tulingan* are usually cut up into fish steak. Large ones are sold whole to Japanese restaurants to be cut into *sashimi.* Fresh fish heads make a delicious soup. Most of the *tulingan* caught end as canned tuna.

UNREFINED SUGAR ∘ Panocha

Panocha are dark, solid cakes of raw, unrefined sugar made from the juice of the sugar cane. The juice is collected and boiled down until concentrated, leaving a thick, natural sugar syrup that is poured into whole or half coconut shells and allowed to harden. It is used as a sweetener and flavoring for *sago* coolers, *gulaman* and *kakanin*. Mixed with peanuts, almonds, and/or cashews it is made into round, flat brittle candies similar to peanut brittle.

WATER CHESTNUTS ∘ Apulid

Water chestnuts come from plants that grow in wet or swampy soil. The brown bulbs must be peeled to reveal the white pith. *Apulid* are the size of walnuts with a taste and texture similar to that of jicama. Water chestnuts are available in some Oriental stores fresh but are more widely available canned. Although slightly sweet in flavor, their real charm is that they lend a crunchy texture to any vegetable dish.

WATER SPINACH ∘ Kang kong

This is a versatile and beautiful green, leafy vegetable, grown in fields with lots of water and mud. The tender stems and leaves are commonly used as a vegetable either eaten steamed or added to soups and stews.

WINGED BEAN ∘ Sigarilyas

Sigarilyas is a four-cornered vegetable pod, known as the winged bean or asparagus bean. It is delicious simply sautéed with bits of pork and shrimp. When not over cooked, it has an interesting mouth-feel with its four-winged shape and desirable crunch.

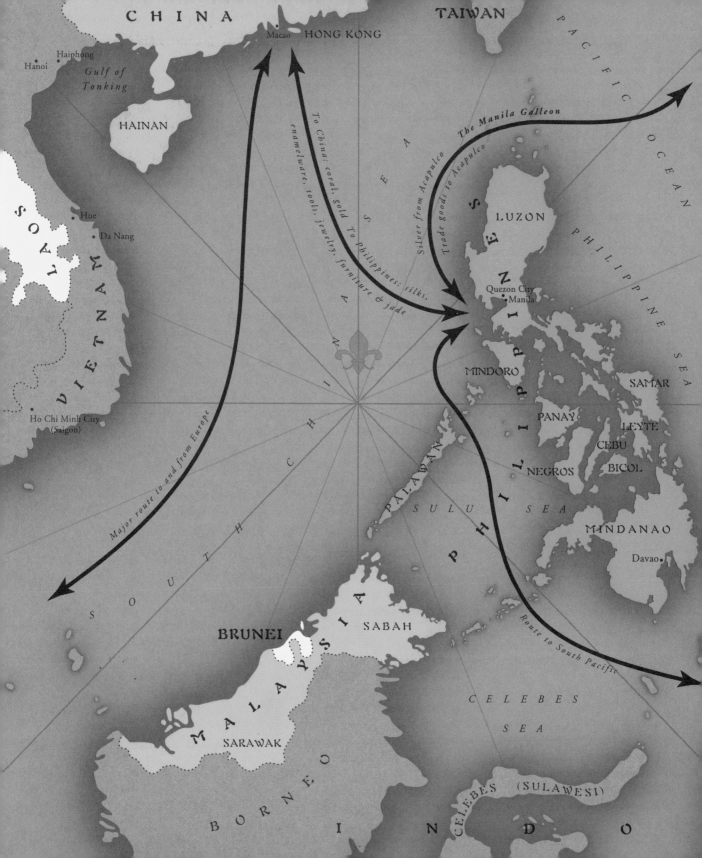